Pragmatics

Edinburgh Textbooks on the English Language – Advanced

Titles in the series include:

A Critical Account of English Syntax: Grammar, Meaning, Text
Keith Brown and Jim Miller

English Historical Semantics
Christian Kay and Kathryn Allan

A Historical Syntax of English
Bettelou Los

Morphological Theory and the Morphology of English
Jan Don

Construction Grammar and its Application to English
Martin Hilpert

A Historical Phonology of English
Donka Minkova

English Historical Pragmatics
Andreas Jucker and Irma Taavitsainen

English Historical Sociolinguistics
Robert McColl Millar

Corpus Linguistics and the Description of English
Hans Lindquist

Contemporary Stylistics: Language, Cognition, Interpretation
Alison Gibbons and Sara Whiteley

Modern Scots: An Analytical Survey
Robert McColl Millar

Visit the Edinburgh Textbooks in the English Language website at
www.edinburghuniversitypress.com/series/etoteladvanced

Pragmatics

Chris Cummins

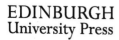
EDINBURGH
University Press

Edinburgh University Press is one of the leading university presses in the UK. We publish academic books and journals in our selected subject areas across the humanities and social sciences, combining cutting-edge scholarship with high editorial and production values to produce academic works of lasting importance. For more information visit our website: edinburghuniversitypress.com

Edinburgh University Press Ltd
The Tun – Holyrood Road, 12(2f) Jackson's Entry, Edinburgh EH8 8PJ

Typeset in Janson MT by
Servis Filmsetting Ltd, Stockport, Cheshire,
and printed and bound in Great Britain.

A CIP record for this book is available from the British Library

ISBN 978 1 4744 4002 8 (hardback)
ISBN 978 1 4744 4004 2 (webready PDF)
ISBN 978 1 4744 4003 5 (paperback)
ISBN 978 1 4744 4005 9 (epub)

Contents

Figures

Acknowledgements

For the existence of this book, thanks are due to Heinz Giegerich, for initially encouraging its development, and to Laura Williamson and Richard Strachan at the EUP for shepherding me patiently through the production process. For the content, thanks are predominantly due to Hannah Rohde, who largely designed the course upon which this book is loosely based, and was tremendously forthcoming with encouragement and useful advice, asking nothing more in return than the pleasure of not having to write it.

Among the many colleagues and co-authors who have shaped how I think about the topics in this book, I would like to single out my PhD supervisor, Napoleon Katsos, without whose influence I might well be studying functionalist syntax. I owe him a tremendous debt of gratitude for all he taught me about pragmatics, about research collaboration, and about a general academic attitude of mind. This acknowledgement is submitted way behind schedule in his honour.

1 What is pragmatics?

Jack. Charming day it has been, Miss Fairfax.
Gwendolen. Pray don't talk to me about the weather, Mr. Worthing.
Whenever people talk to me about the weather, I always feel quite
certain that they mean something else. And that makes me so nervous.
Jack. I do mean something else.
Gwendolen. I thought so. In fact, I am never wrong.

(Oscar Wilde, *The Importance of Being Earnest*)

How do we communicate with one another? One apparently straightforward answer to this is that we do so by exchanging signals that
each have a meaning associated with them. These signals might include
words, signs, gestures, facial expressions, and so on. The relationship
between the signals and the meanings is agreed by all the members of
a particular group of people, what we might call a speech community.
In order to communicate, one person – let's call them the speaker –
chooses the signal that is associated with the meaning they wish to
convey, and produces that signal; another person – let's call them the
hearer – identifies the signal and can thereby figure out the meaning
that the speaker meant to convey.

This straightforward account of communication is essentially the one
described by Shannon and Weaver (1949), in which communication
takes place as a result of a message being successfully encoded, transmit-
ted and decoded. This model of communication has been enormously
influential and is very important for a number of fields. And it does have
implications for human communication – for instance, it's obviously
crucial that the signals can be correctly identified, and this might not be
possible if there are physical disturbances in the communication chan-
nel. This kind of disturbance is what Shannon and Weaver call 'noise',
and it's useful to be able to think of 'noise' as something that doesn't just
mean unwanted sound but also includes distortion, interruptions, and
so on, and as something that applies to visual as well as auditory signals.

However, in one particular way, Shannon and Weaver's (1949) account runs into major difficulties when applied to human interaction: and that is because the signals that we use are systematically ambiguous.

Consider a simple sentence such as *I have a credit card*. As discussed by Gisladottir et al. (2012), this can be understood in several different ways: in (1), as an answer to a question; in (2), as a way of declining an offer; and in (3), as a way of making an offer.

(1)   A: How are you going to pay for the ticket?
       B: I have a credit card.
(2)   A: I can lend you money for the ticket.
       B: I have a credit card.
(3)   A: I don't have any money to pay for the ticket.
       B: I have a credit card.

In each of these contexts, B seems to assert the same fact – that they have a credit card. We know this because we can decode B's utterance, using our knowledge of the relevant language (in this case, English). Specifically, we rely on what we know about the meaning of the words (**lexical semantics**), how words are put together into grammatical sentences (**syntax**), and how the meanings of the words need to be combined, given how the words are arranged in this specific instance (often called **compositional semantics**).

Already there's a slight complication here. The meaning of the pronoun *I* depends upon who is speaking. Contrary to the assumptions of the Shannon and Weaver model, what *I* means to the speaker is not the same as what *I* means to the hearer, and if that's true we can't encode and decode the utterance by using our shared knowledge about the relation between signal and meaning. Still, we might be able to get around that: we could propose, for instance, that *I* is to be understood as 'the person who is speaking' throughout. Then our generalisation would be that *I have a credit card* always serves to state the fact that the person who is speaking has a credit card.

But having addressed that minor complication, we're faced with a major complication. What B is actually trying to communicate, when they utter *I have a credit card*, seems to vary very substantively between the three situations presented. In (1), B means to convey that they intend to pay for the ticket with a credit card; in (2), that they don't need to be lent money because they have a credit card; and in (3), that they are willing to use their credit card to buy the ticket for A.

These three meanings are readily available to the hearer, based on the same signal. Yet it would be somewhat implausible to suppose that the meanings are all somehow built into the semantic meaning of *I have a credit card*. Actually, we would run into all sorts of difficulties if we did try to come up with an account of the syntax and semantics of *I have a credit card* which specified all these possible meanings. To labour this point, if *I have a credit card* means 'I will use my card to pay for the ticket', we would have difficulty accounting for B's utterance in (4), in which this meaning is removed, or **cancelled**, by the continuation. B's utterance should seem self-contradictory, but it doesn't. Similarly, if *I have a credit card* means 'I decline your offer of a loan', B's utterance would be incoherent in (5), and if it means 'You can use my card to pay for your ticket', B's utterance would be incoherent (or at least rather unhelpful) in (6).

(4)   A: How are you going to pay for the ticket?
      B: I have a credit card, but actually I'll use cash this time.
(5)   A: I can lend you money for the ticket.
      B: I have a credit card, but if you're sure you don't mind I'll take you up on that offer.
(6)   A: I don't have any money to pay for the ticket.
      B: I have a credit card, but I'm afraid it won't be accepted here.

Alternatively, we can admit that B's utterances in (1)–(3) are understood to convey additional meanings that are not usually associated with the particular words that they uttered. The challenge that we're faced with, then, is to figure out what the speaker means, given that this does not correspond precisely with what they are saying, and that we can't simply look this up in some special decoding manual.

In some cases like this, the actual words that are uttered are not important, in that they aren't associated with any conventional meaning at all. In (7), Martin's ostensibly meaningless utterance conveys a specific message, namely that what the previous speaker is saying makes no sense to him: but it does so without being directly decodable in any way. In (8), a real-life example, R's silence also seems successfully to convey a message, namely that R will not be in the office on Monday, even though this is not a fact that someone could normally convey just by being silent.

(7)   Niles: He's clearly the one dealing with repressed material, not to mention the obvious Oedipal issues.
      Martin: Argle, gargle, gooble, goop.
                                    (Rob Hanning, *Frasier*, s7e1, 'Momma Mia')
(8)   C: So I was wondering would you be in your office on Monday by any chance?
      R: [silence, 1.86s]
      C: Probably not.
                                    (quoted by Levinson 1995: 237)

As these examples suggest, having inconsistent relationships between signal and meaning is not merely a source of additional complication – it can be an advantage. A speaker who can master this system, and who is talking to a similarly adept hearer, can communicate meanings without having to send all the signals that would usually be necessary. Under the right circumstances, we can say very little – potentially nothing at all – and still convey complex and subtle meanings by doing so. We can rely on the hearer being able to shoulder their share of the burden and derive interpretations that go far beyond anything that was explicitly said. In (1)–(3), speaker B probably would be successful in conveying their intended meaning: in fact, we know this because these are materials used in an experiment by Gisladottir et al. (2012), and their adult participants were consistently successful in deriving the interpretations discussed above.

How widespread is this pattern of speakers conveying meanings that don't correspond to the apparent semantic content of their utterances? Once we start looking, it turns out that there are all kinds of examples in which the speaker means more than they explicitly say. In (9), we assume that the speaker is referring to their own finger, although they do not say so. In (10), we probably assume that they mean that Anna and Bez are married to each other. And in (11), we would usually interpret Edina's question to refer only to the hours immediately prior to the time of utterance.

> (9)   I broke a finger.
> (10)   Anna and Bez are married.
> (11)   Edina: Have you eaten something?
>   Patsy: No, not since 1973.

> (Jennifer Saunders, *Absolutely Fabulous*, s2e3, 'Morocco')

These kinds of enrichment of meaning are so commonplace in language use that it sometimes seems odd or contrary for a hearer to miss out on one and interpret an utterance in accordance purely with its semantic meaning, as seems to happen in (11). The speaker of (10) might conceivably just mean that both Anna and Bez are married, without intending to convey that they are married to each other – but in practice, that interpretation probably isn't going to be the one that the hearer arrives at, because they will probably assume that the speaker intends to convey the richer 'to each other' meaning.

For this reason, as Bach and Harnish (1979) point out, it's not just that we need to think about the speaker's intention on those occasions when they mean to convey something that's different from what they 'literally' say. Rather, we have to think about the speaker's intention every time, so that we can distinguish the cases where they mean something extra from the cases in which they don't.

If we're not just relying upon the words that the speaker uses, and their meanings, what else goes into helping us understand what the speaker intends to convey? The very general answer is: **context**. As hearers, we take into account the circumstances under which an utterance is made – including such things as who is speaking, what the interaction is about, what has already happened in the interaction, what the speaker knows, and so on – in order to better understand what the speaker means. As we've also seen, speakers can exploit this tendency in order to communicate more efficiently – they know how their words will likely be interpreted in the specific context in which they are uttered.

The discipline of pragmatics is concerned with meanings that go beyond those that are usually – semantically – associated with the signals that are being used in communication. In linguistic terms, this means that it is concerned with the meanings of linguistic signals that are not simply part of their semantic meaning. We are interested in how speakers convey these meanings and hearers recover them. And for the reasons discussed in the preceding paragraph, pragmatics is concerned with meaning in context. But in order to be more precise about this, it will be helpful to introduce some definitions.

1.1 Definitions

First, we need to distinguish between sentences and utterances. A **sentence** is an abstract linguistic object, whereas an **utterance** is a unit of speech, produced by a particular speaker on a particular occasion.

Note on terminology
For convenience, I'll adopt the convention of referring to the individual who produces a linguistic utterance as the **speaker** and the one who interprets it as the **hearer**, whichever mode of communication we're dealing with. Of course, the production and comprehension of linguistic signals needn't involve speaking and hearing; it might involve signing and seeing those signs, or writing and reading text. The hearer is sometimes referred to as the **addressee** – that is, specifically the person the speaker is addressing, rather than just someone who happens to hear what is said – but that distinction won't be relevant in this book.

The issue of precisely what constitutes a sentence isn't going to be a particularly important one for us in this book. We might think of it as a unit of language that expresses a complete thought, or we might think of it just as a unit of syntax that admits a particular definition within a theory of grammar. By the same token, we won't make much specific use of the notion of **sentence meaning**, which we could think of as the meaning carried by a sentence (in the absence of context). We will, however, make use of the broader notion of **semantic meaning**. Linguistic semantics is concerned with the meanings of words (**lexical semantics**) and how these meanings contribute, along with syntax, to establishing the meanings of more complex linguistic units, such as sentences. Traditionally, semantics focuses on stable, context-independent meaning: in the case of a word, for instance, we might think of its semantic meaning as the contribution it makes to the meanings of all the phrases and sentences in which it appears.

Note on terminology
We might think of semantic meaning as roughly equivalent to **literal meaning**. But we have to be careful here, particularly in cases such as idioms. A phrase like *kick the bucket* has two possible meanings, one which is predictably connected to the meanings of *kick* and *bucket*, and one which is associated directly with the whole expression ('die'). We might say that the former meaning is literal, and the latter non-literal. However, both are semantic rather than pragmatic (although we might rely on context to figure out which of these meanings a speaker intended, just as in other cases of lexical disambiguation). I'll therefore reserve the term **non-literal** to make this kind of distinction, as in Chapter 6, and will not refer to pragmatic meanings in general as 'non-literal'.

I'll occasionally use the term **pragmatic meaning** to refer to meaning in context, as implicitly contrasted with semantic meaning: that is, it will refer particularly to the aspects of meaning that are contextually determined. However, it's usually going to be helpful to be more specific about this. Assuming that the hearer's goal is to understand what the speaker is attempting to communicate, the focus is on this meaning, which we can refer to as the speaker's **communicative intention**. I will avoid the term 'utterance meaning', because it's not clear whether that should refer to the meaning that the hearer actually recovers, the meaning that the speaker intended, or the meaning that we (as observers) think the utterance ought to have conveyed.

Much of the meaning that we are interested in is **propositional** in nature. Different philosophical traditions vary in their understanding of precisely what a proposition is. For our purposes, we can think of a proposition as being some statement about the world that may be true or false. In (1)–(3), B conveys the proposition that 'B has a credit card', which is part of the semantic meaning of the sentence *I have a credit card* – assuming that *I* refers to the individual B – and also part of the speaker's communicative intention. In (2), B also conveys the proposition that 'B does not need to borrow money from A', which is not part of the semantic meaning of the sentence that they used, but is again part of the speaker's communicative intention. We could call this the pragmatic meaning of the utterance (2).

1.2 Ways of defining pragmatics

Having defined various subsidiary pieces of terminology, what about defining pragmatics itself? This is a surprisingly complex undertaking – many book chapters, and at least one whole book (Ariel 2010), have attempted to do this – so I'm not going to try to resolve that issue here, or offer any prescription as to what pragmatics ought to be, as a field. However, I will try to make clear what I take pragmatics to mean, for the purposes of the present volume.

In the first part of this chapter, I tried to explain the need for pragmatics by pointing out that there is more to linguistic meaning than just semantics – if by semantics we mean the stable, context-independent relations between forms and their meanings. In that spirit, one long-standing approach to pragmatics is to adopt a purely negative definition and declare it to be the study of linguistic meanings that are not semantic. However, one question that naturally arises is whether that makes pragmatics a coherent field in its own right, or whether we're simply treating it as the 'linguistic wastebasket' (Bar-Hillel 1971) – the place to dump all the phenomena that we can't explain more systematically.

Even so, this negative definition of pragmatics has been highly relevant to a lot of research on meaning, in that – as we shall see – a recurring question is whether particular aspects of meaning are best treated as semantic or pragmatic in origin. In considering implicature (Chapters 2 and 3), presupposition (Chapter 4), and speech acts (Chapter 8), among other topics, we will be repeatedly asking to what extent the meanings associated with specific utterances are traceable to the semantic meanings of units of language, such as words, and to what extent they require a distinct pragmatic explanation.

A more positive approach to defining pragmatics is to ask what would constitute a pragmatic explanation of meaning. That is, what unifies pragmatic approaches to these diverse phenomena? As mentioned above, one important aspect of this is appeal to the context of utterance as a contributory factor in linguistic meaning. However, it is difficult to identify precisely which contextual factors should be subsumed into pragmatics, without encroaching on other subfields of linguistics. As a brief illustration of this point, consider (12)–(14).

(12)   Mary admired Elaine because she . . .
(13)   Mary asked Elaine to entertain her.
(14)   Mary asked Elaine to entertain herself.

In each of these examples, we have a pronoun (*she, her, herself*) and two individuals to whom this pronoun might in principle be referring, Mary and Elaine. In (12), the preferred interpretation of *she* is 'Elaine', and this has something to do with the use of the verb *admired*, a point which we'll discuss in more detail in section 5.1.4. In (13), the pronoun refers to Mary, and in (14) it refers to Elaine. In all of these cases, we could honestly say that the interpretation of the pronoun is determined by the prior linguistic context – specifically, the structure of the sentence that contains it – but we would normally think of the interpretations of (13) and (14) as being determined by syntax and semantics rather than by pragmatics. Therefore, simply saying that pragmatics is about how context determines meaning appears to be too broad a definition.

Another positive definition of pragmatics simply identifies it as the study of how we use language. This naturally allows us to include aspects of language that are relevant to the performance of social actions (as discussed in Chapter 8) alongside those that have to do with the more specific task of conveying propositional meaning. However, once again, this is a very broad construal. Sociolinguistics and stylistics seem naturally to fall into this category, and syntax and semantics are clearly also relevant to the performance of social actions through language, so this definition seems rather more inclusive than we would like.

The approach that I will adopt in this book is to focus on those cases in which we are able to intentionally communicate meanings that go beyond what is literally said. I will specifically aim to focus on the cognitive processes that underpin this capability. This approach in fact fits quite well with the conclusions advanced by Ariel (2010). A recurring idea will be that several, if not all, phenomena traditionally regarded as pragmatic have certain points in common, which may be ultimately connected to similarities in the underlying reasoning processes by which speakers decide how to encode their meanings and hearers understand the speakers' intended meanings. I will aim to discuss these various distinct pragmatic topics while also pointing to some of the parallels, both in the phenomena and in their theoretical treatment.

The general approach retains the traditional pragmatic outlook, in that the focus is on speakers, hearers, and how they use language, rather than the structure of language itself. However, an important goal of the enterprise is trying to discover things about human cognition by examining how we reason about meaning. With this goal in mind, I will be interested not only in descriptively adequate accounts of how particular meanings arise in appropriate contexts, but also on psychological evidence concerning the processes by which hearers recover (and speakers encode) those meanings.

1.3 Pragmatics and linguistics

The description of pragmatics as the 'linguistic wastebasket' is emblematic of its rather marginal status within much modern linguistics. Perhaps a significant driver of this has been Chomsky's influential view that linguistics should be concerned with competence rather than performance: that is, that our aim is to study the individual's capacity for language, and not 'the actual use of language in concrete situations' (Chomsky 1965: 4). Given that pragmatics is fundamentally about utterances, it seems clearly to fall on the 'performance' side of this dichotomy, and therefore outside the scope of linguistics as construed by the Chomskyan tradition.

One way of defending pragmatics as a linguistic discipline, then, would be to argue that separating the study of performance and competence is undesirable, or even impossible in practice. This view has many noted adherents and has often been forcefully expressed. However, another option, going back to Hymes (1966), is to argue that there is more to linguistic competence than merely the ability to produce and detect syntactically well-formed sentences, and that we should be thinking in terms of the much broader notion of communicative competence.

On the approach taken in this book, it's completely reasonable to think of pragmatics as being concerned with competence, as opposed to performance, in the Chomskyan sense. The goal of pragmatics is to understand the cognitive abilities that speakers and hearers can employ when conveying and understanding meaning in context – what we might call their **pragmatic competence**. Importantly, what an individual does on any particular occasion isn't necessarily going to be a perfect reflection of their pragmatic competence. In Chapter 3, we'll see experimental data which suggests significant variability in individuals' performance on certain linguistic tasks, but we will not necessarily interpret that as evidence for a difference in their pragmatic competence. In order to understand pragmatic competence, we should in principle need to abstract away from pragmatic performance in just the way that Chomsky articulates for syntax.

So, if our object of study is competence rather than performance, does that make pragmatics a discipline of Chomskyan linguistics after all? Not necessarily. Chomsky's object of study is the human language faculty, which can be defined in a couple of distinct ways. Hauser et al. (2002) distinguish the faculty of language in the broad sense (FLB) from the faculty of language in the narrow sense (FLN). The FLN comprises just the recursive computational system that they take to be fundamental and distinctive to human language, while the FLB includes other subsystems, including a 'conceptual-intentional' system. However, they distinguish the FLB from the even broader category of 'components of the nervous system [that] are recruited in the use of language in its broadest sense' (ibid.: 1570). They go on to argue that FLN is uniquely human, and reflects recent evolutionary developments unique to our species, while FLB as a whole 'has an ancient evolutionary history, long predating the emergence of language' (ibid.: 1573).

It's pretty clear that pragmatics doesn't enter into Hauser et al.'s (2002) idea of FLN — although it could be argued that fundamental pragmatic capabilities are perhaps species-specific and essential to the nature of human communication in much the same way (see for instance Hurford 2007; Scott-Phillips 2014). But it can easily be seen as part of FLB, and therefore potentially part of the linguistic object of study.

Hauser et al. (2002) also note that even the study of FLN can benefit from considering other domains in which the same competencies are potentially relevant, such as number, navigation and social relationships. In that spirit, it is not necessarily a problem that pragmatic reasoning appears to surface in other domains that don't involve human language: in fact, this might also tell us something useful about the underlying pragmatic competence. Consider for instance the much-quoted fictitious example (15).

> (15)   Gregory: Is there any other point to which you would wish to draw
>   my attention?
>   Holmes: To the curious incident of the dog in the night-time.
>   Gregory: The dog did nothing in the night-time.
>   Holmes: That was the curious incident.
>   (Sir Arthur Conan-Doyle, *Silver Blaze*)

Here, Sherlock Holmes interprets the silence of the dog as meaningful: specifically, he realises that the dog would have barked if a stranger had approached, and consequently its failure to do so informs us that no stranger did so. There appears to be a parallel with example (8), discussed earlier, in which a speaker interprets their hearer's silence as an implicit rejection of their request: they realise that the other person would have said 'yes' if they were able to meet the request, and consequently their failure to do so informs us that they cannot.

In short, the pragmatic reasoning process appears to be very similar between these two cases. But, of course, they are very different cases from a linguistic point of view. The hearer in (8) could have employed any one of a multitude of complex utterances, drawing upon the full richness of their linguistic capabilities. By contrast, the dog in (15) could presumably be regarded, as far as the humans in the story are concerned, essentially as a switch with just two possible outputs, 'barking' and 'not barking'. This tiny, finite system of signals is not the kind of thing that modern linguistics is concerned with, and yet we seem to be able to apply the same kind of pragmatic reasoning to it and arrive at appropriate and useful results.

Bearing in mind that pragmatic processes may not just be applicable to language, is it possible to function without pragmatic competence? As far as language is concerned, without pragmatic competence we would still be able to extract the rich semantic meanings that the system makes available to us, although – given how widespread pragmatic enrichment is – presumably this kind of restriction would render our communication much less efficient. In other domains, we might encounter more difficulties. This is not a purely hypothetical question: autism spectrum disorder (ASD) is often considered to involve a selective impairment in pragmatic, but not linguistic, competence. However, in practice, many apparently pragmatic processes turn out to be relatively unproblematic for people with ASD, which suggests that the precise nature of the relevant impairment is more nuanced than the popular view suggests. We'll touch upon this point in Chapter 6.

Finally, given that pragmatics potentially extends beyond the scope of linguistics, why focus our attention on linguistic pragmatics? That's certainly going to be the approach taken in this book, even though some of the experiments discussed here explore the use of signals that aren't obviously representations of natural language. Part of the motivation for focusing on the linguistic angle is to contribute to the general programme of understanding language better, and because the pragmatic interpretation of linguistic material is of enormous practical consequence in all sorts of domains. But from a purely theoretical point of view, natural language is a superb testbed for pragmatics, because of the sheer complexity and sophistication of meanings that can be conveyed and pragmatic enrichments that can arise.

For these reasons, even while taking the view that pragmatics overlaps with but is not necessarily contained within linguistics, this volume will focus on the pragmatics of natural language. But I take it that a certain amount of what follows will also be applicable to more general communicative systems.

1.4 Overview of the book

This book is predominantly organised thematically, with chapters covering the major topics in various different areas of pragmatic research. However, before that, I'll introduce some more general theoretical ideas that have informed the direction of work in pragmatics, which I'll be calling back to at various stages.

Chapter 2, Pragmatic theories, presents a brief introduction to some of the major lines of thought in pragmatic research, and attempts to explain their motivation and how they can potentially be distinguished and validated. It explores the overarching idea that speakers are understood to be cooperative, and that this enables hearers to draw additional inferences about what speakers mean to communicate.

Chapter 3, Implicature, examines one broad category of pragmatic meaning, that in which the speaker conveys an additional meaning by virtue of what they didn't say. Focusing particularly on quantity implicatures – in which the hearer infers the falsity of a stronger statement that the speaker could have made – we look at the various ways in which these could possibly be recovered by hearers, and how experimental evidence has informed the debate about which analysis to adopt.

Chapter 4, Presupposition, considers how utterances have logical prerequisites, and how speakers can exploit this to convey additional information efficiently. We look at some of the competing proposals as to how presupposed meaning can be classified, which make different predictions about the precise status of these meanings and how they are recovered, and consider the advantages and disadvantages of the competing accounts.

Chapter 5, Referring, explores how we use language to refer to entities. We're frequently confronted with a choice about how to refer to a person, place or object, and we're also often confronted with referring expressions that are potentially ambiguous to some extent, such as pronouns. This chapter considers how speakers and hearers coordinate their usage of referring expressions, and what that can tell us about our general tendencies and preferences in pragmatic reasoning.

Chapter 6, Non-literal language, looks at various forms of speech in which the speaker intends to communicate something that is directly contradictory to what they are saying – irony, metaphor, metonymy and hyperbole. We consider to what extent these are violations of normal pragmatic principles and to what extent they can be explained by the same mechanisms that are invoked in cases such as implicature.

Chapter 7, Arranging information in coherent discourse, is about the relationships between units of meaning in longer coherent utterances. Both within and between clauses, speakers can convey additional meanings by structuring the information that they present in particular ways. We look at what kinds of meanings can be communicated in this way, and how hearers understand the relations that speakers try to encode.

Chapter 8, Speech acts, takes a broader perspective, thinking of communication not just as about the flow of information but also as involving the performance of specific social actions. We will see that many of the same issues arise, and need to be resolved, at this level of analysis: what kinds of actions are possible, and how do we resolve the ambiguous relations between utterances and the actions that they are used to perform?

1.5 Summary

Human communication is uniquely complex, not only because of the versatility and expressive power of syntax and semantics, but also because of the non-obvious relationship between the speech signal and the speaker's intended meaning. Pragmatics is concerned with speaker meanings, and explores how speakers express and hearers infer meanings that go beyond the usual meanings of the signals involved. Whether or not we think of this as an aspect of linguistics as such, it is highly relevant to the workings of human communication, and is also part of the human cognitive capacity; moreover, it is potentially worth studying because of its practical implications. In this book we'll consider some of the major ideas about how pragmatics works, and explore how these can be applied to a wide range of topics, ranging from determining the meaning of a pronoun to understanding the social purpose of an utterance.

Exercises

Answers to the following are available at <edinburghuniversitypress. com/pragmatics>.

1. What kinds of pragmatic meanings might be associated with the following utterances? Why is semantics insufficient in helping us understand these utterances?
    a. I haven't had lunch.
    b. I haven't had my holidays yet.

    c. It is what it is.
    d. If John turns up, I'll eat my hat.
    e. I don't think John will come.
    f. Mary saw the man with the binoculars.

2. Suppose that the hearer of the following remarks failed to respond (that is, they 'produced' a silence). How might the speaker interpret that, and why?
    a. You're thinking about *her* again, aren't you?
    b. You're not listening, are you?
    c. Hang on – just give me a second, and then you'll have my full attention.

Discussion questions

1. In section 1.3, I speculated that humans would be able to communicate somewhat effectively relying purely on semantics, in the absence of any pragmatic competence. But what about acquisition? In what ways could we expect a lack of pragmatic ability – broadly construed – to obstruct or slow down the acquisition of language?

2. What kinds of communication difficulties might we expect to run into if we were talking to – or even trying to design – an automated system for understanding language? How many of these difficulties are essentially 'pragmatic' in nature?

2 Pragmatic theories

Headmaster: Of the ten staff who teach Giles, seven of them think that his presence is having a seriously damaging effect on other pupils in the group.

Parent: What about the other three?

Headmaster: Well, they think so too. I'm sorry – I was trying to break it to you gently.

(John Morton, People Like Us, s1e2, 'The Headmaster')

In the mid-nineteenth century, there was a disagreement between two prominent scholars, Sir William Hamilton and John Stuart Mill, about the meaning of the word *some*. Hamilton argued that *some* should be understood logically to mean *some and some only*. Mill argued that this was a mistake, and that what Hamilton proposed to adopt into the logic was actually merely a consequence of common practice in conversation. He observed that:

> If I say to any one, 'I saw some of your children to-day,' he might be justified in inferring that I did not see them all, not because the words mean it, but because, if I had seen them all, it is most likely that I should have said so: though even this cannot be presumed unless it is presupposed that I must have known whether the children I saw were all or not. (Mill 1867: 501)

This is a very early example of an argument over the nature of a particular linguistic meaning, concerning whether we should treat it as semantic or pragmatic. For Hamilton, the 'not all' interpretation of *I saw some of your children today* is a matter of the semantics of *some*. For Mill, it is a matter of pragmatics. In support of his argument, Mill appeals to ideas about how a speaker is expected to behave, and to be understood. Specifically, he argues that the speaker would have said *I saw all of your children today* if that had been (known to be) true: and that because we can assume that this would have happened, we can infer from the speaker's failure to produce this utterance that the stronger proposition is in fact false.

Unfortunately for us, Mill didn't really pursue this idea: his concern was with how to analyse the meaning of *some* (and a handful of other examples involving apparently logical operators in natural language). Consequently, the idea that similar reasoning might apply to all utterances – and that we can appeal to expectations about how speakers are going to behave in order to obtain richer understandings of what they say – wouldn't really be articulated in general terms for another century. In this chapter, we look at several of the main proposals that were eventually put forward about how this process occurs, starting with the first and most influential, due to H. Paul Grice.

2.1 Grice's Cooperative Principle

In his lecture on 'Logic and Conversation', given in 1967 but not published until 1975 (and reprinted in a different collection in 1989), Grice set out to systematise how conversation works. His particular focus was on better understanding a class of meanings that go beyond the semantic content of what is said, which he calls **conversational implicatures**. Much like in Mill's account of *some*, Grice argues that hearers can appeal to generalisations about how speakers tend to act in conversation in order to obtain richer understandings of the speakers' intended meanings. Thus, in order to understand how these richer meanings come about, we first need to understand what those generalisations are that we can make about how speakers act.

For Grice, the heart of the matter is that we expect speakers to be cooperative, and that other expectations about their behaviour naturally flow from this, concerning the quality and quantity of information that they provide, how they provide it, and how it relates to the current discourse purpose. Specifically, he proposes an overarching principle which he calls the **Cooperative Principle** (CP):

> Make your conversational contribution such as is required, at the stage at which it occurs, by the accepted purpose or direction of the talk exchange in which you are engaged. (Grice 1989: 26)

He unpacks this as a series of maxims under the four headings of Quantity, Quality, Relation and Manner, which I will quote directly as follows:

Quantity:
1. Make your contribution as informative as is required (for the current purposes of the exchange).
2. Do not make your contribution more informative than is required.

Quality:
Try to make your contribution one that is true.
1. Do not say what you believe to be false.
2. Do not say that for which you lack adequate evidence.
Relation:
Be relevant.
Manner:
Be perspicuous.
1. Avoid obscurity of expression.
2. Avoid ambiguity.
3. Be brief (avoid unnecessary prolixity).
4. Be orderly.

(Grice 1989: 26–7)

According to Grice, our general expectation is that a cooperative speaker will adhere to the CP and, as far as possible, to these maxims. This provides a possible basis for our subsequent reasoning about their likely communicative intentions, as we shall see.

2.1.1 Reasoning with Grice's Cooperative Principle

On a Gricean account, a hearer can use the assumption that the speaker is cooperative in the relevant sense in order to recover conversational implicatures: that is to say, additional inferences about the speaker's meaning that go beyond the semantics of what they said. The reasoning involved is essentially of the same character as that sketched out by Mill – in fact, the example Mill discusses is potentially a paradigm case of conversational implicature. To illustrate this, we can recapitulate Mill's account of his example in Gricean terms, as follows:

*   The speaker (S) tells the hearer (H) 'I saw some of your children today'. Mill argues that *some* has purely existential meaning, so all that S is saying is that there exist individuals among H's children whom S saw today.
*   S's utterance potentially violates the first submaxim of Quantity: it would have been more informative to say *I saw all of your children today*. Note that under Mill's assumption about the meaning of *some*, S has not explicitly stated whether or not they saw all of H's children today, hence replacing ... *some* ... with ... *all* ... would make the utterance more informative: it would still contain all the information it did before, along with some extra information.
*   H notes this violation of Quantity and looks for an explanation of why S, while being cooperative, should have said ... *some* ... instead

of ... *all* ..... H infers that saying ... *all* ... would have violated another maxim.

- The only possible maxim that *I saw all of your children today* could have violated is Quality. Therefore, H concludes that this utterance would have violated Quality, and therefore that S doesn't know this statement to be true.
- Given that S knows who they saw, if we can further assume that they know how many children H has, S must also know whether or not they saw all of them. If S knows this and doesn't know that *I saw all of your children today* is true, they must know that it's false.
- Hence, H can conclude (under these assumptions) that S did not see all H's children today.

The chain of reasoning, spelled out at this level of detail, seems complex, but the upshot of it is fairly straightforward: by the use of one utterance, the speaker conveys that the use of a more informative one would have resulted in them saying something false. This form of implicature is usually referred to as a **quantity implicature**, which reflects the fact that it could be explained with reference to Grice's quantity maxim, as in the above example. However, Chapter 3 will also go into more detail about other possible explanations for some varieties of quantity implicature.

We can also appeal to Grice's maxims to help us towards an explanation of the more complex non-literal interpretations discussed in Chapter 1. Consider two of the exchanges from Chapter 1, repeated here as (16) and (17).

    (16)   A: I can lend you money for the ticket.
             B: I have a credit card.
    (17)   A: I don't have any money to pay for the ticket.
             B: I have a credit card.

In both of these cases, B's utterance appears, on its semantic meaning, to violate the maxim of Relation. However, assuming that B is cooperative in the Gricean sense, we are entitled to assume that they intend to communicate something that is relevant to the current discourse purpose. In (16), if we can assume that A's utterance is an offer, what would be relevant to the current purpose is for B to indicate whether or not they wish to accept that offer. Hence, bearing in mind the maxim of Relation, it would be sensible for us to try to interpret B's utterance as one that either accepts or declines this offer. By the same token, A's utterance in (17) conveys that there is an obstacle in the way of A fulfilling a particular aim (paying for the ticket). It would therefore be relevant for B to try to address that obstacle, and, again assuming that B is cooperative, it would be sensible for us to try to interpret B's utterance as one that somehow addresses that obstacle.

Of course, the above analysis only gets us part of the way there: it tells us that B's utterance in (16) is probably intended to accept or to decline A's offer, but it doesn't say which. And it tells us that B's utterance in (17) is probably intended to do something about A's inability to pay for the ticket, but it doesn't say what. So we have a bit more to do in order to figure out how we arrive at the specific interpretation that we ultimately do, in both cases. Chapter 8, on speech acts, goes into more detail about the interpretation of utterances of this kind.

A further category of examples discussed by Grice (1989) are often termed **manner implicatures** because, on a Gricean account, they rely upon reasoning that involves the manner maxim. An example that Grice (1989: 37) offers is (18).

(18)   Miss X produced a series of sounds that corresponded closely with the score of 'Home Sweet Home'.

As in the case of the quantity implicature, we can first observe that (18) appears to violate cooperativity: specifically, it is unnecessarily verbose compared with the alternative (19), also from Grice (1989: 37).

(19)   Miss X sang 'Home Sweet Home'.

The hearer can follow essentially the same reasoning as for quantity implicature, and will be led to the conclusion that the speaker is not sure that (19) is true. Thus they arrive at the conclusion that the performance described in (18) is, for some reason, not one about which the word *sang* could truthfully be used, presumably because the performance was defective in some major way by the standards of what constitutes singing. Grice argues that this interpretation is sufficiently obvious to be recoverable by the hearer, and could therefore count as an implicature of (18).

Of course, if it's already clear that Miss X is not attempting to sing in any sense of the word, but is producing sounds in some other way for which we lack a verb (for instance, by playing a glass harp), we wouldn't expect this reasoning to go through. In that case, there wouldn't be any shorter alternative utterance that would do the job of conveying the meaning of (18). Therefore, even though (18) appears somewhat verbose, it wouldn't violate the manner maxim, and hence it wouldn't give rise to any implicature about the quality of the performance.

2.1.2 *The status of conversational implicatures*

In discussing these examples, I've focused almost entirely on the role of the hearer in attempting to calculate the pragmatic meaning that arises from the utterances that they encounter. But what about the speaker? On a Gricean account, the speaker is assumed to be pragmatically competent both with respect to what they do and with respect to what the hearer is going to do. That is to say, they will obey the CP and the maxims; but they will also be aware that the hearer expects them to do this, and will be able to appeal to the CP and maxims in order to perform pragmatic enrichments, in the ways sketched out in the previous subsection.

This is an important point because of the status it gives to implicatures. In the Mill example, a speaker who says *I saw some of your children today* not only permits the hearer to infer that they mean ... *not all* ..., but actually intends the hearer to draw this conclusion. This is fundamental to Grice's conception of conversational implicature. A fully-fledged conversational implicature is something that the speaker deliberately aims to convey – it is part of the speaker's communicative intention. And the speaker typically intends this by producing an utterance that will cause the hearer to perform this kind of pragmatic reasoning in order to recover the speaker's intended meaning. That is, the speaker who says *some* intends the hearer to notice that they could have said *all*, and to draw the relevant conclusions about precisely what they mean to convey.

Conversational implicature à la Grice therefore represents an example of the speaker exploiting the pragmatic system in order to do more with less. By assuming that there is shared knowledge about the conventions that govern conversational interaction, the speaker can communicate additional propositional information without needing to encode it explicitly, relying instead on the hearer's ability to recover it by inference.

It sounds, on this account, as though the speaker is being selfish by deliberately withholding information and forcing the hearer to work it out instead. However, this might be a sensible thing to do for both parties, if we assume that the limiting factor in conversation is how rapidly words can be spoken, rather than how rapidly hearers can understand meanings. If the main limitation is the bandwidth of speech, as argued by Levinson (2000), it would be eminently sensible for both parties to limit the amount of speech that has to take place, even at the cost of requiring more inferential work on the part of the hearer. We will see a similar trick that a speaker can use in Chapter 4, when we discuss the accommodation of presuppositions, which also seems to burden the hearer but which might also have advantages in terms of reducing the number of words that need to be uttered.

2.2 Clarifying the Gricean account

Grice's CP and maxims are enormously widely quoted in the pragmatics literature, but are also frequently misunderstood in some ways. So before we start looking at alternative conceptualisations of cooperativity in conversation, it's worth taking a moment to note some of the subtleties of Grice's formulation, and some of Grice's own concerns about its limitations.

2.2.1 Is the CP a rule?

Grice's CP and maxims are worded as though they are prescriptive statements about how we have to act in order to qualify as cooperative interactors. Nevertheless, it's clear that Grice's purpose in formulating them isn't a prescriptive one. Rather, his point is that these are principles which 'participants will be expected (ceteris paribus) to observe' (Grice 1989: 26): that is to say, 'the assumption ... we seem to make [is] that talkers will in general ... proceed in the manner that these principles prescribe' (ibid.: 28).

In short, these are not rules set out to enable us to judge whether or not someone is being properly cooperative – they are merely generalisations about how we expect people to behave, given that they are cooperative. So while Grice entertains the idea that observance of these maxims might indeed be part of some kind of implied social contract, the crucial point as far as pragmatics is concerned is merely that it is 'a well-recognized empirical fact that people do behave in these ways' (ibid.: 29). Crucially, it's assumed to be something that both the speaker and hearer recognise in a given interaction, which is what makes it a possible basis for the kinds of pragmatic enrichment discussed above.

2.2.2 The content of the maxims

The CP and maxims are enormously widely cited, and often taken to constitute the essence of Grice's philosophy of language. But it's worth adding a note of caution: in the original text, Grice seems to be far from convinced that these are essentially correct in the form in which he gives them. He describes the CP as a 'first approximation to a general principle' and proceeds to enumerate the maxims '[o]n the assumption that some such general principle as this is acceptable' (Grice 1989: 26). He uses the very brief summary description of the maxim of Relation as a placeholder, and says of it that 'its formulation conceals a number of problems that exercise me a good deal' (ibid.: 27). And he takes the Manner maxim to include 'various maxims such as' the four listed above, adding that 'one might need others' (ibid.: 27). So, although Grice is evidently of the view that there are constraints applicable to Relation and Manner that fit within the CP, his own formulation leaves things intentionally vague. It's difficult to tell whether or not a particular instance of usage actually complies with these maxims as they are originally stated.

2.2.3 The relative importance of the maxims

In a similar spirit, most citations of Grice's maxims have retained the headings of Quantity, Quality, Relation and Manner. We can sometimes end up with the impression that Grice intended each of these categories to have roughly equal status. But this is not Grice's view at all. In fact, the existence of these four categories is due to Grice deliberately – but tentatively – echoing a theory of categorisation due to Immanuel Kant. In discussing the maxims, Grice wonders aloud whether the maxim of Quality even belongs in this system, on the basis that it is so much more fundamental to the working of communication than the others: he argues that 'other maxims come into operation only on the assumption that this maxim of Quality is justified' (1989: 27). His decision to retain it seems ultimately to stem from the idea that it is more convenient to have Quality built into the system rather than acting as an overarching principle. It certainly isn't intended to downplay the importance of Quality as compared with the other maxims. As Grice indicated, and as we shall see in Chapter 6, the extent to which a speaker can ever violate Quality, while still being 'cooperative' in a general sense, is somewhat unclear.

In a similar spirit, we might wonder whether Grice intended each of the submaxims to have equal status: and given how provisional the list of submaxims of Manner is, we would be entitled to assume that he did not. For Quantity, Grice makes it quite clear that he does not consider the two submaxims equal. Violating the first submaxim of Quantity (thereby being underinformative) is a potentially serious breach of cooperativity, but violating the second submaxim of Quantity (thereby being overinformative) is barely a violation of the CP at all. In fact, if we did insist upon treating overinformativeness as a violation of the CP, we could analyse it instead as a violation of the maxim of Relation, as it involves the speaker conveying additional information that is not necessary for the current discourse purpose. Corresponding to this difference in importance, a broad class of implicatures arise from apparent violations of the first submaxim of Quantity (as discussed in detail in Chapter 3), whereas the implicatures that could arise from violations of the second submaxim of Quantity are much scarcer and subtler, as we shall see in sections 2.3 and 2.4.

2.2.4 The justification for not having more maxims

Another question is whether the set of maxims that Grice posits is sufficient, or whether there are other things going on in conversation that also need to be accounted for. Grice is aware that there is a strong case for extending the system. As he observes, participants typically follow a range of other principles, such as observing politeness: and moreover, hearers can draw on this awareness to derive interpretations of utterances that go beyond what is literally stated, just as they can use the maxims that he specifies in this way.

Grice's precise justification for excluding politeness from his canon is that he has chosen to focus on things that are what he calls 'specially connected ... with the particular purposes that talk (and so, talk exchange) is adapted to serve and is primarily employed to serve' (1989: 28). This is fair enough if we see talk as being used primarily for the goals of conveying information and directing, or at least influencing, the actions of other people. However, if we construe conversation as being 'talk for the sake of building and maintaining social relationships' (Warren 2006: 102), we would surely have to think of politeness as being deeply connected to that particular purpose.

There are undeniably many occasions on which it is necessary to factor in politeness when attempting to understand the communicative decisions made by a speaker, and how these relate to the meanings that they wish to convey. There is much relevant work on this topic within semantics and pragmatics (see Holtgraves in press for a recent review). However, taking Grice's lead, I will not be focusing on the communicative consequences of politeness in this book (although the topic will briefly feature in the discussion of indirect speech acts in Chapter 8).

2.3 Horn's functionalist approach: Q- and R-principles

Following Grice's example, but taking into account the provisional nature of his account, subsequent researchers have attempted to capture the same kinds of insight in various different ways. One notable attempt to do so is made by Laurence Horn in a 1984 paper.

Horn argues that we can treat conversation within a more general functionalist approach to language articulated by Zipf (1949), in which there are two competing forces, unification and diversification. Unification, also termed Speaker's Economy, is 'a drive towards simplification' (Horn 1984: 11), which if left to its own devices would ultimately cause us to have just one, completely ambiguous, verbal signal with which to express all meanings. Diversification, also termed Auditor's Economy, leads us 'toward the establishment of as many different expressions as there are messages to communicate' (ibid.: 11). The tension between these two forces leaves us with an intermediate kind of system that economises in complexity by allowing some ambiguity, but leaves us with enough different expressions to make communication possible.

Horn takes Grice's hint and sets aside Quality as a *sine qua non* of communication: but then, in the spirit of Zipf's approach, he proposes to reformulate the other maxims under two headings, which address the needs of the hearer and the speaker respectively (ibid.: 13):

> **The Q-principle** (Hearer-based)
> Make your contribution sufficient.
> Say as much as you can (given R).
> **The R-principle** (Speaker-based)
> Make your contribution necessary.
> Say no more than you must (given Q).
>
> (Horn 1984: 13)

The choice of the labels Q and R for these principles is deliberately intended to evoke the Quantity and Relation maxims in Grice's account, but leaving some room for manoeuvre. In fact, Horn sees his Q-principle as recapitulating Grice's first submaxim of Quantity, but his R-principle as embracing Grice's second submaxim of Quantity in addition to his maxims of Relation and Manner. He follows Grice in noting that the obvious reason why a contribution could be considered more informative than is required for the current discourse purpose (and thus a violation of Quantity-2) would be that it presents information that is irrelevant to the current purpose (and is thus a violation of Relation).

Under Horn's account, the Q-principle does essentially the same job as Grice's maxim of Quantity in enabling the speaker to convey and the hearer to recover quantity implicatures. But for Horn, there is a neat symmetry between the implicatures that arise from the Q-principle and those that arise from the R-principle. In the Q-implicatures, like in the case of Gricean Quantity implicature, the speaker who asserts some proposition p means to convey *at most p* (that is, the falsity of additional propositions). In the R-implicatures, the speaker who asserts some proposition p means to convey *more than p*, like in the case of Gricean Manner implicature.

An important feature of this account is how it resolves the conflict between the Q- and R-principles. Horn argues that the general answer to this involves what McCawley (1978) calls the 'division of pragmatic labor'. Under this account,

> the use of a marked (relatively complex and/or prolix) expression when a corresponding unmarked (simpler, less 'effortful') alternate expression is available tends to be interpreted as conveying a marked message (one which the unmarked alternative would not or could not have conveyed. (Horn 1984: 22)

Horn argues that this pattern arises in language as a consequence of unmarked forms being associated with unmarked meanings through R-based inference, and marked forms being associated with marked meanings through Q-based inference.

Although the motivation for it is a bit complicated, the division of pragmatic labour offers a potentially more direct account of some pragmatic meanings: for instance, the Manner implicature discussed earlier. In the examples from Grice (1989: 37), repeated below, (18) is marked by comparison with (19), in that it is more complex and verbose. According to Horn, the utterance of (18) should therefore encourage the hearer to infer that it conveys something other than the meaning of the unmarked (19) – in this case, that something other than typical singing has taken place.

(18)   Miss X produced a series of sounds that corresponded closely with the score of 'Home Sweet Home'.

(19)   Miss X sang 'Home Sweet Home'.

In a similar spirit, the utterance of *I broke a finger*, mentioned in Chapter 1, invites R-based inference to the unmarked interpretation, namely that the finger broken is the speaker's own.

2.4 Levinson's Q-, I- and M-heuristics

Still another way of describing cooperative conversational behaviour is offered by Stephen Levinson, who develops a system that posits three principles, labelled Q-, I- and M-heuristics. In terms of their scope, these heuristics broadly map onto the Gricean maxims. Levinson's Q-heuristic roughly corresponds to Grice's first submaxim of Quantity, the I-heuristic to Grice's second submaxim of Quantity, and the M-heuristic to (parts of) Grice's maxim of Manner. The heuristics are summarised briefly by Levinson as follows:

> Q: 'What isn't said, isn't.'
> I: 'What is simply described, is stereotypically exemplified.'
> M: 'What's said in an abnormal way, isn't normal.'
>
> (Levinson 2000: 31–3)

This account differs from Horn's in how it separates out the component parts of cooperativity. But Levinson's motivation for doing this is not merely to articulate the notion of cooperativity more clearly, and his decision to label these as 'heuristics' is not merely a cosmetic difference from Horn's account. Levinson proposes that these three heuristics in fact directly guide our interpretation and are respectively 'invoked by the kinds of linguistic expressions employed' (2000: 136), a point we'll return to shortly.

Each of Levinson's heuristics can be unpacked as a maxim directed towards the speaker, specifying how they should act in conversation, and a corollary for the hearer, specifying the inferences that they are entitled to draw. In the case of the Q-heuristic, the speaker's maxim requires them to refrain from providing a statement that is 'information-ally weaker than your knowledge of the world allows' (ibid.: 76), subject to the need to obey the corresponding maxim for the I-heuristic. The hearer's corollary is that the speaker can be taken to be making the strongest statement consistent with what they know. Thus, again, the Q-heuristic explains the classic scalar implicature, in that the speaker's utterance in Mill's example (*I saw some of your children today*) directly entitles the hearer to infer that the speaker does not know the stronger alternative (. . . *all* . . .) to be true.

Levinson's M-heuristic instructs the speaker to 'indicate an abnormal, non-stereotypical situation by using marked expressions that contrast with those you would use to describe the corresponding normal, stereo-typical situation' (ibid.: 136). The hearer can correspondingly assume that a marked message corresponds to a marked situation. In this way, for instance, the utterance of (18) immediately directs the hearer to assume that there was indeed something about Miss X's performance that rendered it a non-stereotypical display of singing.

Finally, in Levinson's I-heuristic – which is perhaps the most striking departure from earlier accounts – the speaker is required to 'produce the minimal linguistic information sufficient to achieve your communicative ends (bearing Q in mind)' (ibid.: 114). The hearer is correspondingly entitled to enrich the speaker's utterance, unless the speaker has used a marked expression that violates the I-heuristic. As an example of the type of enrichment he has in mind, Levinson suggests that the hearer can 'assume the richest temporal, causal and referential connections between described situations or events, consistent with what is being taken for granted' (ibid.: 114). This suggests, for instance, that the minimal and rather non-specific utterance *I have a credit card* produced by B in (16) and (17) should naturally attract pragmatic enrichment, because of the way in which it can be understood to relate to the preceding utterance context. It also accounts for why the speaker's use of an unmarked expression such as *I broke a finger* attracts a referential enrichment to the effect that the finger is the speaker's own.

The reason that Levinson proposes to retain the I-heuristic as a separate entity – when it is articulated as part of the maxim of Quantity by Grice, and is rolled up into the R-principle by Horn – is that, in Levinson's account, each of the three heuristics is invoked by a specific, different kind of expression. When an utterance is produced that contrasts with a more informative utterance, the Q-heuristic is invoked and the hearer can thereby infer that the more informative version of the utterance is not available. When a marked expression is used, the M-heuristic is invoked and the hearer can thereby infer that an opposing interpretation is intended to that which would have arisen from the corresponding unmarked expression. And when a minimal expression is used, the I-heuristic is invoked and the hearer can thereby infer that a maximal interpretation is called for. (When more than one heuristic is potentially invoked, Q takes priority, then M, then I.)

Levinson articulates these ideas within a general framework that he calls Generalized Conversational Implicature (GCI). He focuses upon a distinction that is suggested (and named) by Grice (1989) but not fully elaborated there, which is between conversational implicatures that arise only in specific contexts and conversational implicatures that usually arise unless there are specific contextual reasons why they should not. Levinson proposes that there is a categorical distinction between these two types of implicature. On his view, this latter category of implicatures, GCIs, arise through the use of heuristics, whereas the former category (Particularized Conversational Implicatures or PCIs) rely on contextually bound reasoning of the kind that might involve consideration of Grice's maxims. As we'll see in Chapter 3, this naturally implies a difference in the time-course on which these two categories of meaning become available, which – particularly in the case of quantity implicatures – has been the subject of much experimental investigation.

2.4.1 Two ways of enriching some

For Levinson, an inference like that from *some* to *not all* is naturally construed as a GCI, which is incidentally why it is so easily mistaken for a semantic meaning of *some*. Notably, sentences involving *some* that give rise to the GCI *not all* interpretation may also give rise to PCIs, but these are considerably less robust.

To illustrate the distinction between Levinson's GCIs and PCIs, we can look at a trope of socio-political discourse, termed the '"Some of my best friends" defense' by the New Republic (https://newrepublic. com/article/90059/gop-rick-santorum-best-friend-defense). (20)–(22) present examples of this.

(20)   Some of my best friends are Republicans, and although we have had our political fights, we have never fallen out and quarrelled. (John Worth Kern, 1908)

(21)   Understand I am not a foe of the Catholics. Some of my dearest friends are Catholic. (John Roach Straton, 1928)

(22)   Hacker: I think you're a sexist.
       . . . Sir Humphrey: I'm not anti-feminist! I love women! Some of my best friends are women! My wife, indeed.
       (Antony Jay and Jonathan Lynn, *Yes Minister*, s3e1, 'Equal Opportunities')

In this trope, a speaker asserts that some of their best friends possess a particular characteristic, or are members of a particular group, that has traditionally been the object of prejudice. It's understood that the speaker's intended purpose in using the phrase is to deny an implicit or explicit accusation that they themselves are prejudiced against that group. Of course, given the widespread suspicion that the 'some of my best friends' defence is used only by people in denial about their prejudices, the hearer may be unlikely to believe this denial, but that doesn't preclude the speaker from trying to convey it.

Taking it that the speaker's objective is to communicate a message to the effect of 'I am not prejudiced against members of this group', what kind of meaning is this? In the first place, it's a meaning that is context-dependent: the same kind of utterance in a neutral context wouldn't convey the message that the speaker was attempting to deny their prejudice, as shown by (23). We would therefore be obliged to treat this implicature as a PCI, in Levinson's terms.

(23)   A: Are any of your best friends black?
       B: Yes, some of my best friends are black. What's your point?

However, at the same time, all these examples are also predicted to give rise to a GCI as a consequence of the use of *some*, and thereby yield the interpretation that *not all* the speaker's friends are Republican, Catholic, women, or black, respectively. And this interpretation does seem to be available, irrespective of the context. In fact, it's available even though it could be argued to run counter to the speaker's main objective – surely the speaker who is denying prejudice doesn't intend to point out to their hearer that 'not all their friends are X'? The idea that this is a GCI explains why the interpretation of *some* as 'some but not all' still seems to arise even in a discourse context that would be unsupportive of it, if we were to focus solely on the speaker's intention.

Levinson's proposal, then, not only carves up the space of cooperative conversational moves slightly differently, but offers a distinctively different account of how these moves lead to pragmatic consequences, which seems to reflect some distinctions that are observable in practice. We now turn to another influential proposal that argues for yet another distinct way of deriving pragmatic enrichments.

2.5 Relevance Theory

Relevance Theory (RT), developed by Dan Sperber and Deirdre Wilson and first published in 1986, is perhaps the most consequential departure from Grice's approach to cooperative communication. For Sperber and Wilson, the crucial aspect of cooperation is relevance, and a fully-fledged account of what this means in practice will be the central plank of a theory of communication. They hold that 'utterances raise expectations of relevance not because speakers are expected to obey a Co-operative Principle and maxims or some other specifically communicative convention, but because the search for relevance is a basic feature of human cognition, which communicators may exploit' (Wilson and Sperber 2002: 250–1).

Within an RT framework, an 'input' to a hearer's reasoning – for instance, an utterance – will be by definition more relevant if it yields greater cognitive effects, and (separately) if it requires less cognitive effort to process. The precise definition of 'cognitive effect' has been a topic of research within RT: Wilson and Sperber settle on the formulation that 'a positive cognitive effect is a worthwhile difference to the individual's representation of the world – a true conclusion, for example' (2002: 251). Processing effort, meanwhile, is to be measured in terms of the 'effort of perception, memory and inference required' (ibid.: 252).

Relevance Theory argues that hearers have an automatic tendency to maximise relevance because this is how our cognitive systems have evolved. This observation is termed the Cognitive Principle of Relevance. The existence of this principle creates a communicative opportunity for the speaker, because they can exploit this tendency by creating stimuli that will attract the hearer's attention, prompt the hearer to reason about them in a particular way, and thus derive the conclusion that the speaker means them to. The specific kind of stimulus that is intended to attract the hearer's attention is called an **ostensive** stimulus.

RT also proposes that 'every ostensive stimulus conveys a presumption of its own optimal relevance', an axiom that Sperber and Wilson term the Communicative Principle of Relevance (ibid.: 256). On this account, the very fact of an utterance being made tells the hearer two things: first, that it is worth processing, and second, that it is the most relevant utterance that the speaker was willing or able to produce. Importantly, the Communicative Principle of Relevance doesn't guarantee that the speaker's utterance is necessarily the out-and-out best, or most relevant, one that could possibly be made under the circumstances: it's merely the best one that the speaker can come up with. After all, the speaker doesn't know precisely what the hearer knows, or how the hearer is going to reason about the utterance, and therefore can't be sure precisely what cognitive effects their utterance will bring about.

Another reason why the speaker's utterance might not be objectively optimal in terms of relevance is that it might be hard for the speaker to formulate the optimal utterance, and the speaker has a limited amount of time and effort to expend on trying to do so. In Chapter 5, when discussing referring expressions, we'll see some specific examples of cases in which the speaker might not be inclined to waste effort in formulating a truly optimal utterance. But more general examples are all around us. For instance, I'm attempting to make this book optimally relevant, in that I'm doing the best I can to ensure that it maximises the positive cognitive effects for the reader and minimises the cognitive effort involved in achieving these effects. Yet it's undeniable that I could do better, and certainly if I spent the rest of my life rewriting it I would hope to do better – so there's implicitly a trade-off between the effort spent in formulating utterances and their effectiveness at achieving relevance. In short, we have to agree that by 'optimal relevance' we can only really mean 'optimal relevance subject to the other constraints on the speaker'.

The hearer's comprehension procedure, as articulated by Wilson and Sperber, then calls for them to 'follow a path of least effort in computing cognitive effects', and 'stop when [their] expectations of relevance are satisfied' (ibid.: 259). The ultimate destination that the hearer arrives at, by following this reasoning process, will constitute the hearer's best guess as to what the speaker's communicative intention was. Bearing this in mind, the task of the speaker is effectively to guess at the route that the hearer will take through the reasoning process, consider where that process will terminate, and select an utterance that will cause the hearer to terminate at the correct interpretation (the one that actually does correspond to the speaker's communicative intention).

We can exemplify this by considering a pair of exchanges discussed in Chapter 1, repeated below as (24) and (25).

(24)   A: I don't have any money to pay for the ticket.
       B: I have a credit card.
(25)   A: I don't have any money to pay for the ticket.
       B: I have a credit card, but I'm afraid it won't be accepted here.

In both of these cases, A volunteers a piece of information. B, automatically looking for optimal relevance, arrives at the conclusion that A is not merely providing a piece of information for their benefit but wants them to do something about it. Presumably B reasons that, if A didn't want them to take an action, this piece of information simply wouldn't be worth providing at all, and hence A's utterance would fail to adhere to the Communicative Principle of Relevance.

In (24), B responds with an assertion, which A, now in the role of hearer, interprets, again assuming that the utterance adheres to the Communicative Principle of Relevance. Again, the semantic content of the assertion on its own seems insufficient to justify B producing the utterance at all, so A attempts to derive a richer intended meaning. As A has implicitly asked B to pay for the ticket, an obvious line of reasoning for A to follow is to look for a way in which B's utterance is relevant to this request: and in this case, it's easy to see its potential relevance, because it suggests that B is able to pay for the ticket. However, this still doesn't satisfy A's expectations of relevance – the fact that B is able to pay for the ticket doesn't itself resolve A's problem, unless B is actually willing to pay for the ticket – so they are licensed to go further and infer that B is in fact willing to pay for the ticket, thus interpreting B's utterance as an offer.

By contrast, in (25), B's assertion can again be interpreted as optimally relevant, but this time it suggests that B is not able to pay for the ticket. Although this interpretation obviously doesn't satisfy A's request, it does satisfy their search for relevance in B's utterance: it is useful to A to know that B is unable to pay for the ticket, not least because it precludes the need for further discussion. On this analysis, the difference with (24) is not merely that (25) hedges around the offer by suggesting that it might not be able to solve A's problem; rather, by adding this additional information, B arguably prevents their own utterance from getting as far as being interpreted as an offer at all. (It is not clear whether B is willing to try to buy the ticket with their card, although they don't explicitly rule this out.)

Relevance Theory also differs from a Gricean approach in the way it characterises the status of pragmatic meanings. Sperber and Wilson (1986) identify a level of meaning that they call **explicature**, which captures the fact that, on their view, pragmatic reasoning processes can contribute to the truth-conditional meaning of the utterance – that is, the proposition that is explicitly communicated, rather than the implicature. To repeat one further example from the first chapter, the utterance of (26) usually gives rise to the meaning (27), an understanding that requires some kind of pragmatic inference. On an RT account this is usually regarded as an explicature, which is unproblematic because there is no reason why pragmatic reasoning cannot contribute to an understanding of the explicit content of the sentence; however, this is controversial in approaches that assume that 'literal' propositional meaning has a privileged status. From a Gricean point of view, we might say that (26) means exactly what it says, but implicates the additional meaning encoded in (27).

(26)   Anna and Bez are married.

(27)   Anna and Bez are married to each other.

The assignment of reference to pronouns is also usually considered part of the explicature, in RT terms: so for instance the explicature of B's utterance in (24) makes reference to the proposition 'B has a credit card' rather than 'I have a credit card'. However, I won't make any particular use of this point in the discussion of referring expressions in Chapter 5.

2.6 Comparing and testing these approaches

The preceding sections present several different ways in which we can try to describe and model cooperative human interaction. The insight that motivates all of these approaches is that we can communicate meanings that go far beyond what is explicitly said, and that this capability is somehow associated with the fact that typical conversational behaviour predictably adheres to certain principles. Where different accounts disagree is on precisely what these principles are, and how speakers and hearers actually make use of this shared knowledge to arrive at richer understandings of utterances in conversation. There may consequently also be differences of opinion as to which specific interpretations can possibly arise through pragmatic processes: we'll see one such example in section 3.3.2, where we discuss so-called 'embedded implicatures'.

Grice's maxims represent a first attempt to formalise the conversational system, and they offer an explanation of how several major categories of non-literal meaning can arise as a consequence of reasoning about literal meanings. Although Grice didn't intend his account to constitute a psychological theory of utterance interpretation, it can be understood as one with relatively few auxiliary assumptions (Geurts 2010: 66–7). As a psychological theory, it typically posits a process in which the hearer is expected first to understand the full literal meaning of the sentence that is uttered, and then to consider whether to draw additional inferences about the speaker's meaning, based on consideration of the maxims.

From this point of view, Horn's (1984) contribution in terms of reformulating the maxims is an attempt to elucidate that reasoning process. Levinson's (2000) reformulation, however, goes further, in that he commits to the idea that the maxims can in fact be regarded as heuristics, and that certain forms naturally invite the hearer to draw pragmatic inferences based on alternatives that could have been used instead. Crucially, Levinson's account doesn't oblige the hearer to consider the full literal meaning of the utterance before engaging in pragmatic enrichment. As we shall see in Chapter 3, much of the recent debate around certain forms of quantity implicature in particular has been between two viewpoints: one in which the implicature is based upon traditional Gricean post-propositional reasoning, and one in which it relies upon shortcuts that involve or abstractly resemble Levinson's Q-heuristic.

Relevance Theory offers another construal of the reasoning process, although it still draws upon Grice's insight that the speaker's task is to enable the hearer to reconstruct their communicative intention. As inferences in RT rely on context, we can see it as patterning with Grice's approach against the heuristic account of Levinson (2000), and in experimental work since then it has often been taken as the paradigmatic modern version of a contextual account of implicature.

Considered as a framework, Relevance Theory has certainly proved useful: it provides an elegant way to describe the communicative advantages and disadvantages of particular utterances. Considered as a specific account of the psychological processes by which we draw pragmatic inferences, it is harder to evaluate. The crucial difficulty with trying to verify the claims of Relevance Theory is that its predictions about what should happen in specific cases are often unclear. In RT, the hearer's interpretative process is left deliberately theoretically unconstrained. As Kent Bach rather critically puts it, 'What it amounts to, really, is to consider hypotheses about what the speaker means in the order they occur to you – how else? – and to stop as soon as a sufficiently plausible one comes to mind' (2006: 3).

We can see some of the difficulties here with reference to the example *Some of my best friends are X*. As discussed earlier, in a context in which the speaker is accused of being prejudiced, this seems to admit two potential kinds of pragmatic enrichment, one in which the hearer is attempting to convey the message 'I am not prejudiced against people who are X', and another in which they convey 'Not all of my best friends are X'. This latter inference from *some*, however precisely it arises (see Chapter 3 for further discussion), is presumably a very routine inference and available at low cost, because it's the usual kind of inference that we derive when we encounter the word *some*. Moreover, it does contribute information that could be relevant to the hearer: as pointed out earlier, knowing that 'not all' the speaker's friends are X might weaken their argument about not being prejudiced, and in that respect it's a useful thing for the hearer to know. Nevertheless, our intuition is that the former inference – that the speaker intends to convey that they are not prejudiced – seems to be the one that we tend to arrive at. And this meaning is certainly important, in the context of utterance; but against that, it's a highly context-specific inference, involves quite elaborate reasoning and is altogether presumably much more costly to derive than the simple 'not all' reading. In short, as hearers, we're invited to make a choice between a low-cost inference with modest cognitive effects and a high-cost inference with high cognitive effects. RT doesn't offer a good way of comparing these options, and doesn't make a clear prediction about which route the hearer is expected to take.

Sperber and Wilson are clearly aware of these issues. They note that not all utterances can be satisfactorily compared in terms of the relevance they achieve, in practice, and perhaps even in principle. In fact, they take the view that it would be unrealistic to quantify relevance thoroughly, given the many factors that bear upon it: as they remark,

> while some aspects of human cognitive processes can already be measured 'from the outside' (e.g. processing time) and others may be measurable in principle (e.g. number of contextual implications), it is quite possible that others are not measurable at all (e.g. strength of implications, level of attention). (Wilson and Sperber 2002: 253)

Sperber and Wilson nevertheless hold that RT is essentially testable, with the caveat that 'as with other theories of comparable scope, its most general tenets can be tested only indirectly, by evaluating some of their consequences' (ibid.: 278). However, were RT to be essentially wrong, falsifying it would still pose a considerable challenge. Wilson notes that the hearer-referring Cognitive Principle of Relevance would be falsified by '[e]vidence that attention is *systematically* allocated on some other basis: e.g. to inputs which are informative without being relevant, which yield many associations but few inferential effects, which are cheap to process regardless of any expected effects, etc.' (2012: 4). But of course, if it should transpire – as Wilson and Sperber (2002) foreshadow – that the level of attention is not actually measurable, trying to demonstrate how it is allocated seems impossible, and falsification of this principle appears to be closed off.

In any case, the goal of this book is not to advocate for one or another general approach to pragmatic theory. The different accounts presented in this chapter will recur in different forms throughout this volume, with some approaches appearing particularly well suited for particular phenomena. It is perhaps an oversimplification to imagine that any one of these accounts could ultimately be regarded as definitive to the exclusion of the others. In practice, fully understanding linguistic communication appears to involve the kinds of inference about conversational goals and speaker intentions shared by these accounts, along with other kinds of reasoning that we will say less about in this book, for instance concerning how linguistic expressions are typically used by speakers.

2.7 Summary

Grice's characterisation of cooperative conversational behaviour has been enormously influential, and offers a framework for explaining how various kinds of pragmatic meaning come about. Subsequent researchers have drawn upon these insights and offered several different potential advances on Grice's account, typically positing a different array of conversational principles or maxims from those offered by Grice. These accounts can generally be interpreted as making different claims about the precise nature of the pragmatic enrichment process. In the following chapter, we shall begin to see how some of these claims can be clarified theoretically and tested experimentally.

Exercises

Answers to the following are available at <edinburghuniversitypress. com/pragmatics>.

1. Which Gricean maxims are being violated by the utterances in bold in the following exchanges?

a. A: Should we start now, or should we wait?
B: **Yes.**
Frasier: By calling her so many times you give her all the power.
You're much better off coming from a position of strength.
Niles: **Don't pour that sherry on your shirt, it will stain.**
Frasier: What?
Niles: I'm sorry, I thought this was the portion of the afternoon
where we gave each other patently obvious advice.
(Michael Kaplan, *Frasier*, s4e8, 'Our Father Whose Art Ain't
Heaven')

b. Jim Hacker: When you give your evidence to the Think Tank,
are you going to support my view that the Civil Service is over-
manned and feather-bedded, or not? Yes or no? Straight answer.
Sir Humphrey: **Well, Minister, if you ask me for a straight
answer, then I shall say that, as far as we can see, looking
at it by and large, taking one thing with another in terms of
the average of departments, then in the final analysis it is
probably true to say that, at the end of the day, in general
terms, you would probably find that, not to put too fine a
point on it, there probably wasn't very much in it one way
or the other.**
(Antony Jay and Jonathan Lynn, *Yes Minister*, s1e5,
'The Writing on the Wall')

2. What would be the 'unmarked' form corresponding to the following utterances? How do the marked and unmarked forms differ in
meaning?
a. Mary made the car stop.
b. The general caused the soldier to die.
c. I don't disagree with you.

3. What are the limitations of Grice's maxims in explaining the utterances in bold in the following?
a. Motorist: Can I park here?
Passer-by: **It's all the same to me.**
b. A: Isn't the food wonderful?
B: **Yeah.**

Discussion questions

1. Grice's account of communication proposes a clear difference
between what a speaker means to communicate and what the hearer
might actually infer from their utterance. Is that a clear-cut issue?
Are there cases in which it's difficult to tell whether a speaker meant

to convey something or merely did so accidentally? (Consider for example the instances of silence discussed in the exercises in Chapter 1.)

2. If we included politeness in the system, hearers would presumably want to take account of differences between speakers in terms of how disposed they are to be polite, in various social environments. Do we have to take account of individual differences in people's adherence to Grice's original maxims?

3 Implicature

> When I say *everybody*, I mean some people, and when I say *always*, I mean some of the time. Like everybody always does.
>
> (Daniel Kitson)

In Chapter 2, we looked at some of the different theoretical accounts of pragmatics, which ultimately set out to explain how hearers go about understanding what speakers mean, when this goes far beyond what they actually say. The crucial observation that underpins these ideas is that speakers are, in some sense, cooperative. Hearers know this and can use that fact to infer additional information about what the speaker intends to communicate.

In this chapter, we focus on one broad class of the meanings that arise from this process, those which are traditionally called implicatures. We will look at the defining qualities of implicature, and see how different kinds of implicatures can be distinguished from one another, drawing principally on Grice's account but also considering some of the competing proposals discussed in Chapter 2.

It is worth bearing in mind that many theoretical accounts of pragmatic meaning are *post hoc* explanations, in the sense that they are formulated after the data are already known, and are thus designed to fit those data. Take for example the inference from the word *some* to the meaning 'some but not all'. Mill's (1867) account of how this inference arises was perhaps the first time anyone had offered a pragmatic explanation of it, but hearers had presumably been interpreting *some* that way for centuries (which is why Hamilton thought that it might be part of the semantic meaning).

In a lot of cases like this, there is little dispute about the actual facts concerning how hearers tend to interpret particular utterances: the theoretical disagreements concern what kind of knowledge hearers rely on, or which mechanisms they use, in order to derive these interpretations. Consequently, we aren't always able to choose between rival theories on the basis of how well they explain the hearer's ultimate interpretation – most of the time, all the theories that are under serious consideration do this perfectly well. For this reason, part of the theoretical debate in recent years has focused on tracking down those few rather rare and unusual circumstances in which the theories do make different predictions about which interpretations should be available to hearers. But a larger part of the debate has focused on the question of whether there is psychological evidence for the existence of the type of processing that each theory posits. Many prominent theorists within the various traditions have ultimately come to endorse the idea that this kind of psychological evidence is what we will need in order to draw definitive conclusions about how implicature works.

With this psychological angle in mind, the latter part of this chapter will specifically examine one type of implicature: the subclass of quantity implicatures known as scalar implicatures. Scalar implicatures have been the focus of a particularly long-running and sometimes illuminating theoretical and experimental debate. However, before narrowing our focus in this way, we will examine implicature more generally, looking at what its various forms have in common and what distinguishes them from one another.

3.1 Defining and distinguishing implicature

What precisely is implicature? Grice introduces implicature as a cover term for any kind of meaning that is part of what a speaker 'implied, suggested, [or] meant' (1975: 24) as opposed to what they actually said. However, he is immediately aware that this distinction is problematic because it depends on an appropriate understanding of what it means to 'say' something. For Grice, what someone has 'said' is 'closely related to the conventional meaning of the words (sentence) . . . uttered' (ibid.: 25). However, on his account, even if something is 'closely related to the conventional meaning of the words . . . uttered', that does not automatically make it part of 'what is said'. The first example Grice gives of a conventional meaning that does not contribute to 'what is said' in this sense is repeated here as (28), while another classic example is given as (29).

(28)   He is an Englishman; he is, therefore, brave.
(29)   Martha is poor but happy.

Grice argues that the speaker of (28) is committed to three distinct claims about the person being spoken of: that he is an Englishman, that he is brave, and that the fact of him being brave follows logically from the fact of him being an Englishman. However, although the speaker is committed to all these meanings, the last one is – for Grice – not part of what the speaker has explicitly *said*. In a similar vein, the speaker of (29) is expressing three things: that Martha is poor, that Martha is happy, and that there is some kind of contradiction, or at least tension, between being poor and being happy. But again, this last meaning is not part of what the speaker has said. For Grice, these 'unsaid' meanings are **conventional implicatures**: they count as implicatures by virtue of being outside what is explicitly said, and as conventional because they are irrevocably attached to the words that give rise to them (*therefore* in (28), *but* in (29)).

The distinction between conventional implicatures and semantic meaning is rather subtle in cases like this. In drawing that distinction, we rely on the assumption that it would be possible for an utterance like (28) or (29) to be judged as true if the conjuncts are both true, even if the conventionally implicated meaning is judged to be false. Suppose that you know that Martha is indeed both poor and happy, but you reject the idea that there's any tension between poverty and happiness. Could you declare (29) to be false? According to the conventional implicature account of *but*, you might be unwilling to do so, because the part of the meaning that you are objecting to (the supposed conventional implicature) does not have the same logical force as the parts of the meaning that you agree with.

The crucial contrast here is between implicature and the logical notion of **entailment**. The relation of entailment holds between two propositions if the truth of one guarantees the truth of the other: that is, we say that 'p entails q' if the proposition q is true in all the cases in which the proposition p is true. To put it another way, if the semantic meaning of an utterance entails something that is false, that utterance is false as well. (31), for instance, is an entailment of (30), on the basis of the semantic meaning of the lexical item *assassinated*. Consequently, given that we know that (31) is false, we know that (30) is also false.

(30)   John Hinckley Jr assassinated Ronald Reagan in 1981.
(31)   Ronald Reagan died in 1981.

Similarly, (28) entails that 'he is an Englishman' and also entails that 'he is brave', and if we know that either of these claims about the person being described is incorrect, we wouldn't hesitate to judge (28) false. However, according to Grice, (28) merely implicates that being English indicates bravery: so if we know that not all Englishmen are brave, that doesn't necessarily constitute sufficient reason to judge (28) false.

Conventional implicatures are often considered to be part of pragmatics because they deal with meanings that go beyond what is literally said. On the other hand, they don't appear to rely on context to any very pronounced extent, and the hearer doesn't seem to need to engage in any very elaborate reasoning process in order to recover them. In these respects, conventional implicatures are somewhat marginal to pragmatics, as defined in Chapter 1. And it's certainly not obvious that studying conventional implicature will tell us much about pragmatic competence in humans, which is the central object of study for this book. Hence, I don't propose to discuss conventional implicature further here.

By contrast with conventional implicatures, **conversational implicatures** of the kind described in the last chapter are assumed by Grice to be context-dependent. As Grice notes, they need to be calculable, in the sense that the hearer has to be able to recover the meaning that the speaker intends to communicate, which is not necessarily a trivial matter when the speaker's intended meaning has nothing to do with the conventional meaning of the words uttered. More importantly, even in the case of Generalized Conversational Implicatures (GCIs), the meaning conveyed by a conversational implicature may be cancelled, or fail to arise in a particular context.

On Grice's account, it has to be possible for a conversational implicature not to arise, because the calculation of any conversational implicature relies upon the assumption that the speaker is observing the Cooperative Principle, and this is something that the speaker can opt out of. Failing to obey the Cooperative Principle doesn't necessarily make the speaker a liar, or make their utterances deficient, but it does mean that the usual conversational implicatures cease to be available. (32) is a classic example.

(32)   A: I'd like to write to John. Where does he live?
        B: Somewhere in France.

If we assume that B is cooperative, their utterance would suggest that they don't know precisely where John lives. In Gricean terms, they are apparently violating the first submaxim of Quantity, in that they are not providing enough information for A's needs. A can infer that this is because any statement that B could make that is specific enough not to violate Quantity would violate some other maxim, so it's likely that B is ignorant of John's exact location, and therefore if they attempted to make a precise statement about it they would violate Quality. However, there's an alternative possibility: we might think that B is opting out of cooperativity, because B doesn't want to tell A where John lives, for whatever reason. Under this assumption, the rest of the Gricean reasoning falls through – B is violating Quantity because B has elected not to be cooperative, and this has nothing to do with whether or not they possess precise information. So the implicature that B is ignorant of John's exact location – a Particularized Conversational Implicature (PCI) – disappears if cooperativity is not assumed.

In fact, as Geurts (2010: 20–2) discusses, it appears that conversational implicatures can also fail to arise even when the speaker is fully cooperative. (33)–(35) represents cases of a speaker explicitly disclaiming a conversational implicature (reusing examples from Chapter 2), while (36) demonstrates the difficulty of attempting to do that for conventional implicatures (and (37) shows that this is completely out of court for entailments).

(33)   I saw some, and perhaps all, of your children today.
(34)   Some of Bob's friends are black, but even so, he's a racist.
(35)   Anna and Bez are married, but not to each other.
(36)   ?? He is an Englishman; he is, therefore, brave, although most Englishmen are not brave.
(37)   *John Hinckley Jr assassinated Ronald Reagan, but Reagan didn't die.

A convenient way of categorising conversational implicatures is in terms of the Gricean maxims that would be involved in their calculation (assuming, if only for the purposes of classification, that they are calculated in the kind of way that Grice proposed). As Grice noted, the Quality maxim has a privileged status, and arguably all other inferences assume that the Quality maxim is upheld – so there isn't a clear category of Quality-based implicatures as such. (We could analyse metaphor and irony as inferences triggered by Quality violations, but there might be a bit more going on in those cases: see Chapter 6 for more detailed discussion.) However, Grice's schema does enable us to draw a broad distinction between Relation-, Manner- and Quantity-based implicatures, as discussed in the following subsections.

3.1.1 Relation implicatures

As we've already seen, the requirement that a speaker's utterance should be relevant to the current discourse purpose – whatever precisely that means – invites the hearer to draw additional inferences about what the speaker means to convey. We previously considered some examples involving indirect speech acts (which will be discussed in more detail in Chapter 8). One of Grice's own examples (1975: 32) is as follows.

(38)   A: I am out of petrol.
       B: There is a garage around the corner.

Here, B does not explicitly communicate that the garage is open, or that it sells petrol, but these are both reasonable inferences for A to draw, as they provide an explanation of how B's utterance is relevant to the apparent discourse purpose. Knowing this, B can refrain from spelling out these details, allowing A to infer them: and if that's what's going on, we can see them as being communicated by a Relation-based implicature.

Grice postulates a further, rather elusive subcategory of implicatures in which a meaning is conveyed by deliberate violation ('**flouting**') of the maxim of Relation. In his example, a speaker flouts Relation by deliberately changing the subject in order to deflect attention from a previous speaker's *faux pas*. (39) reports a fictional example of a speaker deliberately changing tack in the middle of a conversational exchange.

(39)   The first day I met her she said, 'I'm a radical feminist lesbian.' I thought, what would the Queen Mum do? So I just smiled and said, 'We shall have fog by tea-time.' (Victoria Wood, *Kitty*, 3)

Still, even in a case like this, the second speaker's utterance could be said to adhere to Relation in some sense: although it doesn't relate in content to what the first speaker says, it could be defended as the second speaker's most cooperative attempt to keep the conversation afloat. By changing the subject, the second speaker seems to convey their unwillingness or inability to contribute to the discourse topic proffered by the previous speaker, a meaning that could arise as a standard relation implicature. So, while Grice separates implicatures derived from reasoning about the Relation maxim from those triggered by an apparently gratuitous violation of that maxim, we can potentially do without that distinction.

3.1.2 Manner implicatures

Previously we considered cases where an apparent violation of the Manner maxim triggers an implicature, for instance because a form is unnecessarily verbose. (40), presented in modified form in the exercises in Chapter 2, is a much-discussed example, as its semantic content appears to match that of the briefer alternative (41).

(40)   John caused the car to stop.
(41)   John stopped the car.

In Manner terms, the fact that the speaker of (40) has chosen to use a more verbose form of words than (41) suggests that they intend to convey a meaning that goes beyond the one that would be conveyed by (41). Specifically, (40) is taken to convey that John stopped the car in some non-stereotypical way, and this can be analysed as a manner implicature.

However, because of the breadth of the Manner maxim, we can obtain various other pragmatic enrichments from it, even in cases where the utterance appears to respect the maxim. A notable instance of this occurs in the case of (42) and (43), originally discussed by Wilson (1975: 151).

> (42)   They had a baby and got married.
> (43)   They got married and had a baby.

Both of these are equally brief, and both express the conjunction of two propositions. However, the Manner submaxim 'be orderly' invites us to think that the order in which these two propositions are conjoined could be significant. In this case, the obvious inference is that the events should be presented in the order in which they occurred. By exploiting this expectation, the speaker can convey that order of events efficiently and economically. Thus, we could think of this interpretation of 'and' as 'and then' as potentially a manner implicature.

3.1.3 Quantity implicatures

The remaining broad class of conversational implicatures arises through the speaker's use of an utterance that appears to be wilfully underinformative, in violation of Grice's first submaxim of Quantity. B's utterance in (44) is a classic example.

> (44)   A: Did you meet Jake's parents?
>   B: I met his mother.

We can see B's utterance as underinformative in that, judged purely by its semantic content, it fails to address the current discourse purpose of fully answering A's question – it provides only a partial answer. However, given B's utterance, A would be entitled to reason that B could have given a more informative answer (*I met them both*, or simply *Yes*, for instance). Assuming that B is cooperative, and that B knows whether or not the stronger statement is true – that is, that B knows who they met – the most likely reason for B not giving one of these more informative answers is that these particular more informative answers would have been false. Thus, in this case, B's utterance gives rise to an implicature that it would have been false simply to say *Yes*, and hence that B did not meet Jake's father. By combining the semantic meaning that is explicitly stated and the additional meaning that is pragmatically conveyed, it turns out that B has given a complete answer to A's question after all.

We can also turn this situation around and look at it from B's perspective. Suppose that B wishes to communicate that they met Jake's mother but not Jake's father. They could say so explicitly, but that would involve having to state two separate propositions. Alternatively, they can express either one of these propositions, and the hearer will naturally be able to reason about the alternatives and draw the appropriate conclusion about the other one. If B says *I met his mother*, A will reason in the way described in the previous paragraph; if B says *I didn't meet his father*, A can similarly reason that B could have said *No* if B hadn't met either parent, and therefore it must be the case that B met Jake's mother. Thus, from B's point of view, stating either one of these propositions is enough to answer A's question fully, given these shared assumptions about how A will reason. Thus, we can think of B as intentionally implicating the proposition that they do not express directly.

Implicatures of this kind are usually referred to as quantity implicatures. Their characteristic feature is that the speaker makes an assertion and thereby conveys the falsity of an informationally stronger assertion that they could have made. (We'll come back later to the question of what exactly 'stronger' means in this formulation.) Note that, on a Gricean account, a quantity implicature relies not only on the first submaxim of Quantity but also on the maxim of Quality, because we have to assume that the speaker is unwilling to make a false statement. It also relies on either the second submaxim of Quantity or the maxim of Relation – depending on precisely how we define these – because we have to assume that the stronger statement that the speaker could have made would have been relevant to the current discourse purpose. In (45), B does not necessarily implicate that they did not meet Jake's father, because it is not clear that talking about Jake's father would have been relevant to the current discourse purpose – for instance, perhaps A and B both know that B has already met Jake's father, or they both know that Jake's father wasn't at the party.

(45)   A: Did you meet anyone new at the party?
        B: I met Jake's mother.

As noted above, fully-fledged quantity implicatures are also dependent upon the assumption that the speaker is knowledgeable about the truth of the stronger proposition that could have been uttered. The implicature arising from B's utterance in (44) relies on the assumption that B knows whether or not they met Jake's father. If that fact cannot be assumed – for instance, we're not sure that B knows who Jake's father is – then the best we can do in Gricean terms is to interpret B as conveying that they do not know that they met Jake's father. This is sometimes referred to as an **ignorance implicature**: the speaker is taken not to convey the falsity of a stronger proposition, but just to convey their lack of certainty about the truth or falsity of that stronger proposition.

3.2 Scalar implicatures

In the previous subsection, we looked at the general recipe for a quantity implicature: the speaker says something, and the hearer understands that as an attempt to convey the negation of some stronger alternative statement. The key feature of this is that the speaker doesn't even have to mention the stronger alternative statement, which is what makes this such an efficient way of conveying information.

But as a general recipe, this is actually a bit too general. Most of the time, when a speaker doesn't say something, it's pretty clear that they're not denying that thing, even implicitly. To illustrate this, let's take an uncontroversial fact – that Paris is the capital of France, say – and see what happens when we conjoin it with a statement that a speaker might make, such as (46).

(46) I like tennis.
(47) I like tennis, and Paris is the capital of France.

The resulting conjunction (47) is a stronger statement than (46) – it entails (46) – and therefore our recipe for quantity implicatures predicts that a speaker who utters (46) implicates the falsity of (47). But that's obviously wrong: the speaker who says that they like tennis isn't usually trying to convey anything about Paris, much less trying to deny a universally admitted fact about it.

In this case, we could perhaps say that we know the speaker of (46) isn't trying to implicate that Paris is not the capital of France, because everyone (the speaker presumably included) knows that it is. But in other cases, our general recipe for quantity implicatures still fails, even though the meaning that it predicts is a perfectly reasonable one. To illustrate this, let's consider (48)–(50).

(48) John ate some of the cakes.
(49) John ate all of the cakes.
(50) John ate some of the cakes, and Mary ate the others.

Under our usual assumptions about the meaning of *some*, the semantics of (48) merely specifies that John ate a non-zero number of cakes. (This is specifically assuming that *some* has a purely existential semantic meaning, rather than having the semantic meaning 'some but not all'; we won't get into the question of whether *some* necessarily means 'more

than one'.) On this interpretation, (49) entails (48), because if John ate all
the cakes then he must have eaten a non-zero number of them (unless
there never were any cakes in the first place, in which case (49) would be
a very odd thing to say). (50) also entails (48): it's simply a conjunction
and therefore entails each of its conjuncts. Semantically, then, neither
(49) or (50) could possibly be true unless (48) is true, and both (49) and
(50) assert something additional to the content of (48).

Based on the standard recipe for quantity implicature, we might
expect that the speaker who utters (48) implicates the falsity of both (49)
and (50). But, in practice, it seems that the speaker of (48) implicates
the falsity of (49) but says nothing about whether or not (50) might be
true. And unlike the second conjunct of (47), the second conjunct of
(50) – *Mary ate the others* – isn't obviously true or false, so in principle it
could be something that the speaker means to convey a message about.
Therefore, in this case, the failure of (48) to implicate the falsity of (50)
must have some other explanation: and a good candidate is the potential
lack of relevance of (50). More precisely, the second conjunct of (50)
isn't necessarily relevant in the same circumstances in which (48) is
relevant. And this seems to be the crucial observation in explaining why
quantity implicatures of this type don't generally arise – that is, why the
utterance of p doesn't normally invite us to reason 'the speaker could
have said p *and* q; they didn't do so; therefore they must intend to convey
that q is false', for just any other proposition q.

To flesh this out a little, suppose that the context for (48) is that a
question like (51) has been asked.

(51) Did John eat any of the cakes?

In this kind of context, (48) is an appropriate answer: it gives the questioner the information that they're asking for. (50) entails (48), so by
uttering (50), a speaker would give the questioner the information that
they're asking for: but they would also give them additional information
which isn't obviously relevant to what they want to know. If we asked
the question (51) and got the answer (48) back, it wouldn't occur to us
to wonder why the speaker didn't say (50) instead – we didn't express
any interest in knowing about who else ate the cakes, so the additional
information provided by (50) is probably of no particular use to us. And
if it did occur to us that the speaker could have said (50), and we did
start to wonder why they didn't say it, we could rapidly conclude that
it was in order to avoid violating the second submaxim of Quantity, or
some equivalent principle.

Now, (51) is just one of the many possible questions that could elicit
a cooperative reply of (48). The crucial point is that, for most such

questions, where (48) is an appropriate reply, (50) is not, because it presents irrelevant information. Thus, considering (48) as an utterance on its own, we can easily see that it is often appropriate in circumstances in which (50) would not be entirely appropriate. And this is sufficient reason for us not to take the utterance of (48) to implicate the falsity of (50).

However, the comparison between (48) and (49) is rather different. The tendency of the utterance of (48) to implicate the falsity of (49) is altogether much more robust. Indeed, this is another instance of the *some–all* case discussed at the beginning of Chapter 2: as we saw, the tendency of *some* to convey the meaning 'not all' is sufficiently strong that it is tempting to consider this to be part of *some*'s semantic meaning. But, in fact, this kind of semantic account turns out not to be attractive on closer inspection: as (52) demonstrates, the 'not all' component of *some*'s meaning can be cancelled without a sense of self-contradiction.

(52)   John ate some, perhaps all, of the cakes.

In this respect, the 'not all' meaning is less central than the purely existential meaning of *some* – when we try to cancel the existential meaning, we do get a strong feeling of self-contradiction, as in (53).

(53)   * John ate some, perhaps none, of the cakes.

On the basis of these examples, we're led to the conclusion that utterances with *some* implicate, but do not entail, the corresponding 'not all' meanings. However, as pragmatic enrichments go, this particular kind of implicature seems to have a privileged status, as indicated by the comparison between (49) and (50). Several ideas have been advanced as to how and why it is special, the first of which – due to Horn (1972) – being the most influential.

3.2.1 Horn scales

Horn (1972) proposes that the crucial feature of lexical items such as *some* is that they stand in a special kind of relation to specific other lexical items (for instance, in this case, *all*). When we encounter an utterance containing *some*, because we know about the relation between *some* and *all*, we are immediately aware that *some* could be replaced by *all* to create a more informative utterance – that is to say, one that would be true under fewer circumstances than the utterance with *some* would be. In effect, the use of *some* draws our attention to the speaker's non-use of *all* and invites us to infer that the speaker is implicating the falsity of the corresponding utterance with *all*.

Put differently, we can think of <*some, all*> as constituting an entailment scale. Positive declarative sentences with the stronger term (*all*) entail the corresponding sentences with the weaker term (*some*). Correspondingly, utterances of positive declarative sentences involving the weaker term implicate the falsity of the corresponding sentences with the stronger term. In Horn's honour, scales of this type are often referred to as **Horn scales**; the implicatures that arise from them are called **scalar implicatures**.

What constitutes a Horn scale? Well, we might first ask what kind of lexical items can potentially enter into such a scale. According to most accounts, Horn scales can occur with a very broad range of lexical items, including representatives of various different grammatical classes. There are scales of quantifiers such as <*some, all*>, modals such as <*may, must*>, adverbs such as <*sometimes, often, always*>, adjectives such as <*warm, hot*>, and even connectives such as <*or, and*>. Of course, we would expect all the terms in a given scale to belong to the same grammatical class, as otherwise we would not be able to substitute one for another while preserving grammaticality. In principle there can be more than two terms in a scale: we might argue that *some* and *all* are in fact just two terms drawn from a larger scale such as <*some, many, most, all*>. In that case, the utterance of a weak term from a scale will implicate the falsity of the corresponding utterances with all its stronger scalemates.

In addition to the requirement that stronger terms in a scale should entail weaker terms, Horn also requires that the terms relate to the same semantic field. For example, as Levinson observes, <*know, regret*> do not constitute a scale, even though regretting something entails knowing it, on the grounds that '*regret* introduces semantic parameters additional to those involved in *know*' (2000: 80).

Beyond this, we need to impose yet another constraint on Horn scale membership in order to explain why we don't seem to observe scalar implicatures corresponding to scales such as <*hot, very hot*> or <*if, if and only if*>. That is to say, we wouldn't normally take (54) to implicate the falsity of (55), or (56) to implicate the falsity of (57). (In practice, we would normally interpret (56) as meaning something rather like (57), an inference known as **conditional perfection** and first described by Geis and Zwicky (1971).)

(54) This water is hot.
(55) This water is very hot.
(56) I'll give you $10 if you mow the lawn.
(57) I'll give you $10 if and only if you mow the lawn.

For Horn, the relevant constraint is that the terms of a scale should be equally lexicalised, and belong to the same register. This captures the presumed fact that a speaker making a weak statement doesn't usually implicate the falsity of a stronger statement if that stronger statement would involve using terms that were more marked, or wordy, or otherwise complex.

We can explain this observation straightforwardly from a Relevance Theory perspective. From this point of view, the use of a more complex form to convey a more informative meaning wouldn't necessarily result in increased relevance, because the extra cognitive effects arising from that information might not be enough to compensate the hearer for the extra cognitive costs they incur in processing it. Taking (54) as a potential warning, for instance, the addition of *very* might not do much to intensify the speaker's meaning, but it would delay the completion and understanding of the utterance. And comparing (56) and (57), the additional *and only if* serves to emphasise the point that the speaker won't give the hearer $10 if they don't mow the lawn – a point that could probably be assumed by both parties, without needing to be explicitly articulated.

If the terms of the scale are truly equally lexicalised – however we define that – then there is a sense in which Horn scales are reversible. Indeed, an attractive feature of this account is that, if we reverse the entailment direction of the scalar terms – for example, by placing them under the scope of negation – we can still predict the scalar implicatures that arise. For instance, just as (58) implicates the negation of (59), (60) implicates the negation of (61): that is, it implicates the meaning of (58).

(58)   You can have dinner at 7.
(58)   You must have dinner at 7.
(60)   It's not the case that you must have dinner at 7.
(61)   It's not the case that you can have dinner at 7.

3.2.2 Using Horn scales in implicature

Scalar implicatures represent a hotly contested area of pragmatic research, with several competing theories on the market as to precisely how they come about. Although these theories are rooted in contrasting pragmatic approaches, as outlined in Chapter 2, to some extent we can think of the differences between them as corresponding to different understandings of exactly what a Horn scale is (or what it means for lexical items to be members of a Horn scale).

On the one hand, there's the traditional Gricean approach to Horn scales, which is nicely articulated by Geurts (2010). From that perspective, a Horn scale is just a way of representing a fact about the simultaneous relevance of two or more lexical items in the contexts in which one of them is typically uttered. As Geurts puts it, 'Horn scales represent hearers' expectations in the sense that if β is a scalemate of α's, β is taken to be relevant in a context in which α is used' (2010: 52). Specifically, what distinguishes Horn scales from things that are not Horn scales is simply that the former express relevance relations that are somewhat more stable across contexts. For instance, if we compare <*warm, hot*> and <*hot, very hot*> as candidate scales, the fundamental difference is that *hot* would reliably be a better thing to say, if it were true, in contexts in which *warm* is used, whereas *very hot* wouldn't so reliably be a better thing to say, even if it were true, in contexts in which *hot* is used. Hence, *hot* can be substituted for *warm* wherever that is factually possible, whereas *very hot* can't always be substituted for *hot*. Similarly, <*know, regret*> isn't a scale, because *regret* wouldn't necessarily be a better thing to say, even if it were true, in the contexts in which *know* is used.

We can express this more succinctly in Relevance Theory terms: <*warm, hot*> is a Horn scale because *hot* would be more relevant than *warm* in cases where both are true; <*hot, very hot*> is not a Horn scale because *very hot* wouldn't necessarily be more relevant than *hot* in cases where both are true; and <*know, regret*> isn't a Horn scale because *regret* wouldn't necessarily be more relevant than *know* in cases where both are true.

In short, for both a traditional Gricean account and a Relevance Theory account, Horn scales are not considered to have any privileged status, in terms of the inferences that they license: they merely express a generalisation about the circumstances in which quantity implicatures are expected to be available. From both points of view, the hearer of (62) is expected to draw a pragmatic enrichment by considering that the speaker could have said (63). Saying that <*warm, hot*> is a Horn scale just amounts to saying 'the hearer can assume that (63) would be more relevant than (62), if both are true'. As a consequence, on hearing (62), the hearer is entitled to assume that (63) is not true (as far as the speaker knows).

(62)   The coffee is warm.
(63)   The coffee is hot.

On the other hand, as discussed in Chapter 2, Levinson (2000) proposes to account for a set of quantity implicatures in terms of his Q-heuristic.

Corresponding to this heuristic, there is an obligation on the speaker to avoid producing a statement that is informationally weaker than their world knowledge allows, unless producing a stronger statement would contravene the maxims associated with the I-heuristic. And by hypothesis, replacing one term in a Horn scale for another would not contravene those maxims. Consequently, the Q-heuristic entitles the hearer to draw scalar inferences, as long as the sentential context is appropriate (that is, there is no scalar reversal or anything of that kind). According to Levinson, on encountering (62), the hearer can immediately infer the falsity of (63), on the basis that <*warm*, *hot*> constitutes a Horn scale.

Crucially, on this approach, we don't have to wait until we have processed the whole utterance, and extracted its propositional meaning, to find out whether we will be entitled to draw an implicature. In (64), when we reach *some*, we already know that the context is appropriate for scalar implicature, in that it's a positive declarative sentence. Thus, at this point, we are already permitted to infer the falsity of the corresponding utterance with the stronger scalar alternative(s), in this case *all*. The same is true for *can* in (65), where the stronger scalar alternative is *must*, or in (66), where the stronger alternative is *and*, and so on.

(64)   John ate some of the cakes.
(65)   You can leave early.
(66)   Anita or Mary will teach the class.

In this respect, Levinson's account differs strikingly from the traditional Gricean and Relevance Theory approaches. On those accounts, it would not be possible for the hearer to consider the alternative utterances, and start drawing inferences about the speaker's intention based on the speaker's decision not to utter them, until the utterance is complete.

Levinson's approach offers a potential explanation of that intuition that a weak scalar term actually contains the negation of its stronger scalemates as part of its meaning: that *some* actually means 'some but not all', that *warm* means 'warm but not hot', that *or* means 'one or the other but not both', and so on. Another approach that captures that intuition, termed the 'grammatical' approach to scalar implicature, has been pursued by Gennaro Chierchia and colleagues (see for instance Chierchia et al. 2012). Their approach posits that scalar implicatures are represented in the syntactic structure of utterances, and arise due to the presence of a silent exhaustification operator in the sentence structure. This operator, *exh*, has a meaning that can roughly be glossed as 'only'. It can appear freely in sentences – it's silent, and could be anywhere – but only occasionally has effects on the resulting meaning. One of the cases in which *exh* does influence meaning is when it takes scope over a weak scalar, such as *some*: in this case, it causes that scalar to be interpreted exhaustively ('only some'), which has the effect of denying all the stronger scalar alternatives. With *exh* inserted above *some*, for instance, (64) has approximately the same meaning as (67).

(67)   John ate only some of the cakes.

From the perspective of the grammatical account, we can see a Horn scale as articulating what precisely is denied when the operator *exh* acts on a weak member of the scale. Saying that <*some, all*> is a Horn scale amounts to saying that *exh(some)* entails *not all*. Similarly, saying that <*can, must*> and <*or, and*> are Horn scales amounts to saying that *exh(can)* entails the negation of *must* and *exh(or)* entails the negation of *and*.

Broadly, it makes sense to think of this debate as being between researchers who consider scalar implicature to be a common variety of quantity implicature that proceeds via post-propositional reasoning about the speaker's intention (including Griceans and Relevance Theorists) and those who consider scalar implicature to be a special kind of pragmatic enrichment that proceeds via some form of specialised mechanism (notably including Levinson, Chierchia and colleagues). The former view is often labelled **contextualist**, and the latter **defaultist**.

Note on terminology
Another way of describing this distinction is that defaultist accounts predict **local** enrichment – the richer pragmatic meaning can arise at the trigger word – while contextualist accounts predict **global** enrichment, in which the richer meaning can arise only at the sentence level. For consistency, I'll stick to referring to these accounts as defaultist and contextualist wherever possible.

There are nevertheless some broad points of agreement between these two parties. It appears to be common ground to both sides that some form of post-propositional reasoning (which could be traditionally Gricean in character) is sometimes required for pragmatic interpretation. We seem to need this in cases like (44), repeated below as (68).

(68)   A: Did you meet Jake's parents?
       B: I met his mother.

Here, B's utterance implicates that B didn't meet Jake's father, but we can't easily read that off a default or grammatical account. It's certainly not true in general that saying *his mother* invites the inference 'and not

his father'. And although it's true in this case that the interpretation of
only his mother would convey 'and not his father', it would also convey
'and not anyone else' – which isn't the interpretation that B intends. (B
is not implicating that they didn't meet anyone at all other than Jake's
mother; they are merely implicating that they didn't meet any other
of Jake's parents.) So at the very least we would need some kind of
additional pragmatic mechanisms to explain the precise reading that we
get in cases like this.

As a general theoretical principle, most researchers would prefer
to posit just a single mechanism if that were capable of accounting for
the relevant data – thus, an active research question concerns whether
scalar implicatures can arise in a way that is inexplicable to a contextualist account. Of course, if it transpires that we do require default
mechanisms for scalar implicature, this might encourage us to posit
similar mechanisms for other forms of pragmatic inference, such as
Levinson's Q- and M-heuristics.

It is also common ground among theorists that scalar implicatures
sometimes fail to arise, or at least don't always form part of the final
interpretation of an utterance. Where the speaker is ignorant of the
truth or falsity of the stronger proposition, or generally uncooperative,
contextualist accounts predict that these implicatures will fail to arise.
Defaultist accounts have to offer an explanation of how, and when, the
implicatures that arise automatically are to be disposed of when they are
unwanted, such as in cases like this.

Importantly, the view is also broadly shared among theorists that a
successful theory of scalar implicature should have psychological reality. That is, although it's crucial for the theory to make the right predictions about the pragmatic interpretations of utterances, we also want
it to make the right predictions about the processing stages involved,
which can be validated by appeal to psycholinguistic evidence. In effect,
we are not going to judge theories as entirely successful just because
they offer especially elegant, economical or intuitive explanations of
how pragmatic meanings can be recovered: we would ideally require
evidence that they describe the processing pathways that humans actually use.

In recent years, a wealth of experimental evidence has been brought
to bear on the question of how scalar implicatures arise. Some of this
has been concerned primarily with trying to demonstrate the presence,
or absence, of the stages in reasoning that are posited by competing
theories. Other work has examined unusual contexts for implicatures, in
which the availability or non-availability of a particular interpretation
might itself be theory-critical. Still other work has looked critically at

the question of whether or not scalar implicatures are truly a coherent concept, or whether different rules could apply to different scales. In the following section, I will briefly review some of the relevant findings.

3.3 Evidence on scalar implicature processing

Out of the several categories of experimental evidence that are potentially relevant to the debate about whether scalar implicatures are contextual or default in nature, evidence about the time-course of processing is perhaps the most central. There is now a rich and burgeoning array of experimental research on this issue. However, much recent attention has also been focused on how weak scalar terms are interpreted in embedded positions, as it has been argued that the different accounts make categorically different predictions about which interpretations are possible in certain cases. This debate too has been informed by a wealth of experimental evidence, but, just as is the case for the time-course of processing, the experimental evidence has largely been derived from work involving just a handful of the possible scales. Thus, a third point that is worth considering is whether the claims that we can make about scalar implicatures on the basis of this evidence can safely be generalised to all potential scales, or whether we might have focused too much of our attention on atypical cases and ignored the diversity involved. Examination of this point has also led to some interesting recent experimental work. In the following three subsections, we will look at these lines of enquiry and see how they have informed our collective understanding of the nature of implicature.

3.3.1 The time-course of scalar implicature

Given that the defaultist view of scalar implicature holds that weak scalar terms can immediately trigger implicatures, while the contextualist view holds that scalar implicatures arise post-propositionally if the circumstances permit, the theories seem to make different predictions about the time-course of this implicature. Specifically, it would be strong evidence in favour of a defaultist view of scalar implicature if it could be shown that hearers obtain implicature readings immediately upon encountering weak scalar terms.

Obviously it's difficult to tell whether a hearer has derived a particular interpretation while they are in the middle of reading or hearing an utterance. One popular approach to testing the predictions of the competing accounts has been to examine the hearer's interpretation immediately after the utterance ends. On a default account, the implicature should certainly be available at this stage; on a contextual account, it will still not be ready immediately at the utterance end because the hearer won't yet have completed the post-propositional reasoning that delivers that implicature.

Moreover, we know that an utterance with a weak scalar term may or may not convey an implicature, depending on the broader context: for example, we might ultimately understand an utterance of *some* to convey the meaning 'some but not all', or just 'some (and possibly all)'. On a contextualist account, the initial meaning available at the end of the utterance is the latter meaning – that is to say, the purely semantic, existential meaning of *some* – and subsequent pragmatic reasoning will deliver the implicature 'not all', but only when the necessary contextual conditions for implicature are satisfied. Thus, the semantic meaning comes first, followed (with some kind of delay) by the pragmatic meaning, when that arises at all. By contrast, on a defaultist account, the initial meaning available at the end of the utterance is the pragmatic meaning (e.g. 'some but not all') – and if the contextual conditions for implicature are not satisfied, the hearer will have to unpick this reasoning and revert to the purely semantic meaning. Thus, the pragmatic meaning comes first, followed (again with some kind of delay, assuming that the post-propositional reasoning is once again somewhat time-consuming) by the purely semantic meaning. In both cases, the delay that we're talking about is potentially very small – perhaps some hundredths of a second – but large enough to be detected by psycholinguistic means.

Thus, under the assumption that the default inference is immediate but the deliberative post-propositional reasoning takes time, we derive nicely conflicting predictions from the two theories. According to the contextual account, readings without implicatures are available first, and readings with implicatures take longer. According to the default account, the reverse is true.

These predictions have been tested in numerous experiments since the early 2000s, initially in experiments using truth-value judgement (TVJ) tasks.

Methodology: truth-value judgement (TVJ) tasks

In a TVJ, participants are typically asked to judge each experimental item as true or false, usually by pressing the appropriate button or key. The items may be free-standing, for example presenting encyclopaedic (non-)facts, or they may concern a short story or scenario that has already been read by the participants. The participants may or may not be given feedback about whether their answers are correct: often they are not, as the experimenter wants to know how they judge the materials, without imposing an idea of what would be 'correct'.

The experimenter typically measures response time, sometimes called **latency**, as well as the response itself, and both may be analysed. In the case of response time, the measurement may start from when the material is presented – in which case, for written stimuli, the response time will include reading time – or from some other appropriate point (for instance, the end of a verbal stimulus).

Participants are typically instructed to respond as quickly and accurately as possible. Experimenters can also manipulate this trade-off: for instance, in a **speeded TVJ**, participants are required to respond within a particular time, and instructed to do so as accurately as possible.

The TVJ may be combined with other methods, such as eye-tracking and reading time measures. It's also common to use TVJ on non-critical, filler items within a long experiment, in order to verify that a participant is still paying attention to the content of the items.

Bott and Noveck (2004) conducted a TVJ study in which they asked participants to judge written sentences expressing taxonomic relations. (69) is an example of a true sentence from their study, (70) a false one. Their critical items were sentences such as (71), which are true if we interpret *some* as purely existential but false if we interpret it as meaning *some but not all*.

(69)   Some mammals are elephants.
(70)   Some elephants are insects.
(71)   Some elephants are mammals.

Bott and Noveck (2004) tested these sentences in several experimental conditions. In the simplest of these (their Experiment 3; see also Noveck and Posada 2003), a straightforward TVJ with no other instructions, sentences such as (71) divided opinion: they were judged true in 41 per cent of responses and false in 59 per cent of responses. Critically, the 'true' responses were significantly faster, on average, than the 'false' responses, suggesting that the enriched 'some but not all' reading (under which the sentence is false) takes longer to derive than the unenriched existential reading of *some*, 'some and possibly all' (under which the sentence is true). Bott and Noveck interpreted this as support for the contextual view of scalar implicature.

The other versions of Bott and Noveck's experiment also supported this conclusion. In their Experiment 1, they explicitly asked participants to interpret *some* as either 'some but not all' (the 'Pragmatic' condition) or as 'some and possibly all' (the 'Logical' condition) throughout the study.

Participants in the Logical condition were faster to respond than those in the Pragmatic condition, which again suggests that the pragmatic enrichment takes time (even when it is made routine, as in this case). Bott and Noveck's Experiment 4 was a speeded TVJ: participants given less time to respond were more inclined to produce purely existential interpretations of *some*. Once again, these results appear to support the contextual view over the default view: there is no evidence here that scalar implicature readings of *some* as 'some but not all' are available more quickly or less effortfully than non-implicature interpretations of *some* in which it has purely existential meaning.

Subsequent work has generally replicated these results, finding that participants are consistently split on whether sentences such as (71) are true or not, and that they tend to give faster responses when relying on 'logical' rather than 'pragmatic' judgements. However, some caution persists about exactly what we are measuring when we look at the outcome of a TVJ task like this, because performing the task involves making a decision as well as interpreting the linguistic stimulus. One major concern is that sentences such as (71) are problematic for TVJs, in that there are arguments in favour of judging it true and arguments in favour of judging it false: there's a sense in which it's technically true (in that *some* encodes a purely existential meaning) and at the same time there's a sense in which it's seriously misleading (presumably because of the implicature that it conveys). However, in Bott and Noveck's set-up, there is a straightforward binary choice, which doesn't offer participants any opportunity to escape having to label (71) as either true or false, or to express any unease about doing so.

Katsos and Bishop (2011) provide rather striking evidence that this unease might be a factor in participants' behaviour in Bott and Noveck's (2004) experiments. Katsos and Bishop's study uses a three-way (ternary) TVJ, modified to be accessible to young children. Participants in their experiment are asked to judge how well a cartoon character, 'Mr Caveman', described a particular scene, by giving him one of three different sizes of reward. In the critical conditions, Mr Caveman described a scene by using *some* instead of *all* – for example, a mouse picks up all the carrots in the display, and Mr Caveman says *The mouse picked up some of the carrots*. Even at age 5, Katsos and Bishop's participants are already assigning a middle rating to these critical items, reserving the biggest reward for the production of fully informative utterances and the smallest reward for the production of semantically false ones.

It seems likely, therefore, that participants in Bott and Noveck's (2004) experiments are already aware that items such as (71) aren't exactly true and aren't exactly false. It's therefore possible that their delay in the acceptance of underinformative *some* might be purely an artefact of the decision-making process, rather than a reflection of how long it takes them to compute the implicature. Maybe the participants are in fact immediately aware of both possible readings of *some*, and it just happens that the ones who settle on the conclusion that 'the sentence is technically true' tend to make their minds up a little faster than the ones who settle on the conclusion 'the sentence is so misleading that it's really false'.

Another strand of evidence on the time-course of scalar implicature has attempted to avoid the need for conscious reasoning about truth-values by focusing instead on reading times. These can be measured most straightforwardly using a self-paced reading experiment.

Methodology: self-paced reading

In a self-paced reading task, participants are presented with a written text one chunk at a time. They are instructed in advance to read the text, pressing a key to proceed to the next chunk each time. Each chunk may consist of a single word or multiple words, depending on the purpose of the experiment.

The experimenter typically measures the time taken between key presses (again called latency) as a guide to how long the participant took to read each chunk. Comprehension questions will typically also be included to ensure that the participant is actually reading all the material, and the analysis of the data may exclude unnaturally short intervals that could arise from the participant unintentionally holding the key down for too long (or unnaturally long intervals that might indicate a break in the participant's concentration).

It's possible to run other tasks such as TVJ in conjunction with self-paced reading: you could ask a participant to read a sentence under self-paced reading conditions and then to give a truth-value judgement on it.

Generally the experimenter will be interested in the time taken to read chunks that contain theoretically critical material, which can be taken to indicate the level of difficulty that the participant had in processing this material. However, the experimenter may also be interested in the time taken to read chunks that immediately follow this, as those may disclose a slowdown in reading associated with the participant continuing to process the material they have already read. This is often called a **spillover** effect, and the question of how to interpret such effects is much debated in the literature.

Breheny et al. (2006) ran a self-paced reading experiment with a design in which the same material is encountered in the presence or absence of an earlier scalar implicature. Consider the contrast between (72) and (73).

(72)   The director had a meeting with some of the consultants. The rest did not manage to attend.

(72)   The director had a meeting with only some of the consultants. The rest did not manage to attend.

In (73), where *only* is explicit, the first sentence entails the existence of consultants with whom the director did not meet. These consultants are referred to by the phrase *The rest* in the second sentence. Breheny et al. argue that, if *some* attracts a default scalar implicature, (72) should pattern with (73) – again, the first sentence will convey (this time by implicature) that there exist consultants with whom the director did not meet, and again *The rest* can immediately be understood to refer to these consultants. By contrast, under a contextual account, participants will initially understand *some* as purely existential, and won't yet have calculated the potential implicature when they arrive at the end of the first sentence and encounter *The rest*. Consequently, at this stage, the participants won't have access to a suitable set of individuals for *The rest* to refer to: they will have to pause and figure out that *some* did mean *some but not all*, and hence that *The rest* means 'the rest of the consultants'.

Breheny et al.'s (2006) Experiment 2 used these materials (translated into Greek, and read by Greek native speakers). Participants in their study took significantly longer to read *The rest* in the context of (72) than in the context of (73), which suggests that – in the absence of explicit *only* – there is indeed a delay in inferring the existence of a suitable referent for *The rest*. That is, in Breheny et al.'s view, participants are not inclined to spontaneously interpret *some* as 'some but not all', on first reading, or at least not with the consistency that the default account would predict.

This type of reading study is potentially instructive but also requires some caution in how we interpret the results, because there may be quite a few processes going on that we're failing to take account of. For instance, could it be possible that the reader of (72) computes the implicature from *some* immediately, but then dismisses it before they encounter *the rest* and have to restore it? This may seem unnecessarily circuitous on the part of the participant – but more recent follow-up work (Bergen and Grodner 2012; Politzer-Ahles and Fiorentino 2013) has suggested that the reader may be making quite elaborate calculations as to the speaker's likely intentions.

We might try instead to get at the immediate processing of a weak scalar by using an approach that is more closely time-locked to the stimulus. Huang and Snedeker (2009) use an eye-tracking experiment for this, but again do not find evidence of early pragmatic enrichment. That is to say, their participants' eye movements respond to the semantic content of the stimulus considerably earlier than they respond to the pragmatic enrichments of that meaning.

Methodology: eye-tracking

Eye-tracking refers to any experiment that involves recording a participant's eye movements. A popular approach using eye-tracking is the **visual world paradigm**, originally due to Cooper (1974) and notably developed by Tanenhaus et al. (1995), in which participants look at a visual scene (typically displayed on a computer screen) and hear an auditory stimulus. Participants' attention is drawn to entities that are being talked about: indeed, as shown by Altmann and Kamide (1999), participants will begin looking towards entities that they expect to be mentioned. This makes the technique especially valuable for psycholinguistics because it has the potential to disclose what a participant is thinking while they are in the process of interpreting an ongoing utterance, and it does so without interrupting that process.

Eye-tracking is also valuable because of the relatively precise way that eye movements are time-locked to the stimulus – they are quicker to take place than more complex physical actions such as uttering words. However, eye-tracking data also tends to be noisy, because participants can, and do, look at parts of the scene that are not relevant to the auditory stimulus. There is, of course, no obligation for someone to look at the thing they are thinking about – the preference for doing so is just a robust statistical generalisation.

The analysis of eye-tracking data is also a complex matter, and depends upon the needs of the task. A typical approach is to consider the proportion of the time that a participant spends looking at an item in the immediate aftermath of a relevant portion of the auditory stimulus, or to consider how soon they direct their attention to that item.

Other methods have also been tried in recent work. To take a couple of examples, Hartshorne et al. (2015) present a neurolinguistic study examining participants' event-related brain potentials (ERPs) when processing potentially implicature-triggering materials. They show that a particular neural signature associated with pragmatic enrichment arises only in contexts that support implicature. And Tomlinson et al. (2013) use a mouse-tracking paradigm: they demonstrate an effect of pragmatic enrichment, but show that this is delayed relative to the effect of semantic meaning.

Methodology: mouse-tracking

In a mouse-tracking study, rather than relying on the usual button- or key-press responses, participants are asked to click on their preferred answer, using a cursor controlled by a mouse. Typically, the two options are presented at the top left and top right of the screen. At the beginning of each trial, the cursor is reset to a starting location at the bottom of the screen, in the middle. The experimenter records both the ultimate response and the pattern of cursor movements.

Participants are again asked to respond as quickly and accurately as possible. The general observation is that, if the participant is immediately sure of their preferred answer, they will move the cursor towards it immediately and in a straight line: however, this movement will be deflected if they are drawn towards the other answer. Thus, as applied to a TVJ, mouse-tracking enables the experimenter not only to establish the participant's ultimately preferred answer but also to get a clearer impression of how their preference has developed over the course of their response.

There is not space here to go into all the subtleties of these studies and justify the conclusions that are drawn. But in summary, the overall picture is reasonably clear: there is little sign of the presence of an automatic, rapid, context-independent scalar implicature of the kind that we might expect to see under the accounts offered by Levinson (2000) or Chierchia et al. (2012).

Can we interpret this as a rebuttal of the default account, and a proof of the contextual account? Well, as we'll see in the following subsections, there is other relevant evidence to consider. But it's also true that the results aren't unambiguously supportive of the contextual account: some findings are problematic for both sides (e.g. Politzer-Ahles and Fiorentino 2013; Hartshorne et al. 2015).

More generally, what we see in this research area is that the experimental tests of the competing accounts tend to rely upon extra assumptions that go beyond the core tenets of the underlying theories. We usually assume, for instance, that default inference is cognitively cheap and Gricean-style reasoning is detectably more costly, which conceivably might not be true (although Levinson's (2000) argument for default inferences is motivated in part by the assumption that they should be cheap). We also tend to assume that the contextual account predicts that a purely semantic (or 'literal') interpretation should be available to the hearer first, which also might not be the case (Recanati 1995; Breheny in press), and indeed doesn't seem to be true in other domains of 'non-literal' use (see Chapter 6). And fundamentally we also assume that interpretations arise in hearers' minds in some way that is externally detectable using the experimental tools available to us – which is crucial, because we don't have the technology to detect what someone is actually thinking, in propositional terms, with anything like enough precision to detect something like a scalar implicature. However, it is probably fair to say that, at present, there is no compelling evidence from studies of online processing that would oblige us to abandon a purely contextual account of implicature.

3.3.2 Scalar terms in embedded positions

Another possible argument in favour of a default, rather than a contextual, account of scalar implicature concerns weak scalars in embedded positions. Consider (74) and (75).

(74)   Raj believes that Steve ate some of the sweets.
(75)   Most of the students got some of the questions right.

It seems possible to interpret (74) as conveying that Raj believes that Steve ate some, but not all, of the sweets, and (75) as conveying that most of the students got some, but not all, of the questions right. But if that's so, we can't account for their meanings under a traditional Gricean account. The problem is that the usual recipe for scalar implicature – interpreting the utterance with the weak scalar as conveying the negation of the corresponding utterance with a stronger scalar – doesn't quite work here. Specifically, on a Gricean account, we are predicted to understand (74) as conveying the negation of (76), and (75) as conveying the negation of (77).

(76)   Raj believes that Steve ate all of the sweets.
(77)   Most of the students got all of the questions right.

And this isn't quite good enough. It doesn't follow from (74) plus the negation of (76) that Raj believes that Steve ate 'not all' of the sweets: it only follows that it is not true that Raj believes that Steve ate them all. That is, for all we know (on a Gricean analysis), maybe Raj doesn't have an opinion about whether Steve ate all the sweets. Similarly, (75) plus the negation of (77) would tell us that most of the students got some of the questions right, and that it isn't true that most of them got all of the questions right – but that's still not enough to guarantee that most of the students got some-but-not-all of the questions right. For instance, suppose that 40 per cent of the students got no questions right, 40 per cent got all the questions right, and the other 20 per cent were somewhere in the middle. (75) would be true – 60 per cent of the students got some of the questions right. And the negation of (77) would be true – 60 per cent failed to get all of the questions right. But our candidate interpretation of (75) – 'most of the students got some, but not all, of the questions right' – would be false, because in fact only 20 per cent of the students would have done so.

These examples may be a little tricky to follow, but the point is reasonably simple: default and contextual accounts don't usually predict the same interpretations, when weak scalars appear in embedded positions. Thus, in principle, we should be able to use these contexts to adjudicate between the two theories.

Note on terminology

The enriched readings of weak scalars in embedded positions are sometimes referred to as **embedded implicatures**. Geurts (2010) objects to this description on the basis that implicatures, by definition, can't be calculated with respect to embedded material, but only at a propositional level – so, however these meanings come about, it isn't through what we would properly call implicature. As a consequence, some of the subsequent literature has referred to these interpretations as **embedded upper-bound construals** (UBCs). For the current purposes I will try to avoid committing to a view as to what these pragmatic enrichments should be called.

Geurts and Pouscoulous (2009) present relevant data on this, using a very simple TVJ-type paradigm. In their task, they ask participants to judge whether a particular inference is legitimate, by presenting a piece of information and asking whether or not a specific conclusion is true in the light of that information, as in (78).

(78)   Emilie says: *Betty thinks that Fred heard some of the Verdi operas.*
       Would you infer from this that Betty thinks that Fred didn't hear all of the Verdi operas? (Yes/No) (Geurts and Pouscoulous 2009: 7)

In their critical items, the background information involves a weak scalar (*some*) and the proposed conclusion involves the negation of the stronger scalar alternative (*all*). Both of these appear in an embedded position, in this case embedded under the verb *thinks*.

For this particular example, Geurts and Pouscoulous obtain – in two versions of their experiment – 50 per cent and 65 per cent rates of participants endorsing this inference. For embeddings under *all* and *want*, they obtain rather lower rates of acceptance for this inference, and for the embedding under *must* (or, to be more precise, *have to*), they obtain a very low rate (3 per cent). This is hardly surprising: we would not normally take (79) to convey the meaning expressed by (80), which is the meaning we would get if *some* was interpreted as *some but not all* in this context.

(79)   Fred has to hear some of the Verdi operas.

(80)   Fred is not allowed to hear all of the Verdi operas.

How can we interpret these results in theoretical terms? Geurts and Pouscoulous (2009) argue that their findings disprove the claim of Chierchia et al. (2012) that these strengthened readings of *some* occur 'systematically and freely in arbitrary embedded positions', a claim which would otherwise support a default view of these pragmatic enrichments. Under a default view, it's difficult to explain why (79) so consistently fails to convey (80). (80) is a perfectly reasonable meaning, in principle, and indeed would be conveyed pragmatically by (81), which gives rise to it as a standard quantity implicature on any account.

(81)   Fred is allowed to hear some of the Verdi operas.

To explain the non-availability of (80) as an enrichment of (79), we would perhaps have to say that the insertion of the *exh* operator before *some* is forbidden in (79) for some reason that isn't obvious. Alternatively, we could argue that the *exh* operator may be inserted, but ultimately other pragmatic considerations prevail and the hearer is forced to change their interpretation and remove that operator from their parse of (79). Again, there doesn't seem to be an obvious reason why this should have to happen.

At the same time, the fact that these pragmatic enrichments are sometimes available in cases like (78) – and indeed (74) and (75) – is problematic for a contextual account. Can we explain how these arise? Possibly, but we may have to assume that the hearer is using additional information in computing these enrichments. The enrichments for (74) is available under a standard Gricean account if we assume that the speaker has a belief, one way or the other, about whether or not the stronger proposition is true – that is, that Raj has a view on whether Steve ate all the sweets. This might be a reasonable assumption, although it does not seem to be part of the meaning of the utterance in its own right. Similarly, for (78), there are various potential assumptions that would do the job of delivering the enrichment of *some* by purely contextual means. However, the question of whether hearers really do believe in these assumptions, and use them in order to strengthen the pragmatic enrichments that they derive from these utterances, seems to be an open one.

In summary, then, the initial data on embedded implicatures seem to be inconclusive theoretically: we do not see quite the range of interpretations that we might expect to under a default account, but we do occasionally see readings that are nicely dealt with by the default account and require additional assumptions under a contextual account. More recent work has continued to probe the availability of these enrichments, but again we await definitive evidence as to whether default scalar inferences are being calculated here.

3.3.3 Scalar diversity

Given the multiplicity of potential scales, and their diverse nature in terms of grammatical category (as noted in section 3.2.1), it is striking that so much of the experimental work on scalar implicature has focused on just a handful of these scales, with the majority of it concerning just the scale <*some, all*>. We would like to use those experimental results to say very general things about the nature of scalar implicature, but there's a danger in doing so: perhaps the scales that we are focusing on are somehow atypical, and that could lead us to erroneous conclusions. After all, no one on the default side of the theoretical debate is committed to the view that everything that could possibly be analysed as a Horn scale must give rise to a default implicature: it would be perfectly reasonable to hold a view in which some of the apparent Horn scales are the basis of default inferences, while others are not. We can't really challenge that kind of position just by presenting evidence about a couple of theoretically possible scales that happen not to yield obvious default inferences.

Following earlier work by Doran et al. (2009), Van Tiel et al. (2016) explore whether different potential Horn scales give rise to implicatures at different rates. They used a simple inference judgement task, like that of Geurts and Pouscoulous (2009), but looking at weak scalars in fairly minimal unembedded contexts. They tested 43 candidate scales, and did indeed find widely divergent rates of scalar inference: from 4 per cent in the case of <*content, happy*> to 100 per cent in the case of <*cheap, free*>. Notably, <*some, all*> was very near the top of the range, at 96 per cent, and modals that have sometimes been used in experiments (<*may*>, <*will*>, <*may, have to*>) also scored highly.

The factors underpinning this diversity are not entirely clear, although Van Tiel et al. (2016) examine several possibilities, and Sun et al. (under review) develop this line of enquiry further. But perhaps the most important point to take from this is simply that not all scalar inferences behave similarly. There are indeed many scales which consistently give rise to scalar implicatures, when a weak term from that scale is presented in a positive declarative sentence and no context is provided. There are also many scales that should work perfectly well in principle, but in practice don't seem to give rise to implicatures with anything like the same consistency.

Because <*some, all*> is one of the most robust scales, according to Van Tiel et al.'s measure, it is tempting to think that it should be the scale that gives rise to the best evidence for default inference. That is, in the absence of compelling evidence for default inference in the case of <*some, all*>, we might assume that we would also be unlikely to find such evidence if we tested other scales in the same way. However, this may not be an entirely safe assumption. It would certainly be useful to have more detailed information about hearers' behaviour with other scalar terms – in terms of their usual interpretation, their processing in real time, and their interpretation in embedded contexts – before making confident generalisations about the mechanisms for scalar implicature.

3.4 Alternatives in quantity implicature

In the discussion of quantity implicature in section 3.1.3, we talked about the negation of stronger alternatives, where by 'stronger' we meant that these alternatives entail the weaker statements that were actually uttered. Thus, for instance, (82) is stronger than (83), and thus when (83) conveys the negation of (82) we can treat this as a standard quantity implicature.

(82)   I met her parents.
(83)   I met her mother.

This notion of informational strength is also rolled up into the definition of Horn scales that we've been working with in sections 3.2 and 3.3. However, among the lists of candidate Horn scales we find a few examples which might not fit with this definition. Consider the case of <*cheap, free*> tested by Van Tiel et al. (2016). Their participants reliably interpreted *cheap* as meaning 'not free'. Now this could indeed be a scalar implicature, but another possibility is that the semantic meaning of *cheap* contains the information 'not free', either because it entails it or because it presupposes the existence of a non-zero cost. (See Chapter 4 for more on presupposition.) Similar considerations apply to the scales <*rare, extinct*>, <*difficult, impossible*> and so on.

This certainly bears upon the ability of the proposed scalemates to substitute freely for one another. There are clearly statements that are felicitous with the weak term and odd with the strong, as in (84)–(86).

Presumably this is because one can't 'buy' free software, 'preserve' an extinct species, or 'perform' an impossible task.

(84)   The company only buys cheap / ? free software.
(85)   This charity is devoted to the preservation of rare / ? extinct species.
(86)   We specialise in performing difficult / ? impossible tasks.

Could quantity implicatures still arise even between terms that aren't linked by this kind of entailment relationship? Apparently so – although whether we would still want to call them 'quantity implicatures' is debatable. Consider the following famous movie dialogue.

(87)   **Jess**: So you're saying she's not that attractive.
       Harry: No, I told you she *is* attractive.
       Jess: Yeah but you also said she has a good personality.
       Harry: She *has* a good personality.

       . . .

       Jess: When someone's not that attractive, they're always described as having a good personality.
       Harry: Look, if you had asked me what does she look like and I said, she has a good personality, that means she's not attractive. But just because I happen to mention that she has a good personality, she could be either. She could be attractive with a good personality, or not attractive with a good personality.
       Jess: So which one is she?
       Harry: Attractive.
       Jess: But not beautiful, right?

       (Nora Ephron, *When Harry Met Sally*)

There are obviously several illustrative things going on here. In the last turn, Jess tries to interpret the use of *attractive* as a scalar implicature trigger conveying 'not beautiful', which is somewhat contestable. (Van Tiel et al. tested the scale <*pretty, beautiful*> and found a rate of only 8 per cent implicature readings.) And Harry makes the point that the utterance 'She has a good personality' could be used to answer the question 'What does she look like?', in which case it would potentially convey 'She is not attractive', which we could explain in terms of relation-based implicature. Thus, Harry nicely articulates the pragmatic observation that this particular kind of meaning is only available when the utterance occurs in an appropriate conversational context.

More interestingly, Jess appears to argue that the description 'has a good personality' is 'always' used in characterising someone who isn't judged to be physically attractive. This suggests that, from Jess's point of view, there are a couple of possibilities about how one expects a speaker to describe someone who is both attractive and has a good personality: they could mention both attributes, or they could forget the personality and just describe that person as 'attractive'. On the former analysis, the scale in effect is <*has a good personality, is attractive and has a good personality*>. This is obviously not a Horn scale in the strict sense, because the terms of the scale are not equally lexicalised, but it is potentially the basis for a classic quantity implicature, because the second term entails the first. But on the latter analysis, the scale in effect is <*has a good personality, is attractive*>. The second term doesn't entail the former, so the implicature from *has a good personality* ('is not attractive') can't be a classic quantity implicature. Yet this appears to be the version that matches Jess's expectation of how these expressions work in communication.

How could we explain the existence of that implicature? In essence, it seems to arise from the usual expectation that a cooperative speaker would have made some other statement, if they believed it to be true: the only difference is that, in this case, that alternative statement isn't strictly more informative, in the sense we've been talking about – it just presents a different kind of information. We could think of the implicature as being relation-based, and relying on a shared presumption that this alternative information (about the person's physical attractiveness) would somehow be more relevant to the discourse purpose, and therefore the speaker's refusal to disclose that information indicates that it's not true. Or we could think of it as a quantity implicature, based on the fact that the physical description somehow provides 'more' information, in a sense that we would have to make precise. Or we could adopt a Relevance Theory approach and say that these are essentially the same explanation.

Ultimately, the challenge is to develop a system that has the flexibility to explain – and ideally to predict – implicatures of this kind, but is sufficiently constrained to account for why they don't just happen all the time. As discussed earlier, it's pretty clear that we don't take just any statement to implicitly convey the negation of just any other statement: and it looks as though this ultimately has to do with the relevance of the alternatives to the current discourse purpose. So to figure out how the whole system works in general, we would need to pin down exactly what it is about a given utterance that makes it relevant at a particular moment in time.

To illustrate the challenge involved, let's briefly revisit a problematic example from section 3.3.2, repeated here as (88).

(88)   Most of the students got some of the questions right.

The problem here, at least from a contextualist standpoint, is that there is a candidate interpretation of (88) on which it means that most of the students got some, but not all, of the questions right. This doesn't follow simply from adding the standard pragmatic enrichment, the negation of (89).

(89)   Most of the students got all of the questions right.

(88) plus the negation of (89) only gives us that most of the students got some of the questions right and that it's not true that most of them got all the questions right. That is, it leaves open various possibilities that are incompatible with our target interpretation of (88): for instance, the possibility in which the students are evenly split between the categories 'got no questions right', 'got some but not all questions right' and 'got all questions right'.

Thus, it looks as though we would need to interpret *some* as 'some but not all' in situ in order to explain the target reading. The problem is, as we've also seen, that kind of default/grammatical enrichment of *some* doesn't seem to be available in all contexts, so we would still need to explain why it should be available this time.

However, sticking with a contextual account, we could still arrive at the candidate interpretation if we understood the speaker of (88) to be conveying the falsity of (90).

(90)   Some of the students got all of the questions right.

(90) doesn't entail (88), so this wouldn't be a standard quantity implicature. But it is nevertheless conceivable that (90) would be more relevant, if it were true, in the circumstances in which (88) is being uttered. So it's possible that the utterance of (88) might, under the right circumstances, implicate that (90) is false – and that would give us the 'some but not all' reading of (88) that we want to be able to explain.

The question of whether hearers of (88) are actually conscious of the possibility of (90) being uttered, and able to use that knowledge as part of their pragmatic calculation, still seems to be an open one. To answer this, we would ultimately need a much richer understanding of what is relevant in a particular context of utterance. We can certainly think of Horn scales as capturing some of the relevant facts and generalisations about which alternatives enter into quantity implicature calculations, but we also have to acknowledge that there's still quite a bit of territory left to explore.

3.5 Summary

The term 'implicature' is used to refer to meaning that is conveyed by the speaker indirectly, and goes beyond what is said. We can distinguish conventional implicatures, which are firmly associated with a particular form of words, from conversational implicatures, which are context-dependent. We can further distinguish several different kinds of conversational implicatures, which are often named with reference to the Gricean maxims that would be involved in their derivation – quantity, relation and manner. There are competing accounts as to how conversational implicatures are actually understood by hearers: most experimental testing of these accounts has focused on quantity implicatures, and specifically scalar implicatures, and has looked for evidence of default pragmatic processes. At present, there doesn't appear to be any compelling reason to assume any additional mechanism alongside the usual contextual processes for reasoning about the speaker's intention. However, research in this area has turned up a number of challenges for both contextual and default accounts of implicature.

Exercises

Answers to the following are available at <edinburghuniversitypress. com/pragmatics>.

1. What are the potentially pragmatically relevant stronger alternatives to the following?
   a. This meal is tasty.
   a. This church is old.
   a. Not everything has a price.
   a. All that glisters is not gold.
2. For each of the following, what's the difference between the predicted reading under a default and a contextual account? Is there additional information that we could assume, under a contextual account, that would deliver us the same meaning that the default interpretation predicts?
   a. Exactly five of the snowboarders managed to land some of their tricks.
   b. Rick said that Malia would do decently in the exam.
   c. Mary wants Joe to write most of their Christmas cards.
3. In the following exchanges, what implicatures might we predict to arise, and what contextual factors might prevent them from actually being conveyed?

a. Interviewer: What qualifications do you have – GCSEs, A-levels, a degree?
   Applicant: A degree.
b. Bob: What do you make of the course feedback forms?
   Sue: I've only read two so far. Looks like some of the students are unhappy.
c. Student: I'd prefer to submit my coursework online.
   Lecturer: You can do that.

Discussion questions

1. Katsos and Bishop (2011) do a couple of things differently from Bott and Noveck (2004). They use utterances based on what is happening in the visual display, such as *The mouse picked up some of the carrots*, rather than utterances such as *Some elephants are mammals*. They also present a cover story in which the cartoon character, Mr Caveman, is learning the child's language, and wants help from the child as to whether or not they 'said it right'. What differences might these manipulations make to how a child responds to these experimental items?

2. The lexical item *some* is also used in English as an indefinite determiner (*an apple/some apples*). Does this invite implicature? How might we be able to tell the two senses of *some* apart? How might the presence of the determiner *some* in the system influence our acquisition of scalar implicature?

3. Suppose that our assumption is wrong and that there's actually no difference in cognitive cost between contextual, Gricean-style inference and default inferences. Which of the approaches discussed in this chapter would still be potentially useful in trying to tell these two processes apart?

4 Presupposition

As in previous years, football will be divided into two major sectors, 'college' and 'professional', the difference being that professional players receive money, whereas college players also receive complimentary automobiles.

(Dave Barry, *Sacking the Season*)

In Chapter 3, we discussed implicature, as a broad category of meaning that goes beyond what is literally said. In the case of conversational implicature, we can in principle use our understanding of how cooperative speakers tend to act in order to infer rich pragmatic interpretations of their utterances. However, at least for scalar implicature, we could also rely on how generalisations about how particular units of language – weak scalar terms such as *some* – tend to be used. As we saw, different theories disagree about the extent to which the latter type of reasoning is used.

We also briefly discussed the case of conventional implicature, in which a particular meaning is reliably associated with a form of words, but in some sense is not as robust as a purely semantic meaning would be. One example was *but*: in (91), repeated from Chapter 3, this seems both to conjoin two pieces of information and to convey that there is some tension between them. However, that latter meaning is a bit harder to pin down, and somehow doesn't seem to contribute to the overall communicative effect of the utterance in quite the same way that the former meaning does.

(91)   Martha is poor but happy.

This chapter deals with another major category of meaning, presupposition. Like implicature, presupposition is also not part of the core meaning of the utterance; however, presupposition is dissimilar enough to implicature to merit special treatment.

We can think of presupposition in at least two different ways. From one perspective, a presupposition is anything that is a prerequisite for a particular utterance, in the sense that the utterance would not make sense if the presupposition did not hold. From another perspective, a presupposition is a unit of meaning that the speaker signals that they are taking for granted when they use a particular utterance. In a way, the former is a semantic construal of presupposition, because it considers what is logically necessary; the latter is a pragmatic construal of presupposition, because it is about usage and the speaker's intention. As we shall see, just as in the case of implicature, the pragmatically adept speaker is able to exploit how presupposition works in order to convey additional information to the hearer without having to state it explicitly.

4.1 Projection

Consider the following utterance.

> (92)   Sorry I'm late: my car broke down.

As we've already seen, we can enrich the meaning of this by appeal to the notion of relevance. We infer that there is some connection between the speaker being late and their car having broken down, and a natural way to flesh this out is to suppose that the speaker's car breaking down was a direct cause of their lateness, specifically because they were using it to travel in. As in the examples discussed in the previous chapter, this is an abductive inference and may be incorrect: perhaps the speaker was planning to take the bus anyway, but had to leave home late because they were waiting in for a car mechanic. Nevertheless, the interpretation in which the speaker was travelling by car is sufficiently obvious that they can utter (92) with confidence that this particular enriched meaning will be the one recovered by the hearer.

However, in addition to this, (92) tells us something else: namely that the speaker has a car. We know this because the proposition that the speaker is asserting makes no sense unless they have a car. Put differently, the use of the expression *my car* carries an **existential presupposition**: the existence of this entity is logically necessary in order for the reference to it to make sense.

In the case of (92), we could argue that the existence of the speaker's car isn't a matter of pragmatics at all, because it is entailed by the proposition that was asserted. If their car broke down, it follows that they have a car, and that inference is available to us without any kind of pragmatic processing at all. But in a case such as (93), things are less clear.

> (93)   I didn't bring my car.

Like (92), this utterance seems to suggest that the speaker has a car. But in this case, that does not logically follow from what they said – having a car is, after all, not a prerequisite for <u>not</u> bringing it. Indeed, under certain circumstances, it seems possible for a speaker to say (93) even when they don't have a car. For instance, (94) appears to be a possible utterance that isn't self-contradictory.

(94)   I didn't bring my car, because actually I don't have one.

It seems, then, that the use of the phrase *my car* suggests the existence of the speaker's car even in cases where its existence is not logically necessary in order for the utterance to make sense. We sometimes refer to this as the phrase **triggering** the presupposition, in this case the existential presupposition. For instance, *my car* could be argued to trigger this existential presupposition in (92), (93) and (94). Where it isn't essential to the meaning of the utterance, as in (94), it can subsequently be denied without contradiction.

In (93), the reason that the existential presupposition of *my car* is not necessary for the sentence to make sense is ultimately that *my car* falls under the scope of negation. The fact that the meaning arises anyway is classically taken to indicate its status as a presupposition. To put it more technically, the presupposition persists even when the expression that carries it falls under the syntactic scope of some operator that would cancel entailments, such as negation. This is often referred to as the presupposition **projecting** from under the scope of that operator.

Conditionals are another environment from which presupposition projection can occur. For instance, (95) appears to convey that the speaker has a car. That is evidence that the existential presupposition of *my car* can project from under the scope of a conditional. Just as in the case of (93), the important point is that the existence of the car is not logically necessary in order for (95) to make sense: there is nothing in the utterance of (95) that entails that the speaker must have a car.

(95)   If I brought my car to work, I would have nowhere to park it.

In short, presuppositional expressions of this kind carry meaning in a way that differs in important respects from regular asserted meaning. The presupposed meanings arise when the expressions that trigger them are used in positive declarative sentences, but also when they appear under the scope of negation, in conditionals, in modal contexts ('maybe ...') and so on. This also distinguishes presuppositions from implicatures, which do not standardly arise in these environments. However, when the presupposition-triggering expression does occur in the scope of negation (and conditionals, and modals, and so on), the presupposition is somewhat provisional, in the sense that it can be subsequently denied without contradiction. In fact, whether or not a presupposition eventually projects, after having been triggered in the scope of an operator such as negation, seems to depend on context, thus making it a natural issue for pragmatic investigation.

4.2 Accommodation and backgrounding

Why should we care whether a presupposed meaning ultimately arises from an utterance, if the presupposition is just a background assumption? Certainly, a lot of the time, our background assumptions are already shared by speaker and hearer, and in that case, discussing whether or not those meanings are linguistically signalled as well seems rather redundant. If you already know that the speaker has a car, the existential presupposition carried by (92), (93) or (95) doesn't tell you anything new. In the same way, (96) uses referring expressions that presuppose the existence of two individuals, but the speaker might reasonably assume that the hearer will already know that these people exist. And in (97), a Norwegian soccer commentator addresses an imagined English audience by referring to eight people by name, thus presupposing the existence of each (along with the referent of *your boys*, the England football team that had just lost 2–1), and yet presumably not intending any of these entities to be new to the hearer.

> (96) The Secretary-General of the United Nations will be meeting with the President of the United States.
> (97) Lord Nelson! Lord Beaverbrook! Sir Winston Churchill! Sir Anthony Eden! Clement Attlee! Henry Cooper! Lady Diana! ... Maggie Thatcher ... Your boys took one hell of a beating! (Bjørge Lillelien, 9 September 1981)

However, alongside these uses, a speaker can exploit the way presupposition works in order to convey new information. The speaker of (92), or of (93) or (95), does not require the hearer to know in advance that they have a car: this can be inferred from the utterance. In cases such as this, the speaker is entitled to expect that the hearer will do so. In effect, by acting as though the presupposed information is already mutually known to speaker and hearer, the speaker succeeds in conveying it to the hearer, thus making it mutually known. The process that this relies on – the hearer taking the presupposition to be true – is known as **accommodation**.

What's the difference between getting a hearer to accommodate a presupposition, and simply asserting the corresponding meaning? In practice, sometimes not a great deal: the speaker of (95) could have said (98) instead, for instance. The hearer would probably understand these two potential utterances to be conveying essentially the same meaning, and no obvious consequences would arise from the speaker choosing one option rather than the other.

(98)   I have a car, but if I brought it to work, I would have nowhere to park it.

However, as we just discussed, presupposed meaning – unlike regular asserted meaning – can project from under the scope of negation. This makes a big difference when we want to challenge presupposed meaning, because when we try to negate it, it doesn't go away. Consider a question such as (99).

(99)   Do you spend a lot of time running your drug empire?

This question carries an existential presupposition, through the use of the words *your drug empire*. Yet it is purely a yes/no question. What's more, if the hearer were to respond *yes* or *no*, they would essentially be allowing the presupposition to stand. If they said 'yes', they would be asserting that they spend a lot of time running their drug empire, which obviously entails that they have such a thing. If they said 'no', they would asserting that they don't spend a lot of time running their drug empire, which still presupposes that they have one. Essentially, neither of the usually appropriate responses to this yes/no question serves the hearer at all well if they want to deny that they have a drug empire (which I'm assuming they probably want to do, for one reason or another).

The difficulty of denying presupposed content in cases like this is the basis of one of the widely used diagnostic tests for presupposition, the 'Hey, wait a minute' test (Shanon 1976; Von Fintel 2004). The key observation is that it's felicitous to challenge a presupposition with an utterance like (100) – offered as a response to (99) – but it would be odd to use that kind of utterance to address the main content of the preceding utterance. That is to say, considered as a response to (99), (101) would not only fail to deny the presupposition but would answer the question in a rather odd way.

(100)   Hey, wait a minute, I don't have a drug empire!
(101)   ?? Hey, wait a minute, I don't spend a lot of time on it!

In fact, this test might not be a very specific test for presupposition: as Potts (2012) points out, we can use a 'Hey, wait a minute'-type utterance to challenge other forms of non-asserted content, such as conventional implicatures ('What do you mean, *but?*'). Indeed, to the extent that (101) is an odd reply to (99), it's odd in the fact that it seems confrontational – as though the speaker of (101) has decided that the specific accusation that they spend a lot of time running their drug empire is the unreasonable thing for the speaker of (99) to allege.

That notwithstanding, as far as presupposition is concerned, the 'Hey, wait a minute' test does reinforce an important point: although we can convey new information using presuppositions (and by exploiting accommodation), that information doesn't typically have the same status as asserted information, at least in terms of the role that information plays in the ongoing discourse. (We'll consider the question of whether presupposed information has the same psychological status as asserted information in section 4.5.) It is difficult for the hearer to deny, or even to challenge, that presupposed information; to do so, they have to use some kind of circumlocution, such as in (100). Simply saying *no* or *that's not true* simply won't do the job, because these responses are naturally understood to be directed towards the asserted content of the preceding utterance, rather than its presupposition.

Because presupposed material is difficult to deny, a speaker can use presupposition in order to introduce controversial information, which might be a rhetorically effective device, as well as being a potentially aggressive discourse move, as in (99). (102)–(104) are some attested examples from online sources, using the presupposition trigger *know*.

(102) We all know that Lebanon's economy is in need of serious diversification. (https://www.thenational.ae/business/comment/will-mckinsey-help-lebanon-chalk-out-a-better-economic-model -1.699296)

(103) We all know that better business results come from the diversity of ideas that arise from a diversity of people and perspectives. (https://www.houstonchronicle.com/opinion/outlook/article/Houston-s-future-depends-on-its-businesses-being-12529 534.php)

(104) We all know that Obamacare literally kills people … (https://hazlitt.net/blog/what-went-wrong-week-broccoli)

In each of these cases, responding *that's not true* might invite the interpretation that the responder was challenging the claim that *We all know X* rather than the fact of *X*. We'll consider examples of this type more thoroughly in section 4.3.2.

In the above discussion, I've been contrasting presupposition with 'asserted meaning', and I've tended to rely on an appeal to intuition as to what that means. Ever since Frege (1892), there has been broad agreement that we can distinguish presupposition from this other kind of content. But in certain cases this can be problematic. Consider (105).

(105) I didn't realise that I over-scrutinised every project, telling them exactly what to do on each deliverable. (https://www.theguard-ian.com/seizing-opportunities-with-aldermore/2018/jan/09/top-startup-tips-six-things-i-wish-id-known)

The speaker of (105) seems to be conveying two things: (i) that they over-scrutinised every project, and (ii) that they didn't realise that (at the time, although presumably they do now). Given the context, it's clear that the speaker doesn't expect the hearer already to know either of these things: both are new pieces of information that the speaker is communicating. Formally, there's a difference in the status of these two pieces of meaning. Meaning (ii) is asserted by the speaker. However, *realise* is a presupposition trigger, and meaning (i) is presup-posed, in the expectation that the speaker will be able to accommodate it. In fact, as it stands, the presupposition is projecting from under the scope of negation. If we were to negate (105), cancelling out the exist-ing negation, we would end up with (106), which conveys meaning (i) in exactly the same way as (105) does, but conveys the negation of meaning (ii).

(106) I realised that I over-scrutinised every project, telling them exactly what to do on each deliverable.

In short, we can formally distinguish something that we can call asserted content from something that we can call presupposed content. However, in this case, the asserted content is not really what we could call the 'main content' of the utterance. In fact, the speaker's primary purpose in uttering (105) – just as it would be in uttering (106) – seems to be to convey meaning (i).

In order to discuss cases like this, it's useful to have some kind of functional notion of presupposed content alongside the formal notion. One way of approaching this is in terms of **backgrounding**: a speaker packages information in a certain way when they produce an utterance, making some of it more salient to the hearer and some of it less salient. We could try to articulate that in processing terms, for instance by saying that some of the information (the foreground) is immediately relevant to the hearer when verifying the utterance, and perhaps will also be processed more deeply as a result, while the rest of the informa-tion (the background) is not (see for instance Kim 2008). Or we can try to approach it in terms of discourse functions, for instance by appeal to the notion of **Question Under Discussion** (QUD), as introduced by Roberts (1996). On this view, each utterance is considered to offer an answer, or partial answer, to some question that is either implicitly or explicitly in need of answering at that point in the discourse. We can then distinguish material that is **at-issue**, in the sense that it addresses the QUD, from material that is **not at-issue**, in the sense that it does not.

As a generalisation, presupposed information is backgrounded and not at-issue: we do not expect hearers to consider that information immediately relevant when they are verifying the utterance, and we don't expect it to help in answering the QUD. But, as in examples like (105), there are numerous apparent exceptions to this generalisation. This raises the same kinds of questions that we discussed in Chapter 3 with respect to implicature. Are presuppositions all processed in the same way, or are there potentially different classes of presupposition that receive different treatment? Do presupposition triggers differ in how much, or how consistently, they cause the presupposed meanings to be backgrounded or to be not at-issue – and are these the same thing? And do some presuppositions project automatically from under the scope of operators such as negation – a bit like scalar implicatures, on a GCI analysis – or does this always depend on context?

In order to address some of these questions, it will be useful to have a fuller picture of presupposition. The following section takes a broader look at presuppositions and their triggering expressions, and considers some ideas about how this category of meaning is structured.

4.3 Types of presupposition

In the preceding section we discussed projection and accommodation initially with reference to existential presupposition, and then by briefly considering the presuppositions associated with the specific verbs *know* and *realise*. However, presupposition is a much more widespread phenomenon than this, and accommodation can correspondingly be used to convey a wide range of meanings.

Many different kinds of expressions can be used to trigger different kinds of presuppositions. Zeevat (1992) proposes to sort presupposition triggers into three categories, based on their discourse functions. Although, as we shall see, there are various other ways of categorising presuppositions, Zeevat's taxonomy will give us a useful starting point. His three categories – resolution, lexical and 'bookkeeping' – will be discussed in the following subsections.

4.3.1 Resolution triggers

Zeevat (1992) follows Van der Sandt (1988) in distinguishing presup-position triggers based upon how 'anaphoric' they are: that is to say, the extent to which they refer to pre-existing entities. The most anaphoric category of presupposition triggers, which he calls resolution triggers, are those which 'collect entities from the environment in order to say new things about them' (Zeevat 1992: 397). Definite descriptions, such as *the President of the United States* and *the Secretary-General of the United Nations* in (96), are prime examples. Time-referring clauses involving terms such as *when* and *after* also potentially fit into this category: (107) has one of the latter, and calls back to a past event on the fictional timeline under discussion, which is presupposed to have happened.

(107)   Simon Jones is to reprise his starring role as Arthur Dent, the mild-mannered Englishman who finds himself dragged across the universe, after the Earth is destroyed to make way for an interga-lactic bypass. (http://www.telegraph.co.uk/radio/what-to-listen-to/hitchhikers-guide-galaxy-will-return-new-series-2018/)

Of course, even if we think of resolution triggers as 'collecting entities from the environment', that 'environment' isn't necessarily shared by speaker and hearer. We might think of accommodation, in the case of resolution triggers, as taking place when the speaker uses an expression to collect an entity from their own prior knowledge, and present it to the hearer. If addressing a hearer who knows nothing about the radio series in question, the speaker of (107) is potentially introducing lots of new information through the use of resolution triggers. For instance, *his starring role as Arthur Dent* conveys that Simon Jones had this star-ring role, the phrase *the mild-mannered Englishman . . .* conveys additional information about the character in question, and the *after*-clause details a plot point in such a way as to make it comprehensible to a hearer who doesn't know it already. All this information is presupposed, and might well be familiar to the hearer – in which case it presumably serves merely to remind them of these details – but will be perfectly comprehensible even if it is all new.

Perhaps an even more striking case of accommodation is quoted in (108), which introduces a character in a short story.

(108)   Benedict Farley, that eccentric millionaire, chose not to advertise his choice of residence. (Agatha Christie, *The Dream*)

As Benedict Farley exists only in the realm of this story – and then not for very long – the reader cannot possibly know in advance that he is an eccentric millionaire (although Agatha Christie's stories may have an above-average concentration of eccentric millionaires). But although this fact is introduced using what appears to be a presupposition-triggering expression, there is no difficulty in apprehending it. The point of using this device, as opposed to making this piece of information part of the main content, is perhaps to signal that Benedict Farley's status as an eccentric millionaire is supposed to be widely known in the fictional universe within which the narrative is taking place (hence, the hearer would merely need to be reminded of that fact).

4.3.2 Lexical triggers

At the other end of the scale from resolution triggers, Zeevat (1992) identifies the class that he calls lexical triggers, which are expressions relating to actions and states that trigger presuppositions about their logical prerequisites. In his words, 'the application of a concept is only an option if certain conditions are already met. The conditions that must be met are the lexical presuppositions of the concept' (ibid.: 397).

We've already seen potential examples of this in the use of *know* and *realise*, under the assumption that in order truly to *know* something or to *realise* something, that something has to be true. If so, the truth of that propositional complement of the verb is a lexical presupposition triggered by the verb. *Know* and *realise* can be seen as representatives of a broad class of so-called factive verbs, including *learn*, *regret* and *be ADJ that* for various different adjectives: (109)–(111) all convey presuppositions in this way.

(109)   When will we learn that war is not the answer? (https://www. psychologytoday.com/blog/wicked-deeds/201406/when-will-we-learn-war-is-not-the-answer)

(110)   I regret being so polite about Philip Hammond. (http://www. telegraph.co.uk/politics/2018/01/27/regret-polite-philip-hammond-utterly-unsuited-job/)

(111)   I'm sorry that I made you cry. (John Lennon, *Jealous Guy*)

That said, the status of these verbs is not uncontroversial. Hazlett (2010) disputes the existence of factive verbs, pointing to the fact that *know*, *realise*, and others can be used felicitously with false propositional complements, as in (112), when uttered by someone reporting back on an experience that turned out not to be fatal.

(112)   I knew/realised I was going to die there.

Nevertheless, there is a reasonably clear distinction between verbs of this type and verbs such as *think* that have traditionally been considered non-factive. Using *think* with a false proposition is perfectly OK: one can think something (or say that someone else is thinking something) without being committed to its being true. By contrast, using *know* with a false proposition is open to challenge – did the speaker of (112) really 'know', or 'realise', that? – and many of the attested usages seem to have a metalinguistic character. For example, (113) ironically emphasises the verb *knew*; (114) actually places it in quotation marks. Either option would be odd if the verb had been *thought* instead of *knew*, because the emphasis seems to address a perceived lack of coherence that simply wouldn't arise if *thought* had been used: consequently, (115) seems to be infelicitous, for instance.

(113)   Of course all the pundits and the 'smart' people KNEW that Hillary would win on November 8th. (https://medium.com/@DBCopa/you-cant-handle-the-truth-62b11834c399)

(114)   They 'knew' that Hillary would win so they made it into a horse race. (https://twitter.com/treehouseNY/status/953314441768112128)

(115)   ? They 'thought' that Hillary would win so they made it into a horse race.

Less controversially, verbs like *stop* and *continue* convey presuppositions about the prior state of affairs before the events being described. Adverbs like *still* appear to do the same thing. (116)–(118) all seem to have the same presupposition, namely that Victoria used to smoke at some point prior to the time of utterance. Here again the intuition is fairly clear that the presuppositions in question survive negation: negating (116), (117) and (118) flips their meaning with respect to what they say about the current situation, but the presupposition survives in each case, although it does become potentially amenable to cancellation, as in (119).

(116)   Victoria stopped smoking.

(117)   Victoria continued to smoke.

(118)   Victoria still smokes.

(119)   Victoria didn't stop smoking; she never used to smoke.

Only represents an interesting case. (120), a remark famously attributed to Leona Helmsley, seems to convey two things: that 'little people' pay taxes, and that no one else does. In the negation of this, (121), the meaning that survives is that 'little people' pay taxes, which suggests that this is a presupposition. The remaining content of (120), that no one else does, is negated in (121), indicating that it is not presuppositional in (120).

(120)   Only little people pay taxes.
(121)   Not only little people pay taxes.

4.3.3 Bookkeeping triggers

Zeevat (1992) distinguishes a third category of triggers, which he doesn't name, but which he identifies as playing a role in the 'bookkeeping' of information. He proposes to sort triggers such as *too*, *another*, *also* and *again* into this category. These have a certain amount in common with the resolution triggers discussed in section 4.3.1: they collect, or at least allude to, established entities, such as people or events. However, rather than saying new things about them as such, these triggers relate them to the material that is currently being foregrounded.

In examples (122)–(125), the triggers in the second sentences pick up material that is present in the immediately preceding sentences: for instance, *too* in (122) makes reference to the fact that Esther went to the gym. In these cases, the only effect of using the trigger is to point to some kind of parallel between the events being described in the two sentences, although it does also confer the advantage of making it possible to elide material from the second sentence without causing ambiguity. For instance, *Rita went* wouldn't really serve as a felicitous second sentence in (122) or (123): in the absence of a presupposition trigger (such as *too*, *as well*, *also*), we would have to say *Rita went to the gym*.

(122)   Esther went to the gym. Rita went too.
(123)   Esther went to the gym. Rita also went.
(124)   Jon received a parking fine last week. Today he got another.
(125)   Jon parked illegally last week. Today he did so again.

However, these triggers can reach much further back than this. Consider (126).

(126)   We're due for another ice age, but climate change may push it back another 100,000 years, researchers say. (https://weather. com/news/climate/news/ice-age-climate-change-earth-glacial-interglacial-period)

The first use of *another* in this utterance links a future event with a past event (or events) of a similar nature, but which has not necessarily been mentioned earlier in the discourse. In this case, assuming that it's common ground that there have been ice ages before, it's perfectly reasonable to start a discourse like this – and even if this isn't common ground, the speaker could appeal to accommodation. The second use of *another* is similar, in that it seems to presuppose some period of elapsed time between the last ice age and the present day, and points to a rather vague parallelism between that time and the time that may elapse between now and the next ice age.

In a similar way, it is perfectly reasonable to begin a discourse with (127), presupposing the existence of a past event in which Elaine saw Tim. This past event doesn't have to have been mentioned recently; in fact, it might not have been mentioned at all, and the speaker might be conveying that it happened by appeal to accommodation. And, in much the same spirit, it's reasonable to begin a discourse with (128).

> (127) Elaine saw Tim again last night.
> (128) Women came forward, now more men are too. (http://therepresentationproject.org/woman-came-forward-now-men-are-too/)

In the case of (128), there's an ambiguity which is typical of the use of *too*. The presupposition of *more men are too* in this context might be that 'some previous men came forward', or conceivably just that 'women came forward' (as stated explicitly in the preceding clause). The full vagueness of *too* becomes apparent in an example like (129).

> (129) Martha walked to the store. And Liz cycled to the library too.

In principle, by saying *too*, the speaker of (129) might intend to relate Liz's action to some previous action that Liz performed (perhaps she cycled to the bank, say), or to some previous instance of someone cycling to the library (perhaps Martha did so), or indeed to some previous instance of someone else doing something else. If the context for (129) is the speaker enumerating the ways in which members of the household engaged in healthy activities today, the presupposition of *too* might just be 'Martha walked to the store'.

4.4 Other taxonomies of presupposition

Zeevat's (1992) approach helps us appreciate some of the functional differences between different presupposition triggers. However, there are other ways in which we can distinguish presupposition triggers, and considering those might lead us towards different ideas about how to classify presuppositions taxonomically.

For instance, an important way in which bookkeeping triggers differ from most other triggers is that there is a clear sense in which the foreground content and the background content are potentially independent. In the case of lexical triggers, by definition, the foregrounded content doesn't make proper sense if the presupposition fails. By contrast, for the bookkeeping triggers, the foregrounded content generally makes reasonable sense even if the presupposition fails. We might disagree about whether (127) is true if it turns out that Elaine never saw Tim before last night, but we can agree that it still conveys 'Elaine saw Tim last night', and that might still be true. This point is expounded by Lewis Carroll in the following exchange from *Alice's Adventures in Wonderland*.

> (130) 'Take some more tea', the March Hare said to Alice, very earnestly.
> 'I've had nothing yet', Alice replied in an offended tone, 'so I can't take more'.
> 'You mean you can't take *less*', said the Hatter: 'it's very easy to take *more* than nothing'.

Here, Alice objects to the false presupposition of the March Hare's offer, namely that she has previously had tea. This presupposition is triggered by *more* – a bookkeeping trigger, in Zeevat's terms. The Mad Hatter's reply serves to point out that the failure of that presupposition doesn't actually bear on the offer being made: Alice could perfectly well accept tea without making the point that she hadn't had any already, and indeed it would be prescriptively more polite for her to do just that.

Sudo (2012) and Klinedinst (2012) focus on this kind of distinction, arguing that a major point of divergence between presupposition triggers is whether or not they also entail their presupposed content. Consider *stop* in (116), repeated below in slightly modified form as (131).

> (131) Victoria has stopped smoking.

By common consent, the presupposition of (131) is that Victoria used to smoke. If we take the view that the presupposition and the asserted content mustn't overlap – if, for instance, we were committed to a theory on which the presupposition was necessarily background content and the assertion was necessarily foreground content – then we would have to conclude that the assertion was merely that Victoria doesn't smoke now. However, intuitively, what the speaker is trying to convey in uttering (131) is not merely that Victoria doesn't smoke now but that she recently transitioned from smoking to not smoking. (132) illustrates this: the speaker seems to be proposing that a change in Victoria's status as a smoker is a possible explanation of her observed mood. What they are saying is not accurately paraphrased as 'Perhaps Victoria is tense because she doesn't smoke'.

> (132) Victoria seems tense; maybe she's stopped smoking.

In the case of *stop*, then, it looks as though the presupposition is also entailed by the asserted content of the sentence. We can't really say that the speaker presupposes the previous state and only asserts the current state: rather, they assert a change of state, which entails both the previous state and the current state. But the previous state is also presupposed, which explains why it survives when the sentence is negated, as in (133).

(133)   Victoria hasn't stopped smoking.

Another approach in a similar line is espoused by Glanzberg (2005), namely that presupposition triggers differ in whether or not they require obligatory repair: that is, that for some triggers, presupposition failure leads to expression failure, while in other case it does not. The existential presupposition triggered by the words *that palm tree* in (134) requires obligatory repair in his terms, because the whole expression is ill-formed if the tree doesn't exist; the presupposition triggered by *too* in (135) does not, because the expression is perfectly comprehensible in the absence of that presupposition. This appears to be closely connected to the question of whether the utterance's presupposed content is or is not independent from the rest of its content: where there is independence, the presupposition failure is not catastrophic for the communicative usefulness of the utterance.

(134)   That palm tree is about to fall. (Glanzberg 2005: example (19a))
(135)   John solved the problem too. (Glanzberg 2005: example (19e))

Yet another approach is to focus on the projection behaviour of the presuppositions. Abusch (2002, 2010) draws a distinction between 'hard' and 'soft' presupposition triggers: the former are more robust in their projection behaviour than the latter. Abusch argues that *too* is an example of a hard trigger, while she cites *win* – which presupposes 'participate in' – as an example of a soft trigger. Relevant example utterances are of the form (136) and (137).

(136)   I don't know if John entered the race, but if he won, I'll be surprised.
(137)   ? I don't know if John entered the race, but if Mary did too, they will probably meet up afterwards.

The distinction is perhaps a little elusive, but the claim is as follows: in (136), the presupposition of *won* – that John definitely entered the race – would contradict the speaker's claim of ignorance in the first clause. Nevertheless, (136) seems to be OK, which suggests that no contradiction is perceived to arise. That is to say, the presupposition of *won* doesn't project from under the scope of its conditional.

Note on terminology
The non-projection of a presupposition such as (136) is sometimes called **local accommodation**. The use of the word 'local' reflects the fact that the presupposition does not 'leave' its local environment in such a case (here, the scope of the conditional). The use of the word 'accommodation' reflects a particular theoretical construal of how this process takes place. If the presupposition is not locally accommodated, it projects to the discourse level, which is sometimes referred to as **global accommodation**.

Similarly, in (137), the presupposition of *too* – assuming this to be that John also entered the race – would contradict the first clause for the same reason as in (136), namely that the speaker is avowedly ignorant of whether or not John entered the race. However, in this case, (137) seems awkward, suggesting that there is some sense of a contradiction here, presumably because the presupposition has projected. Abusch argues that there is a systematic difference between presupposition triggers in this respect, with some patterning like *win* in (136) and admitting local accommodation, and others patterning like *too* in (137) and undergoing projection.

Intuitively, we might suspect that these two taxonomies are somehow connected: that is, there is a relationship between projection behaviour and the relative status of presupposed and asserted content. Klinedinst (2012) argues for such an explanation. It's perhaps worth noting again that the role of *too* in (137) is almost purely presuppositional – in this case, the utterance goes through with *too* completely removed, the only difference being the absence of the presupposition – whereas *won* in (136) is being uttered in order to convey its lexical meaning rather than just its presupposition. Consequently, we might think that the use of *too* is more likely to reflect the speaker's deliberate intention to convey a presupposition than the use of *won* is, and hence that the hearer should attempt to understand the presupposition of *too* as projecting, even though it results in the utterance as a whole becoming incoherent.

An alternative and more general account of projection is offered by Simons et al. (2010). They argue that 'projection is a consequence of the scope of sentential operators such as negation, conditionals and modals typically being limited roughly to what is understood as the main point ... of the utterance' (ibid.: 315). They argue that the 'main point' is what is at-issue, in the sense introduced in section 4.2.

Simons et al.'s proposal aims not only to explain the projection of presuppositions, but also of other forms of content. For instance, they note that the content of non-restrictive relative clauses (NRRCs) also projects. From both (138) and its negated form (139), we can derive the interpretation that Kathy is rich, but this doesn't appear to be a presupposition in any obvious semantic sense: it is a parenthetical remark that the speaker asserts in the process of making another point. Simons et al.'s account would characterise this material as being not at-issue and therefore projecting to the discourse level.

(138)   Kathy, who is rich, voted for Trump.
(139)   Kathy, who is rich, didn't vote for Trump.

Notably, although Simons et al.'s account is compatible with there being (for instance) a general tendency for the presuppositions of *too* to project and those of *win* not to, the account also posits that whether a specific instance of a presupposition projects is determined by its relation to the QUD, and is therefore fundamentally a matter of context.

To take a minimal example of how context might make a difference to projection behaviour, consider the effect of changing the stress on (140).

(140)   It's possible that Laura has finished writing her thesis.

Here, the word *finished* is a potential presupposition trigger, the presupposition being that the action in question was started; and it occurs under the scope of modal possibility. With focal stress on the word *finished*, (140) could be interpreted as an answer to a question like (141). But with focal stress on the words *her thesis*, the same utterance seems more naturally to answer a question like (142), and with focal stress on *Laura* it seems to answer (143).

(141)   How is Laura doing with her thesis?
(142)   What is it that Laura has finished writing?
(143)   Who finished writing their thesis?

Correspondingly, we might intuit that the speaker who stresses the word *finished* means to convey the presupposition that Laura has started writing her thesis, and consequently that that projects from under the scope of the modal (*possible*). By contrast, the speaker who stresses *her thesis* appears to be less committed to the idea that Laura has started writing her thesis. And similarly, stress on *Laura* seems to invite the interpretation that, although it may be Laura who has finished writing her thesis, it may be someone else entirely, in which case Laura may not even have started writing her thesis (as far as the speaker knows).

If these differences are reliable, we would have to conclude that a purely semantic account of projection, ignoring context, would be unable to account for the behaviour of this trigger. However, to support such a claim we would ideally need experimental data, and to generalise it as an account of presupposition we would really need to consider a wide range of triggers and contexts. As we shall see in the next section, this is still work in progress, but appreciable headway has already been made.

4.5 Experimental evidence

Let's revisit the questions that were flagged up at the end of section 4.2. Are presuppositions all processed the same way, or are there different classes of presuppositions that receive different treatment? Having looked at some accounts of how to divide presuppositions into classes, we can recast that as a question about whether we can distinguish those classes from one another on processing grounds. Do presupposition triggers differ in how much, or how consistently, they cause the presupposed meanings to be backgrounded or not at-issue? That could be a question about how available the meanings are for being challenged in the subsequent discourse, but on Simons et al.'s (2010) account it becomes a question about whether presupposed meanings associated with different triggers all project equally from under the scope of negation and other operators. And do some presuppositions project automatically, or does that always depend on context? That's certainly a question that seems to invite experimental investigation.

There has been a wealth of experimental work on presupposition in recent years, so I won't attempt to do justice to it all here – see Schwarz (in press) for a thorough recent survey – but I will briefly discuss a few of the studies and methods that seem to offer some progress towards answering the above questions.

4.5.1 The status of presuppositional meaning

One obvious place to start is to ask whether we have evidence that presuppositional content is treated any differently from entailed content, as assumed in section 4.1. This has been the topic of intense philosophical debate for many years, much of it centring on existential presuppositions and how these interfere with our judgements about a sentence's truth-value. The classic examples are (144) and (145), which share the definite description *the King of France*, which is a trigger for an existential presupposition concerning an individual that happens not to exist in the real world.

(144)   The King of France is bald.
(145)   The King of France is not bald.

Strawson (1950) argued that, even granted the non-existence of the King of France, we feel squeamish about declaring that (144) is false. However, what is not clear is whether this is purely a result of the failure of the existential presupposition, or whether other factors are also at play. Strawson (1964) noted that (146) seems straightforwardly false, which might reflect the fact that this is a statement that is verifiable in principle (we could, in principle find out who visited the exhibition yesterday). Of course, our immediate confidence in the falsity of this statement is presumably underwritten by our confidence in the non-existence of the King of France, so to that extent it's puzzling that our intuitions about this could differ from our intuitions about (144).

(146)   The exhibition was visited yesterday by the King of France.

Lasersohn (1993: 116) pointed out that (147) also seems to be uncontroversially false. He explains this in terms of the verification procedure that we can undertake for this sentence: if we can see the chair, we can see either that it's empty or that someone is sitting in it, and in the latter case, we know that the person is not the King of France, because there is no King of France.

(147)   The King of France is sitting in that chair.

In order to gather empirical data on this issue, Abrusán and Szendrői (2013) tested a set of sentences with false existential presuppositions, using a ternary truth-value judgement (TVJ) task: their participants were asked to respond 'true', 'false' or 'can't say'. Among their stimuli were positive and negative versions of sentences with a false existential presupposition: they distinguished straightforward presupposition failures like (144), potentially falsifiable claims such as (146), and directly falsifiable claims such as (147). In the positive case, they included another baseline condition, the not-entirely-presuppositional (148).

(148)   France has a king and he is bald.

Strikingly, in all the positive conditions that Abrusán and Szendrői tested, there was a large majority of 'false' responses: relatively few participants felt squeamish about rejecting sentences such as (144), (146) and (147). By contrast, sentences such as (145) split participants three ways, with 21 per cent 'true', 45 per cent 'false' and 34 per cent 'can't say' responses. Generally, the negative sentences attracted an appreciably higher proportion of uncertain responses.

   The implications of this for theory are quite complex (Abrusán and Szendrői go on to discuss this in considerably more detail). However, at a minimum, we seem to have evidence here for existential presuppositions behaving unlike normal assertions, or entailments, in a TVJ. Here, participants who affirm the falsity of one sentence are refusing to affirm the truth of its negation. Indeed, there are participants who are apparently judging both (144) and (145) false, and if these individuals are being consistent, we would expect them to judge (149) true, which seems problematic (at least with the specific predicate *bald*).

(149)   The King of France is neither bald nor not bald.

Most other presupposition triggers haven't been tested so thoroughly, but the evidence that has been obtained seems to point in the same direction: that is, in favour of presuppositional meaning having a special status as far as truth-value judgements are concerned. For instance, Zehr (2015) tests *stop* experimentally in a ternary TVJ and finds a substantial proportion of participants willing to answer 'neither', even to a positive sentence. His examples involve pictures in which an event has not started happening yet: for instance, (150) is used to describe a picture showing a new, unlit match (ibid.: 165).

(150)   The match has stopped burning.

In this case, presumably there would be grounds to say either 'true' or 'false' – the former if you interpret (150) merely as asserting that the match isn't burning, the latter if you interpret the assertion merely as asserted that the match has progressed from burning to not burning. Perhaps the evidence in favour of 'true' is more compelling here than for examples such as (144), and this is a factor in participants' relative disinclination just to call (150) false.

4.5.2 Access to presuppositions

Schwarz (2007) tested the time-course of the availability of presuppositional meaning, initially focusing on the German trigger *auch* and subsequently using its English equivalent *also*. He used a self-paced reading study, in which participants were timed reading sentences such as (151) and (152) (ibid.: 193). The sentences were divided into chunks as indicated by the / marks.

(151)   The congressman / who wrote to John / had also written to the mayor / to schedule a meeting / for the fundraiser.

(152)   The congressman / who John wrote to / had also written to the mayor / to schedule a meeting / for the fundraiser.

The relevant contrast here is that, in (151), *also* has a clear antecedent, namely the fact of the congressman writing to John. In (152), it does not: the sentence again asserts that the congressman had written to the mayor, but, unlike (151), it doesn't assert that the congressman wrote to anyone else. We can accommodate the presupposition of *also* by inferring that the congressman did indeed write to someone else, or we can understand the use of *also* just as referring to a previous event of writing in general (in which case it could be referring to the fact of John writing to the congressman), rather than a previous instance of the congressman writing to anyone.

These two kinds of items were further contrasted with controls in which *also* was replaced by *just*, which is not presuppositional. The reading time results show an interaction in the *also/just* region, which could be interpreted as indicating that the (152)-type sentences are especially problematic for readers. In short, readers were immediately slower when the presupposition was not satisfied by the prior context. This seems to indicate that the presupposition, once triggered, is immediately available to the reader. In the case of (152), this triggered presupposition compels the reader to start searching for some previous event that the trigger could be referring to.

Tiemann et al. (2011) generalised this result to a broader class of triggers in German, again using reading times to assess the presence of online processing. As well as *auch*, they used *wieder* ('again'), *aufhören* ('stop'), *wissen* ('know') and *sein* ('his') as part of a definite NP. And Clifton (2013) made some additional progress with the role of NP definiteness, showing a processing advantage for definite NPs (e.g. *the stove*) in a context which provided a unique possible referent, and for indefinite NPs (e.g. *a stove*) in a context which provided multiple possible referents (e.g. an appliance store).

Methodology: dual task approaches to working memory

A general approach that can be useful in psychological experiments is to ask a participant to perform two tasks at the same time. In many cases, this will be perfectly straightforward, but in some cases it will be much more demanding to combine these tasks than it is to do each one separately – that is, there will be interference between the two tasks. This is often taken as evidence that the tasks make use of the same underlying cognitive processes. For instance, it's difficult for a person to pat their head and rub their stomach at the same time, and this is taken as an indication of the simultaneous involvement of the same mental processes (connected to the motor cortex) in both actions.

In psycholinguistics, a widely used technique is to ask participants to perform a linguistic task while also retaining certain information in memory – perhaps some words, the output of a simple arithmetic task, or the layout of a physical display. The idea is that this imposes a burden on working memory, and consequently leads to reduced performance in tasks that involve working memory. To put it another way, reduced performance in a task under working memory load might be taken to indicate that that task normally requires working memory – which is often interpreted as evidence that it is not an automatic, default type of process.

More precisely, Clifton (2013) found that participants were initially equally rapid in self-paced reading for the NPs, irrespective of whether the context provided multiple potential referents or just a single referent. However, in a version of the task that imposed memory load (by asking a simple arithmetical question between the reading and the following comprehension question), participants were slower to read definite NPs in the non-uniqueness condition, suggesting that this imposes an additional burden on their reasoning process.

4.5.3 Testing the taxonomies

Jayez et al. (2015) explore the idea derived from the work of Abusch (2002, 2010) that there is a clear distinction between what they call weak and strong triggers. Specifically, they test (using materials in French) whether several putatively strong triggers – including the apparently straightforwardly translatable *aussi* ('too') and *regretter* ('regret') – are resistant to accommodation in the way predicted. (153) is one of Jayez et al.'s (2015: 177) critical items.

> (153)   I don't know whether Paul will go to the party because, if Mary goes too, it will be embarrassing.

In this case, Jayez et al.'s participants do not appear to have any difficulty with the use of *too*, even though the speaker is evidently not committed to the presupposition that is associated with it (namely that Paul will go to the party). Jayez et al. argue that this stems from discourse factors: in this context, the speaker's intended meaning is sufficiently clear that the potentially awkward presupposition trigger is judged to be fine.

For Jayez et al., this is evidence against the potential distinction between weak and strong triggers – or, as they put it, 'there is at the moment no clear empirical evidence supporting the existence of a separate class of *lexically* or *conventionally* strong triggers, and ... it is not clear that triggers in general *encode* directly the strength/persistence/ likelihood of projection' (2015: 184; their emphasis).

Cummins et al. (2013) look at Zeevat's (1992) proposal, focusing on the distinction between lexical and non-lexical triggers (which they broadly term resolution triggers, slightly simplifying Zeevat's three-way distinction). They posit that the two categories of trigger will differ in how acceptable certain assertions involving the triggers are when the presupposition fails. For instance, consider the question (154) and the possible answers (155) and (156).

(154) Did Mary see John again?
(155) Yes, although she never saw him before.
(156) No, because she never saw him before.

The issue here is whether one can and should respond 'yes' or 'no' to a question like (154) if the presupposition (in this case, the presupposition triggered by *again*) doesn't hold. Cummins et al. (2013) show some evidence of a distinction between lexical (*continue, regret, still* and *stop*) and non-lexical triggers (*again, too*) in this respect: for the lexical triggers, responses such as (156) were judged significantly more acceptable than responses such as (155), while there was no significant difference between the kinds of responses for non-lexical triggers. That is to say, for lexical triggers – but not for non-lexical triggers – failure of the presupposition requires a 'no' answer to a question like (154).

Methodology: Likert scales
In cases where experimenters want to gauge the strength of a partici-pant's preference – for instance, how acceptable an utterance is, or to what extent it admits one interpretation rather than another – they will often ask the participant to respond using a scale with some small fixed number of points, often called a Likert scale. Participants might be asked to rate an utterance from 1–5, being told that 1 denotes 'completely unacceptable' and 5 'completely acceptable'.

Judgements elicited using these methods are usually untimed. A concern with timing this process would be that the time taken might reflect how long a participant spends deciding on the precise value to assign to a particular item, rather than how certain they are that it deserves a rating in some general area.

Cummins et al. (2013) interpret this distinction between the two classes of trigger as potential experimental evidence in support of Zeevat's taxonomy, but with some caution: there is still considerable variation among the triggers within each class, and the results are therefore still compatible with a much less clear-cut categorisation of presupposition triggers.

4.5.4 Projection and context

Chemla and Bott (2013) compare the availability of the two alternative interpretations of items such as (157).

(157)   Zoologists do not realise that elephants are birds.

On what they call a global accommodation interpretation, (157) conveys that elephants are birds and that zoologists do not realise that they are: on a local accommodation interpretation, (157) merely conveys that it is not the case both that elephants are birds and that zoologists realise this.

Just like the underinformative utterances in scalar implicature experiments, in a TVJ, (157) receives both 'true' and 'false' responses from adult participants. Chemla and Bott (2013) document that the false responses are delivered faster, on average, than true responses. They take this as evidence that hearers' preference is for global accommodation: that is to say, the presupposition tends to project, and the hearer only later considers an interpretation in which it does not. To the extent that the comparison is meaningful, the evidence for automatic presupposition projection seems rather more compelling than the evidence for the automatic derivation of scalar implicature.

This preference appears to be susceptible to contextual manipulation, though. Tonhauser (2016) demonstrates one way of doing this: she shows that prosodic manipulations can indeed influence the projection of presuppositions, as suggested at the end of section 4.4. Her paper compares three prosodically varied versions of the same utterance: for instance, in the case of (158), one version has a high tone pitch accent (H*) on *discovered*, another version has a complex L-H* pitch accent on *he*, and a third version has an L-H* pitch accent on the stressed syllable of *widow*.

(158)   Perhaps he discovered that she's a widow.

Participants were asked to rate the speaker's certainty as to the truth of the presupposition (in this case, 'that she's a widow'). Judgements of certainty were significantly lower in the conditions in which *widow*, or the pronoun *he*, carries the pitch accent than in the condition in which *discovered* carries the pitch accent. Tonhauser argues that this reflects the role of prosody in conveying information about the Question Under Discussion, although the precise relationship between prosody and QUD is complex and remains a focus of research.

4.5.5 Accommodation

As discussed earlier, speakers can make use of presupposition accommodation to convey information that they would otherwise have to assert. However, given that accommodation is a complex process, is this generally an acceptable communicative strategy? Singh et al. (2016) address this question using a stops-making-sense paradigm.

Methodology: stops-making-sense paradigm
The stops-making-sense paradigm, first used by Boland et al. (1990), is a modified version of a self-paced reading task. In this case, at each word (or chunk), a participant has the choice of pressing one key to continue to the next word or pressing another key if the stimulus no longer makes sense. The relevant measures are both how long it takes a participant to read a word (or chunk) and how frequently the participant decides that the sentence has stopped making sense at that point.

Singh et al. (2015) used definite descriptions of individuals whose existence is or is not plausible in a particular context, as illustrated by (159) and (160), comparing these with a non-presuppositional baseline in which the same individuals were introduced with indefinites (*a bouncer*).

(159) Bill went to a club on Friday night. The bouncer argued with him there for a while.

(160) Bill went to the circus on Friday night. The bouncer argued with him there for a while.

In the implausible condition (160), participants read more slowly and frequently judged the string to stop making sense at the words *the bouncer*. However, in the plausible condition (159), the presupposition – which still required accommodation, because the hearer didn't know that the club had a bouncer – did not cause participants to behave any differently from how they did when reading control sentences. In Singh et al.'s second experiment, they showed a similar effect for *too*, where (161) is the plausible and (162) the implausible context (and the non-presuppositional controls used *tomorrow* instead of *too*).

(161) John will go to the pool this morning. Peter will go swimming too after he gets back from school.

(162) John will go to the mall this morning. Peter will go swimming too after he gets back from school.

Singh et al. (2015) argue that their results reflect the fact that presupposition accommodation is not intrinsically problematic, except when

the presupposition is implausible in the context. Under these conditions, they argue, it is inappropriate for a speaker to attempt to exploit
accommodation: implausible material needs to be introduced as part
of the main asserted content of the utterance. They float the interesting possibility that, 'whatever the nature of the cognitive systems that
decide how much credence to assign to information, they are sensitive
to whether the information has been presented as a presupposition or
not' (ibid.: 624–5).

4.6 Summary

As speakers, we are aware that our utterances have certain logical pre-
conditions, which we call presuppositions. Moreover, we can exploit
this fact in order to convey additional information without asserting
it directly, with the confidence that our hearers will be able to recover
that information. These additional meanings are distinguishable from
asserted meanings and from implicatures, most strikingly because they
continue to arise even when the utterance that conveys them is negated,
placed within the scope of modal uncertainty, or made the antecedent
of a conditional. There is also growing psycholinguistic evidence that
we process these presuppositions differently from asserted content, and
indeed that we process different classes of presupposition differently,
although theoretical debate continues about exactly how we should
try to divide up the rather large and varied class of presupposition-
triggering expressions.

Exercises

Answers to the following are available at <edinburghuniversitypress.
com/pragmatics>.

1. What presuppositions are carried by the following utterances?
   a. Tom managed to pass the exam.
   b. The police remain convinced of the suspect's guilt.
   c. The police discovered the suspect's guilt.
   d. The police didn't manage to prove the suspect's guilt.
2. Which facts have to be presupposed in order for the following to
   make sense? How does that differ from the meanings that the utterances convey?
   a. If Mary doesn't enjoy parties, her husband will probably take
      her to dinner on her birthday.
   b. If Mary is married, her husband will probably take her to dinner
      on her birthday.

3. Which of these utterances are likely to exploit accommodation?
   a. We didn't realise that the hotel is at the top of a big hill.
   b. People are worried that the sky will fall in and the Earth will stop spinning.
   c. Let's come back here after the show.
   d. Marley was dead: to begin with. (Charles Dickens, *A Christmas Carol*)

Discussion questions

1. In an utterance like *Mary had dinner in New York last night too*, the presupposition associated with *too* often appears vague or even vacuous: it's obviously true that Mary wasn't the only person having dinner in New York last night, and hence the use of *too* could be referring to any of millions of other people. Does that mean that it's always acceptable to use *too* in such sentences? If not, why not? And how might the hearer go about figuring out the speaker's specifically intended meaning?

2. Consider an utterance like *John didn't regret arguing with his boss: you're thinking of Bill, his friend who used to work at the bank but later went to work for* . . . In this case, a presupposition ('John argued with his boss') is potentially triggered by the use of *regret*, but the speaker's continuation makes it unclear whether or not they mean to cancel that presupposition. In fact, it seems that they can go on almost indefinitely without explicitly committing to a position on this. What do cases like this tell us about the circumstances under which presupposition cancellation takes place? As hearers, what factors might help us to understand whether or not the speaker does mean to convey a particular presupposition in ambiguous cases such as this?

5 Referring

Father Ted: OK, one last time. [Picks up toy cow] These are *small*, but the
ones out there are *far away*.

(Graham Linehan and Arthur Mathews, *Father Ted*, s2e1, 'Hell')

So far, we've mostly been concerned with propositional meaning. In
discussing implicature, we considered how the speaker can convey
additional propositions – that is to say, claims about matters of fact –
alongside those that are made explicit. In discussing presupposition,
we saw some more examples of this, as well as cases where the speaker
intends to relate new propositional meaning to previously established
facts (using expressions such as *too* and *again*).

But there is more to pragmatics than simply propositional meaning.
At a higher level, pragmatics is also concerned with how language can
be used to perform social actions, which is something we'll discuss
in Chapter 8. And at a lower level, pragmatics is also concerned with
sub-propositional meanings. Consider the following example, repeated
from Chapter 4.

(163)   Sorry I'm late: my car broke down.

As we discussed, the use of the words *my car* can be taken to convey
the fact that the speaker has a car – that is, the existential presupposition. But alongside this, the words *my car* also contribute to the
meaning of the utterance. The speaker is attempting to convey that
something broke down, and presumes that that thing can be successfully referred to, or **denoted**, by the words *my car*. Yet these words
don't have a stable meaning across contexts: if a different speaker
uses the words *my car*, they will likely be using those same words to
pick out a different **referent**, their own car. In just the same way, of
course, the person denoted by the expression *I* depends upon who
is speaking, the person(s) denoted by *you* depend on who is being
addressed, and so on.

Note on terminology
The word 'denotation' is potentially ambiguous in that it can be used to describe the meaning of a word or the things that it refers to. Here I'm using it in the latter sense, but for the most part I will try to avoid confusion by talking about words' reference rather than their denotation.

Thus, the same words can have different reference depending upon the context. And, as a flip side to that, the same entity can be referred to in different ways. This is also obvious in the case of pronouns. If the hearer of (163) responds by uttering (164), they are using *you* to refer to the same individual who was previously referred to as *I*, and *your car* to refer to the same entity that was previously referred to as *my car*.

(164)   Were you able to get your car fixed?

The question of how pronoun meanings are successfully recovered by the hearer seems naturally to fall within the scope of pragmatics. Of course, speakers do not have to rely on the use of pronouns in order to refer successfully to people or things: they can use definite descriptions, and when the entities in question have names, they can use those. To the extent that the speaker has a choice of referring expression, discerning how that choice is influenced by context is also a matter for pragmatics. As we shall see, by studying reference we can potentially learn a lot about how speakers perceive the world and, perhaps most interestingly, how they attempt to understand the mental states of their hearers.

5.1 Resolving pronouns

It's tempting to think that pronoun usage is straightforward: we can use an appropriate pronoun when we wish to refer to an entity that is unambiguous in the context, and by doing so we convey our intended meaning more efficiently. In cases such as (165) and (166), this appears to be true: assuming that Bill is male and Jane is female, the pronoun *she* seems unproblematically to denote 'Jane' in (165), and the pronoun *himself* denotes Bill in (166).

(165)   Bill invited Jane to the dinner because she was successful.
(166)   Jane assumed that Bill was preparing himself for the meeting.

On closer inspection, though, there is a difference between these two examples. In (166), *himself* obligatorily denotes 'Bill', apparently for syntactic reasons: it's a reflexive pronoun, which is to say that we couldn't use it to refer to anyone other than the individual performing the action (in this case, the action denoted by *preparing*). By contrast, in (165), although we know that *she* must denote a female referent (and cannot therefore refer to Bill), the fact that it refers specifically to Jane rather than anyone else is somewhat more negotiable, as we see when we consider (167).

(167)   Bill invited Jane to the dinner because she was unavailable.

Here, we seem to arrive at an interpretation in which *she* refers to another person not mentioned in this utterance (who presumably Bill would have invited to the dinner, had she been available). However, this difference in interpretation doesn't seem to be driven by syntax: in that respect, there are no differences between (165) and (167), with only the final adjective having changed. Instead, the difference seems to arise because of contextual factors. In this case, it follows directly from our understanding that it would be odd to invite someone to dinner because of their own unavailability to accept that invitation, whereas by contrast a person's unavailability constitutes a good reason why someone else should be invited.

To the extent that (167) is felicitous, it also demonstrates that we can use a pronoun to refer successfully even when there are multiple possible referents in play. In this case, we note that *she* could refer to Jane or this other person (who had presumably already been mentioned in the preceding discourse), and that the speaker doesn't cause any real problem for the hearer by using a pronoun that is ambiguous in this way. This point is made even more clearly by (168).

(168)   Mary admired Jane because she was successful.

In this case, there is no syntactic reason to suppose that *she* has to mean Jane rather than Mary, yet that appears to be the salient interpretation. At least, a speaker who meant to convey that Jane was successful and that that caused Mary to admire Jane could do so with (168), whereas a speaker who meant that it was Mary who was successful (and therefore magnanimous enough to admire Jane?) would be in danger of misleading their hearer by uttering (168).

What this suggests is that the correct interpretation of an utterance such as (168) ultimately relies on real-world knowledge, not just an understanding of the grammatical structure of the underlying sentence. The classic examples of this are due to Winograd (1972), who noted the contrast between minimally different pairs of utterances such as (169) and (170).

(169)   The city council refused the demonstrators a permit because they feared violence.

(170)   The city council refused the demonstrators a permit because they
        advocated violence.

In this case, we know that *they* in (169) is very likely to denote 'the city
council' whereas *they* in (170) is very likely to denote 'the demonstrators'. However, in principle, either the city council or the demonstrators could be the ones who fear violence, and for that matter either
could be the ones who advocate violence. To explain our preference
for the interpretations that we actually obtain, we have to dig deeper:
presumably we think that a council fearing violence is quite likely and
that that constitutes a coherent reason for denying demonstrators a
permit, while a council advocating violence is less likely and in any case
wouldn't explain their decision to deny demonstrators a permit. But, of
course, all this draws extensively upon our world knowledge, outside of
linguistics: the fact that councils more often fear violence than advocate
it, and that fearing violence is a coherent reason for denying demonstrators a permit, could hardly be said to be part of our lexical entries for
the words *council, violence, demonstrators* or *permit*, and is obviously not
expressed in any way by the syntactic structure of these examples.

    The pair (169) and (170) constitute what has subsequently become
known as a **Winograd schema**. Classically, a Winograd schema consists
of two short texts, which differ only in a single word, each containing
two noun phrases of the same semantic class (in respect of gender,
animacy and plurality), and a pronoun that may refer to either noun
phrase. In order for something to count as a Winograd schema, it must
be the case that changing a single word (in the above example, *feared* to
advocated) reverses our preference as to which noun phrase the pronoun
picks out. Winograd schemas are important in some areas because of the
way they rely on real-world knowledge. Indeed, Levesque (2014) argues
that the resolution of Winograd schemas poses a particular challenge for
artificial intelligence (AI), and proposes that the resolution of pronouns
in Winograd schemas represents a suitable test for AI systems – better,
in fact, than the long-established Turing test, as a way of demonstrating
the systems' capabilities at emulating humans.

    At the time of writing, no AI system has got anywhere near master-
ing Winograd schemas, which reflects the fact that the kind of world
knowledge deployed by humans when interpreting such sentences is
so rich, multi-faceted, and difficult to formalise. However, we are in a
position to make some useful generalisations about how humans interpret ambiguous pronouns in general, as we shall see in the following
subsections. These interpretative preferences also have implications for
how speakers can use pronouns without risk of being misunderstood.

5.1.1 Syntactic parallelism

The idea that syntactic factors influence the interpretation of ambiguous pronouns is long-established. Consider (171), from Sheldon (1974: 280).

> (171)   John hit Bill and then Sarah kicked him.

According to Sheldon, 'the absence of stress on the object pronoun indicates that it refers to the object NP of the preceding conjunct' (ibid.: 280). That is to say, if (171) is uttered without stress on *him*, the hearer would normally understand the speaker to mean that Sarah kicked Bill, rather than John. (If stress is placed on *him*, things are more complicated.) In a similar way, we would expect *he* in (172) to refer to John, although stress might again interfere with this preference.

> (172)   John hit Bill and then he kicked Sarah.

The general pattern here appears to be a preference for parallelism, in the sense that the pronoun is understood as referring to the referent which has a parallel syntactic role – subject or object – in the preceding clause. Early experimental research on this topic showed that the preference for this kind of parallelism is stronger when the verb phrases are structured similarly in both clauses and the subject and object stand in similar semantic relations in both clauses (e.g. Smyth 1994; but see Kehler et al. 2008 for an alternative explanation of these patterns). Thus, for instance, (173) exhibits much weaker parallelism than (171), because the kinds of relations between subject and object in the two clauses are so different: the *him* of (173) is consequently more ambiguous than it is in (171).

> (173)   John tried to catch Bill and Sarah bored him.

What about this issue of stress on the pronoun – how can we explain that stress may change the interpretation that the hearer understands? It's tempting to think of this as an instance of markedness in action. The speaker knows that, if they utter (171) without special stress on *him*, the hearer is likely to interpret *him* as referring to Bill. Therefore, if they wish to use *him* to refer to John, they have to do something different in order to signal that they don't intend to convey the usual meaning of (171). Stressing the pronoun is one option. We could think of that as triggering an M-implicature, in Levinson's terms (see section 2.4).

Indeed, we could try to go even further and observe that stressing a pronoun might trigger an M-implicature because a stressed pronoun is more effortful, or 'costly', to produce, in much the same way that producing a full noun phrase is more costly than producing a pronoun. We could take this as support for the general idea that costly expressions are associated with relatively non-salient referents (in this case, the dispreferred one of the two possibilities given in the utterance), while less costly expressions are associated with relatively salient referents, much in the spirit of Zipf (1949).

This is an important idea, and worth bearing in mind when we discuss the effect of using pronouns instead of full noun phrases (see section 5.2). However, it turns out that this doesn't look like the right way to analyse the particular case of stress on pronouns. It turns out that sometimes it's natural to place stress on a pronoun even if it's unambiguous, as in (174), where *him* refers to John; and indeed sometimes it's natural to place stress on a full noun phrase, as in (175). These are problematic data for the M-implicature-based or Zipfian explanation proposed above. Kehler et al. (2008) offer a more sophisticated account of pronominal stress that addresses these issues.

(174)   John admires Sarah, and Mary absolutely worships him.
(175)   John admires Sarah, and Mary absolutely worships John.

5.1.2 Subject bias

As noted in the previous subsection, the preference for parallel inter-pretations of ambiguous pronouns isn't always very strong, especially when the parallelism between the clauses themselves is itself relatively weak or limited. Consider the contrast between (176) and (177), drawn from Kameyama (1996).

(176)   John hit Bill. Mary told him to go home.
(177)   Bill was hit by John. Mary told him to go home.

There is an intuition, supported by some experimental work, that *him* in (176) tends to refer to John whereas in (177) it tends to refer to Bill. If so, this is not just a weaker example of parallelism, but a case in which the claim of parallelism seems to make the wrong predictions entirely: in these cases, it seems perfectly possible to use the object pronoun *him* to refer to the subject of the previous sentence without anything in the way of special intonation.

Examples such as these have motivated many researchers to argue for a general subject bias in the resolution of pronouns: that is, all things being equal, we would expect the ambiguous pronoun to refer to the subject of the preceding sentence (see for instance Crawley et al. 1990). Again, this makes intuitive sense – we expect pronouns to refer to salient entities in the preceding discourse, and the subject of the preceding sentence is a highly salient entity in that discourse. It would hardly be surprising if that made it the hearer's default choice as a referent for the subsequent pronoun (assuming that the pronoun matches the referent in gender, animacy and number).

5.1.3 Topicality and recency

There are good reasons to think that both the claim of a preference for parallelism and the claim of a subject bias have an element of truth to them, but it is difficult to reconcile the two. In all the above examples, except (172), the two accounts make different predictions about the interpretation of the ambiguous pronoun. It just happens that the parallelism account works for (171) and (173), while the subject bias account works for (176) and (177). By itself, that isn't much use to us: it suggests that there are some cases in which parallelism appears to be the stronger preference and some in which subject bias appears to be the stronger preference. Unfortunately, when we encounter a new example, we don't know which category it is going to belong to. So we need to dig deeper if we are to come up with useful generalisations about how to interpret utterances like these.

What other factors could be in play? We can try to shed light on that issue by exploring the motivation for the apparent subject bias more thoroughly. Comparing (176) and (177), we might intuit that the subject preference is stronger in (177), and that this has something to do with the use of the passive. For some reason, Bill is important enough to the speaker to have been promoted to subject position in the sentence, even though this involves using a more verbose form of words. If Bill is so important, it wouldn't be surprising if he is now going to be the individual picked out by a pronoun in the following sentence.

One way of capturing the privileged status that Bill has in the first sentence of (177) is to appeal to the notion of **topichood** – that is to say, the question of what the discourse is about. Ultimately, this is a matter for the speaker to determine, but the utterance offers some clues to the hearer: for one thing, the subject position is the usual location for topics in English (Chafe 1976), and this is a particularly reliable signal of topichood in the case of passives (Ward and Birner 2004). In short, given a passive sentence such as the first sentence of (177), we can reasonably expect its subject to be the current topic of the discourse, and hence for the continuation of the discourse to be likely to refer to that individual. To the extent that we can disentangle topichood from the other factors in play, it certainly seems to bear upon the ease with which pronouns are comprehended by hearers: Anderson et al. (1983) found that materials with pronouns were processed faster when the pronouns referred to topical antecedents than when they did not.

Still another relevant factor is how recently the candidate referents were mentioned. At one level, this is hardly surprising: if no male individual has been mentioned for several conversational turns, it would be odd for a speaker to use the word *he* and expect to achieve successful reference by it. In principle, by this argument, we might suppose that there ought to be a preference for the more recently mentioned individual as the referent of the pronoun – which in the above examples would be the object, rather than the subject, of the first clause or sentence. However, in practice, recency effects don't appear to be that strong, at least not for short discourses.

Recency is an important idea, but quantifying it presents a difficult challenge. For instance, can we be sure that the individual who was explicitly referred to more recently – the object rather than the subject, for instance – is necessarily the one who was most recently thought about, in some deeper processing sense? And does it make sense to think of recency in terms of the number of utterances since the individual was mentioned, or does it depend upon the structure of the dialogue? For instance, suppose that the main purpose of our conversation is to discuss Bill, but having done so for a while we drift into a side-topic in which no people are mentioned. Having brought that topic to a close, one of us then begins an utterance *Anyway, he . . .*, intending to refer to Bill. That reference might well be successful, even though the last mention of Bill was many turns previously. So, although it's a reasonable generalisation that we can't use pronouns to refer to individuals who haven't recently been mentioned in the discourse, there are nevertheless occasions where we can: and we would ultimately need a much more sophisticated account of recency in order to explain why this is.

5.1.4 Implicit causality

In the Winograd schemas, we saw how changing one word of a sentence could influence the hearer's preference as to how to understand an ambiguous pronoun. Those examples draw upon specific real-world knowledge. However, in other circumstances, changing a verb can lead to a change in pronoun interpretation that appears to relate much less transparently to that kind of real-world knowledge. Consider (178) and (179).

(178)   Mary annoyed Sue because she . . .
(179)   Mary scolded Sue because she . . .

In (178), when the reader arrives at the word *she*, there is already an expectation that *she* refers to Mary, and that the sentence continuation will describe something that Mary did that annoyed Sue. In (179), there is a corresponding expectation that *she* refers to Sue, and that the continuation will describe something Sue did that annoyed Mary. The unifying feature of both cases is that the ambiguous pronoun is preferentially interpreted as referring to the causal agent of the action of annoying or scolding, respectively.

In this case, it is largely irrelevant that that individual occupies the subject position in the sentence with *annoyed* but the object position in the sentence with *scolded*. Indeed, we could reverse the syntactic roles by making the sentences passive, but the preference in interpretation for the pronoun still tends to point in the same direction: it refers to Mary in (180) and to Sue in (181).

> (180)   Sue was annoyed by Mary because she . . .
> (181)   Sue was scolded by Mary because she . . .

Garvey and Caramazza (1974), who first discussed examples of this type, used the term **implicit causality** to describe the property that these verbs possess, in how they influence the interpretation of the subsequent pronoun. Of course, merely observing that these verbs have this effect doesn't really amount to an explanation of how it comes about. An important observation in this connection is that hearers' expectations about the meanings of the pronouns are bound up with their expectations as to what the following sentence is going to be about. As shown by Stevenson et al. (1994), participants who are asked to continue (active) sentences such with IC verbs exhibit a preference to continue talking about the subject, in the case of *annoyed*, and the object, in the case of *scolded*.

Even so, the effect of IC verbs on the interpretation of a subsequent pronoun still depends on how the sentence is put together. In the above examples, the pronoun is introduced by an explicit *because*, which clearly indicates that the following material is supposed to be an explanation of what came before. If we replace *because* with *so*, as in (182) and (183), the pattern of preferred interpretations seems to be different – now *she* probably refers to Sue in both cases.

> (182)   Mary annoyed Sue so she . . .
> (183)   Mary scolded Sue so she . . .

This interpretative preference is apparently because hearers tend to interpret the pronoun in utterances like this as referring to the individual who bears the consequence of the first clause: we expect that the speaker will continue by telling us what Sue did as a consequence of Mary annoying or scolding her. This effect on pronoun interpretation is sometimes called **implicit consequentiality** (Crinean and Garnham 2006; Pickering and Majid 2007).

In summary, then, it would be an oversimplification to say that implicit causality verbs force subsequent pronouns to be interpreted in a specific way. Still, it is clear that the choice of verb is relevant to pronoun interpretation in cases like this, and (at least for some verbs) this effect seems to be greater than any possible effect of parallelism or subject bias. Yet these effects can be undermined by the choice of connective in the sentence, as we see in examples like (182). In section 7.2.3, we'll return to this question, and see how the types of logical connections that exist between different parts of an utterance can also influence pronoun interpretation.

5.2 Using appropriate referring expressions

In the previous section, we looked at some of the factors that influence hearers' interpretations of ambiguous pronouns. Different theories propose different strategies for the hearer to adopt – they can appeal to parallelism, or subject bias, or recency, and so on – but there is no easy generalisation to be made about how hearers solve the problem in reality. Turning things around and looking at this from the speaker's perspective, it's natural to ask why this challenge arises in the first place: shouldn't a cooperative speaker avoid burdening the hearer with this difficult disambiguation task? And how can we explain their apparent insouciance in allowing this problem to arise for the hearer?

More generally, turning our attention to the role of the speaker invites us to consider the challenge that they face in trying to be cooperative in their use of referring expressions. It's typically the case that the same referent could be picked out in many different ways – by several different descriptions, perhaps by a name, and potentially by a pronoun – and the speaker has to decide upon a strategy that will be communicatively successful. Studying how speakers resolve this problem can tell us a lot both about language processing and about social cognition in general. The following subsections introduce some of the major topics in this area.

5.2.1 Brevity in referring

Why are speakers willing to take the risk of using potentially ambiguous pronouns, when perfectly safe and unambiguous referring expressions, such as proper names, are available? Experimental work by Gordon et al. (1993) points to a potential answer to this. They compared reading times for discourses that differed only in their use of pronouns – for instance, (184) and (185) (ibid.: 318).

(184)   a. Bruno was the bully of the neighborhood.
        b. He chased Tommy all the way home from school one day.
        c. He watched Tommy hide behind a big tree and start to cry.
        d. He yelled at Tommy so loudly that all the neighbors came outside.

(185)   a. Bruno was the bully of the neighborhood.
        b. Bruno chased Tommy all the way home from school one day.
        c. Bruno watched Tommy hide behind a big tree and start to cry.
        d. Bruno yelled at Tommy so loudly that all the neighbors came outside.

It transpires that people are faster in reading (184) than (185). This is not surprising, if we consider that (185) feels slightly awkward as a text, but it is surprising on theoretical principles. For instance, note that the pronoun *he* in (184c) and (184d) is, in both cases, ambiguous until it becomes clear that its referent is not Tommy, whereas the corresponding sentences (185c) and (185d) are unambiguous from the outset. Also, the ambiguity is removed at a very low cost in terms of additional length – it shouldn't take people very long to read the name *Bruno*. Nevertheless, (185) yields a 'Repeated Name Penalty', with reading comprehension slowed down by the use of full names in circumstances in which pronouns would be appropriate (specifically, when the subject of the sentence is the same as the subject of the preceding sentence).

In essence, then, it seems that the use of pronouns has processing benefits for the hearer, even if they have to deal with some ambiguity as a result. However, this assumes that the use of pronouns doesn't impair the hearer's ability to infer the speaker's intended meaning. Presumably it would be costly, and wasteful, for the speaker to create a situation in which the hearer doesn't know who they're talking about – or, perhaps even worse, arrives at the wrong conclusion about who it is. In Gricean terms, the speaker must provide enough information to enable the hearer to recover the intended referent, and shouldn't provide more information than is necessary. But, as we have already seen, failing to provide enough information is a more serious communicative error than providing too much information.

Of course, the speaker's task in choosing a referring expression is often more complicated than merely choosing between a name and a pronoun. Clark and Wilkes-Gibbs (1986) explore the space of possibilities rather more widely, using a director–matcher task.

Methodology: director–matcher task

The director–matcher task is a dyadic (two-person) communication task. In a typical set-up, both participants have copies of the same materials, such as pictures. They are able to communicate in some way, usually verbally, but neither can see the other person's materials. The director is instructed to identify the materials, one at a time, to the matcher – for instance, to get them to arrange their pictures in a specified target sequence.

Experimenters are usually interested in the form of words used to refer to the materials; they may also be interested in how long the task takes and how successful the communication is, as measured by the rate at which the matcher correctly identifies the target items. More specific topics of interest include how often the matcher requests clarification of the director's meaning (in conditions where this is permitted). The task is sometimes implemented using a confederate, usually in the director role: the confederate will (unbeknownst to the participant) produce scripted instructions, allowing the experimenters to focus on how these are understood by the hearer.

Clark and Wilkes-Gibbs (1986) implemented a task using twelve cards showing images created from tangram puzzle pieces, which were semi-abstract and crucially didn't have obviously agreed names. The director's task was to get the matcher to place the cards in the correct order: there were no constraints on what could be said by either party or how many turns they could use. There were six rounds of the task, using the same images each time, but in a different order.

The main finding of the experiment was that the exchanges become shorter through the six rounds of the task, both in terms of the number of conversational turns required to match a card and in terms of the number of words uttered by the director in doing this. Clark and Wilkes-Gibbs quote the following specific example, comprising one director's first utterance on each of the six times they were trying to describe a card that depicts a particular human-like image:

1. All right, the next one looks like a person who's ice skating, except they're sticking two arms out in front.
2. Um, the next one's the person ice skating that has two arms?
3. The fourth one is the person ice skating, with two arms.
4. The next one's the ice skater.

5. The fourth one's the ice skater.
6. The ice skater.

(Clark and Wilkes-Gibbs 1986: 12)

The observation that people shorten their referring expressions when talking repeatedly about the same referent was not itself new to Clark and Wilkes-Gibbs (1986): they credit Krauss and Weinheimer (1964) with that finding. However, the point that Clark and Wilkes-Gibbs emphasise is that the shortening of referring expressions is made possible by the collaborative nature of the referring process. The director is actively trying to help the matcher identify the intended referent – the appropriate card – and wishes to do so in the most economical way possible, so as not to waste everyone's time. The initial steps of the process can be seen as negotiations that establish which referring expressions will work for particular referents. Once the director knows that a particular expression will work, they can use it again with the same matcher: and this realisation makes it possible for them to make a considerable saving in the length of expression that they use.

Importantly, Clark and Wilkes-Gibbs also wish to appeal to the notion of 'least effort' originated by Zipf, but in a slightly revised form. They argue that the traditional interpretation of least effort in referring involves the speaker producing the minimal utterance that will suffice to achieve reference successfully. By contrast, they propose that we should think in terms of the interaction as a whole, and they argue 'that speakers and addressees try to minimize collaborative effort, the work both speakers and addressees do from the initiation of the referential process to its completion' (ibid.: 26). On this view, the speaker has to take into account the implications of shortening the referring expression they use, including the possibility that this will require effortful and time-consuming clarification before it can be successfully understood by the hearer.

5.2.2 Consistency in referring

For Clark and Wilkes-Gibbs, the challenge is to spell out an account of how 'the process of mutual acceptance [of a referring expression] gets initiated, carried through, and completed' (ibid.: 16). In order to study this, it's obviously important to use referents that don't already have an agreed name – hence the tangram task. Presumably if the experiment had involved pictures of people who were already mutually known to both participants, the director could simply have used the people's names, as this is a generally accepted strategy for referring. Similarly, if the experiment had involved pictures of objects that had strongly preferred names, such as *cat*, *dog*, and so on, there would have been relatively little difficulty for the speaker in ensuring that the referring expressions that they used were acceptable to the hearer.

Nevertheless, even in cases where objects' identities are clear, we often still have choices about how we refer to them: given a picture of a poodle, we could refer to it as a *poodle*, *dog* or indeed *animal*. A further long-established observation is that conversation partners tend to converge on how they refer to a particular entity, a process sometimes called lexical entrainment. Brennan and Clark argued, on the basis of experimental evidence, that this process often reflects the formation of a **conceptual pact**: that is to say, 'a temporary agreement about how [a speaker] and their addressees are going to conceptualize an object' (1996: 1491). As a consequence of such an (implicit) agreement being reached, discourse participants will converge on a single expression for a particular object, and there will be no misunderstanding as to what is being talked about.

These two ideas – that we can make our referring expressions shorter once we know that they are going to work, and that we make implicit agreements that we're going to keep our referring expressions stable – appear to impose conflicting requirements on speakers. Should we be reusing the expression that we used before, for a particular referent, or actively looking to abbreviate it in some way? Brennan and Clark (ibid.: 1492) are aware of this tension and note that conceptual pacts are necessarily somewhat provisional and adaptable. They contrast their approach with that of Carroll (1980) in which, as they describe it, 'speakers propose references and, once their partners ratify them, use them consistently thereafter' (ibid.: 1492). That is not something we see happening in the most interesting examples from Clark and Wilkes-Gibbs (1986): in the ice skater case quoted above, a speaker establishes that a particular form of words is successful for referring to the particular card, and then immediately changes it at the next opportunity! However, even here, we could see the speaker as respecting a conceptual pact in a slightly more abstract sense: they continue to conceive of this ambiguous tangram picture as a representation of an ice skater. It's by appealing to that stable notion that they expect the hearer to recognise the card they're talking about.

5.2.3 *Common ground*

A crucial idea linking both of the accounts discussed in the previous sub-sections is that referring is a collaborative process, and that the referring expressions that are used become more appropriate as a consequence of negotiation over the course of a conversation. Initially, one speaker has to initiate this process by attempting to refer to something, but the feedback given by the hearer – for instance, telling the speaker whether or not they have successfully identified the entity which they meant to pick out – is crucial to establishing whether or not the speaker's referring strategy will be successful, or whether they will have to try something else. On subsequent occasions, speaker and hearer will both know which referring expressions have or have not succeeded in the past, and which referents were intended when those expressions were used. This presents the speaker with much richer data about how to refer effectively to the intended object, and the hearer with a much clearer impression of how to interpret the speaker's utterance.

As speakers, we need information of this kind about the hearer's knowledge state in order to use ambiguous referring expressions successfully. Consider a name, such as *Clark* in (186).

(186)   Clark has done a lot of important work on interaction.

There are a lot of people called Clark. It seems clear that the speaker is talking about a specific individual, and evidently that individual is someone who the speaker knows by the name of Clark. But, of course, in order for the reference to be successful, it must relate to someone who the hearer also knows (unless the speaker is trying to convey that person's existence by appeal to accommodation). In fact, the story is even more complicated than this. The hearer will presumably try to resolve the reference by thinking of the people they know who are called Clark. But the individual referred to by (186) can't be just anyone that the hearer knows: it must be one that the speaker also knows. And from the speaker's point of view, this imposes an additional burden, because the speaker has to know that the hearer knows that the speaker knows this person.

It's not easy to talk about this kind of recursive knowledge without making things sound even more complicated than they are, so let's illustrate this with an example. Suppose that you have friends named Amy and Martha, and as far as you know, they don't know each other at all. Amy then messages you to say (187).

(187)   Great night out with Martha.

Amy may intend you to understand that she has been out with the Martha that you know, assuming that the referring expression *Martha* will work because she knows that you also know Martha. But, given that you don't know that Amy knows Martha, your first reaction to (187) might be puzzlement, as you try to figure out which Martha this could possibly be that Amy is talking about. If you don't know that Amy knows Martha, you would have no reason to think that Amy could successfully refer to her by that name.

In fact, we can argue that the recursive knowledge that is required by the speaker goes even deeper than this. Of course, this raises the question of why we bother to try to use referring expressions that rely on this kind of recursive knowledge – surely it would be extremely laborious to check that even these first few levels of it are satisfied.

The shortcut that we need in order to communicate successfully with ambiguous, or potentially ambiguous, referring expressions is a rich understanding of the **common ground**. As discussed by Clark and Marshall (1981), following Schiffer (1972), in principle we need an elaborate and even infinitely recursive amount of mutual knowledge in order to be able to refer successfully (I need to know that you know that I know that you know . . ., etc.) But as they helpfully observe (ibid.: 18), the core of what we actually require is a lot simpler: the speaker needs to know that the speaker and hearer 'mutually know' the relevant referent (in the above example, Martha).

How can we obtain this kind of knowledge? Well, in several ways – the most obvious of which is shared prior experience. Take (186), in the context of this textbook. I've referred several times to work by Clark and colleagues, and I assume that, if you've read this far, you've noticed me doing so. As a consequence of this, we have some shared experience of certain things being said about someone called Clark (specifically, Herbert H. Clark). This entitles me to assume that we mutually know this individual.

How can I be sure that Herbert H. Clark is the only individual named Clark that we mutually know? Well, I don't know who is reading this book, so I have to work on the assumption that the only shared experience we have is of the context of this book. If I can assume that, then I can successfully refer to Herbert H. Clark using the name 'Clark' alone.

If you're reading this, you might know Eve V. Clark (of whom (186) would also be true) – indeed, we might mutually know Eve V. Clark – and in that case you'll have to think a little more deeply, and take into account that I'm saying (186) and expecting to be understood also by people who don't know Eve V. Clark. But of course, in general, if we mutually know both Herbert H. Clark and Eve V. Clark, then I can't simply say (186) and expect that to refer successfully: in that case, we have too much common ground to license the use of that referring expression.

We would expect a common ground-based account also to have something to say about the felicitous use of pronouns, as these are ambiguous expressions *par excellence*. Specifically, it will be appropriate to use a pronoun when the speaker can be sufficiently confident that a unique referent is going to be sufficiently salient to be recovered by the hearer. Typically this will be when a particular individual has just been talked about sufficiently to have established themselves as the salient individual in the conversational context. In this case, we could think of that individual's salience as being part of the common ground between speaker and hearer, established through their common participation in the preceding discourse. However, there are other possibilities: for example, an individual might become sufficiently salient just through past experience on the part of the speaker and hearer. If they customarily talk about one specific person, it might be felicitous even at the very beginning of a conversation to refer to that person with a pronoun, as in (188).

(188)   He called me again last night.

Another important way in which we might end up with the appropriate kind of mutual knowledge to support reduced referring expressions is simply by being co-members of the same community. This could be on a large or small scale, as we see by comparing (189)–(192).

(189)   Message from the new Vice-Chancellor
(190)   PM's full interview with Laura Kuenssberg (http://www.bbc.co.uk/news/av/uk-politics-42917344/pm-s-full-interview-with-laura-kuenssberg)
(191)   The Queen emerges from her winter bunker in a trendy orange coat (https://www.vanityfair.com/style/2018/02/queen-elizabeth-returns-to-london-orange-coat-2018)
(192)   Trump's Palestine deal is a real estate transaction (http://www.aljazeera.com/indepth/opinion/trump-palestine-deal-real-estate-transaction-180208103112105.html)

If I receive an email with the subject line (189), I naturally assume that *the new Vice-Chancellor* in question is that of my home institution. Reading the headline (190), my own default assumption is that *PM* refers to the Prime Minister of the United Kingdom, although to be more confident about whether this assumption is appropriate, I might need to check the source, which in this case is British media. Reading (191), I am more confident that *the Queen* refers to Queen Elizabeth II, even though the source in this case is US-based; and in (192), I can be confident that *Trump* refers to the President of the United States even though the article in question is published by a Qatar-based source.

These four referring expressions all work on the assumption that the speaker and hearer are members of the same community, and therefore possess the relevant common ground. However, different communities, of different sizes, are invoked by these expressions. The first works only among people who share a university affiliation, the second among inhabitants of a particular country, the third among the larger group of people for whom Elizabeth II is the most salient individual who can be described as *the Queen*, and the fourth for the world's populace at large, at the time of writing.

This kind of community co-membership is relevant to the question of how we often manage to achieve successful reference at the first time of asking, even in the absence of any prior shared linguistic experience. A headline writer wants to be brief and to be successful in referring, even when dealing with an audience with which they have not shared any specific experiences. On closer inspection, the terms that they use are often ambiguous – as in the case of *PM* or *Prime Minister* – but it is usually possible for the hearer to arrive effortlessly at the intended understanding. This enables us to better express why Clark and Wilkes-Gibbs (1986) avoided using highly recognisable figures in their experiment: given what appears to be a picture of a dog, we will probably just refer to it as *a dog*, appealing to a general common understanding of what *dog* means and what kinds of things it can successfully be used to refer to.

5.3 Efficiency in referring

In what we've discussed so far, there's been a general assumption that successful reference is about picking out the target referent while exchanging as little information as possible about it, much in accordance with Grice's second submaxim of Quantity. We assume that this will lead to the speaker and hearer engaging in as little processing effort as possible, on the basis that the main cause of processing effort in conversation is having to deal with the linguistic material that has to be produced and decoded. Therefore we expect the speaker to be as brief as possible – or, taking the more balanced view of interaction that Clark and Wilkes-Gibbs (1986) adopt, that the speaker and hearer will want to be as brief as possible between them.

However, there are cases in which the picture is more complicated, either because it's appreciably more laborious for the speaker to produce minimal referring expressions, because it's more laborious for the hearer to comprehend minimal referring expressions, or because the expressions that are used do more than simply refer in that they also provide additional information about their referents. I discuss some of these cases in the following subsections.

5.3.1 Perspective-taking versus egocentricity

In section 5.2, we focused on cases in which speaker and hearer share knowledge to an advanced extent. But there are also cases in which speaker and hearer have a different perspective. We have different perspectives on who should be denoted by pronouns such as *I* and *you*, most obviously. We differ about the location of other entities relative to ourselves, and we differ about how we represent them mentally. If we are facing each other, we differ as to what *left* and *right* mean.

Many experiments on reference have aimed to explore the effect of the difference between the speaker's and the hearer's perspective on a situation. Keysar et al. (2000) set up a director–matcher task in which a four-by-four grid containing various objects is set up between the director and the matcher. Some of the cells in this grid are occluded – that is to say, they are covered over so that one of the participants, the director, cannot see inside them. This creates a difference between the matcher and the director's perspectives, and also makes that difference evident to both of them: the matcher is aware that the director can't see inside the occluded cells, as shown in Figure 5.1.

Keysar et al.'s (2000) experiment explores adjectival modification. If there are two objects in the shared visual field (effectively the common

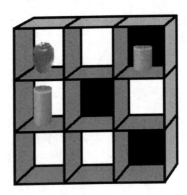

Figure 5.1 Part of a possible matcher's view in a matcher–director task, following Keysar et al. (1998). In this non-critical version of the scenario, there are only two candles, both of which are visible to the matcher. The matcher can also see that the smaller candle is hidden from the director's perspective. Note that this shows a 3-by-3 grid, whereas the original task used a 4-by-4 grid.

ground) that are identical except with respect to one property – such as colour, or size – we expect the speaker to mention this property in order to refer successfully to the intended referent. If there is only one object of a particular kind in the common ground, this kind of adjectival modification won't be necessary. Crucially, Keysar et al.'s critical scenario has one category of object, a candle, that occurs in three sizes – let's call them big, medium and small. The three candles are identical apart from in size. The small candle is in one of the occluded cells, while the other two candles are visible to both director and matcher.

In this scenario, the critical trial is the one in which the director (who is a confederate) asks for the *small candle*. What should happen in this scenario? If the matcher considers the director's perspective, they should conclude that the director is actually asking for what we have called the medium candle. *Small* is a relative adjective, so given that the director can only see two candles, referring to the smaller of them as the *small* one would be perfectly acceptable. By contrast, if the matcher ignores the director's perspective (the shared perspective) and focuses on their own, they should conclude that the small candle in privileged ground (the one only the matcher can see) is the intended referent.

What Keysar et al. (2000) found is that, under these circumstances, the matcher did tend to look towards the small candle in privileged ground – and in a couple of cases went so far as to reach towards it, as if to pick it up. Only subsequently did they correct their error and reorient their attention towards the smaller of the two candles in common ground.

This result suggests that hearers exhibit what Keysar calls **egocentricity** in their interpretation of referring expressions. Hearers initially entertain the possibility that the smallest candle might be the intended referent, only subsequently reasoning that this is unlikely as it is not one of the objects that the speaker can see. Put differently, it appears that hearers' early processing of this ambiguous referring expression takes place with reference to what they can see, rather than what they know the speaker can see: that information only gets taken into account a bit later in processing, just in time to inform the decision they make about which object to pick up.

Note on terminology

In the context of this work, egocentricity or egocentrism merely refers to an individual's tendency to consider what they can see rather than what is in common ground. It shouldn't be read as a synonym for 'selfishness' and is not intended as a criticism of the individual's social behaviour.

To the extent that this is a general pattern – which is hard to be sure about, on the basis of the experimental evidence so far – why might it happen? One obvious interpretation is that taking someone else's perspective is costly, at least when it disagrees with our own. This is an intuitively appealing idea, because presumably to achieve a full representation of what other people can see – and what they know – would require a huge amount of processing effort. Perhaps egocentricity in this sense is a convenient heuristic that usually works. When a speaker asks us for the *small candle*, wouldn't it be reasonable to hand them the thing that we would be most willing to refer to as the *small candle*, given what we know, rather than trying to work out whether that's necessarily the same thing as they would call the *small candle* from their standpoint?

From the speaker's perspective, a related question concerns **audience design**: to what extent should the speaker tailor their utterances to the needs of the hearer, given what they currently know and perceive? This is a very general question, and can encompass the language and register that we choose to use, and the way we articulate our speech, as well as the meaningful content of the utterance. As applied to the case of reference, we might ask: should the speaker choose referring expressions that would also be the hearer's preferred way of referring to those entities?

To make that more concrete, consider again the question of *left* and *right*. If we are facing each other, my *left* is your *right*. If I want to indicate that you should move to my right, I can try either option: I can be egocentric and say *go right*, or I can engage in audience design and say *go left*. Either of these strategies could be successful: the challenge is to coordinate on the strategy that we are using. If I'm being egocentric I place an additional burden on you, but it won't be difficult to work out what I mean. If I'm taking your perspective, you don't have to reason about what my perspective looks like, but if you mistakenly believe that I'm being egocentric, there will be a misunderstanding (and you'll go the wrong way).

In cases such as this – which are quite typical, as speaker and hearer usually differ in their perspective in at least some particulars – it is not straightforward to appeal to notions such as economy, brevity or markedness to justify which approach the speaker should take. Whatever happens, at least one of the participants is going to have to take the other's perspective in order to make this interaction work. It's not easy to determine which of them should take on that obligation. In practice, we might expect this kind of problem to be resolved by some form of explicit negotiation or clarification (*left, that is to say my left*), but even then there is a trade-off between guaranteeing communicative success and minimising the amount of material that has to be explicitly uttered. In short, it's not easy to figure out how to achieve the Clark and Wilkes-Gibbs (1986) objective of minimising the total effort of speaker and hearer in such a case.

5.3.2 Optimising the referring expression

Degen and Franke (2012) conduct an interesting experiment that is designed to explore how deeply we can draw pragmatic inferences based on the choice of a specific referring expression. Their task is a director–matcher task, but under tighter constraints: directors are allowed to choose just one of four signals, in order to convey the identity of one of three potential referents. They have simple and complex scenarios, as depicted in Figure 5.2 (their Figure 1). In both cases, the message recipient (the matcher) knows which three referents are possible, but doesn't know which one the participant has been instructed to identify.

How effective can participants be at conveying the identity of the target referent? Let's assume throughout that they restrict themselves to iconic signals, in that they choose messages that correspond to a property that is relevant to the referent: that is, if it's a fat monster with a dark cap, they choose either the signal for 'dark cap' (m_{d1}) or the signal for 'fat monster' (m_t and m^*_t).

Under this assumption, in the simple scenario, there are two choices that will work for the referent labelled t_d ('thin monster', 'dark cap'),

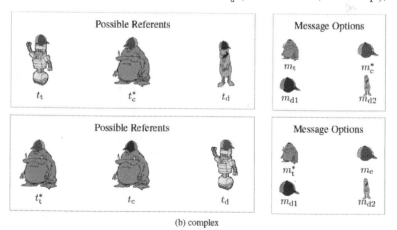

(b) complex

Figure 5.2 Simple and complex referring scenarios from Degen and Franke (2012).

namely m_{d1} and m_{d2}. There is one choice for the referent labelled t_t ('robot', 'light cap'), namely m^*_c ('light cap'). That leaves just one message available to convey the identity of t^*_c ('fat monster', 'light cap'), namely m_t. Therefore it would be rational to reserve the signal m^*_c, the light cap, for the referent that has a light cap and is not describable any other way, which is t_t.

In the complex scenario, things are a little more difficult. If we want to refer to t^*_t ('fat monster', 'light cap'), which signal should we choose – m^*_t, which is also applicable to the competitor referent t_c, or m_c, which is also applicable to the competitor t_d? We can only answer this if we consider the whole system. For t_d, the only appropriate signal is m_c, whereas for t_c, either the signal m^*_t or the signal m_{d1} would be suitable. Thus, we can solve the system, in the sense that we can establish a unique mapping between referents and messages that will work: t_d is signalled by m_c, which forces t^*_t to be signalled by m^*_t, and leaves t_c to be signalled by m_{d1}.

Some of Degen and Franke's (2012) participants are indeed able to solve this system in just this way, and choose to signal in this optimal fashion. Assuming that the message recipient is equally rational, they will be able to recover the signaller's intended meaning, by going through the same reasoning process and thus establishing a one-to-one mapping between referent and signal.

In either of the scenarios, then, it transpires that a single signal should be sufficient to convey the identity of any one of the referents. Moreover, some participants are able to figure out a system that actually does makes this level of efficiency possible. According to Grice's second submaxim of Quantity, this kind of minimal signalling is therefore what we should do. But, of course, that should apply even if we are not restricted to individual signals in the way the experimenters enforce here. If we were being properly Gricean, when asked to refer to t^*_t using words, we shouldn't need to say more than *the one with the light cap*. However, intuitively, we're not that Gricean in this case: we would be much more inclined to say something like *the fat monster with the light cap*.

The reasons for this preference appear straightforward. It's not much work to give a full description, and if we do this, we know that our referring expression will be successful as long as there is no other fat monster with a light cap among the candidate referents. We don't need to consider whether there happens to be a shorter description that would do the job. (Bear in mind that Degen and Franke (2012) deliberately set up their scenario so that there is a shorter description available: in principle, there might not be in a case like this.) And we don't have to worry about whether the hearer would be able to follow our reasoning if we did use a shorter description, and thereby arrive at the referent that we were trying to refer to.

What Degen and Franke (2012) show is that, if we were restricted to a single signal, we would be able to use complex reasoning to solve the whole system and come up with a perfect mapping between referring expressions and referents, in the scenarios presented in their experiment. That is to say, we are (at least some of the time) capable of reasoning in the way that we would need to if we wanted to observe Grice's second submaxim of Quantity. However, notwithstanding this capability, it seems unlikely that we would behave like this in a less constrained communicative situation. In this particular experiment, the speaker's obligation to be properly cooperative in a Gricean sense seems to place an additional and communicatively unnecessary burden upon them.

We can capture this point reasonably well within Relevance Theory, either with reference to the speaker's own production preferences or with reference to the obligations that they may and may not place on the hearer. With respect to the speaker's preferences, recall that the speaker is expected to produce optimally relevant utterances, but with an important caveat: as Wilson and Sperber (2002) stress, this is subject to the abilities and preferences of the speaker. In cases such as this, we could simply observe that the production of optimal referring expressions – as assessed by the criterion of requiring minimal linguistic expression, and therefore reducing the amount of purely linguistic processing to be undertaken by both speaker and hearer – might not be something that the speaker wants to do, or is capable of doing. It's easy to imagine a more complex environment, with a large set of candidate referents – a crowd scene, for instance – in which even a maximally cooperative and economy-minded speaker wouldn't be able to solve the system and figure out what the minimal referring expression was for their target referent.

On the second point, with respect to the obligations placed on the hearer, we've already seen how the production of optimal referring expressions in complex scenarios will oblige the hearer to perform similarly elaborate reasoning in order to decode the speaker's intended reference. It's certainly not obvious that this is a route to optimal relevance: it may impose a greater burden of cognitive effort on the hearer, with no greater cognitive effects to show for it, than they would have had if the speaker had been fully specific in the first place (by using more words). Hence, it's not necessarily the case that utterances that strictly obey Gricean Quantity are always optimally relevant, if we're dealing with sufficiently complex scenarios. That presents even the most obliging speaker with a good reason to avoid excessive brevity.

5.3.3 Doing more than just referring

In this chapter so far, we've tended to assume that the entire purpose of producing a referring expression is to pick out a referent, so that the hearer knows who the speaker is talking about. Under these circumstances, we generally expect referring expressions to go from more to less specific, as they do in (193).

(193)   US President Donald Trump has blocked the release of a Democratic rebuttal of a Republican memo ... The White House said that Mr Trump could not declassify the Democrats' memo because of 'sensitive passages' ... The document alleges the [FBI] abused its power by investigating a Trump adviser ... (http://www.bbc.co.uk/news/world-us-canada-43012430)

However, in practice, referring expressions do not proceed in a smooth gradient from more to less specific. This is particularly striking in sports journalism, as in (194).

(194)   Britain's Andy Murray has had hip surgery in Melbourne ... The former world number one, 30, has not played a competitive match since he was knocked out of Wimbledon in July. The ongoing problem forced the Scot to pull out of the Australian Open ... (http://www.bbc.co.uk/sport/tennis/42602401)

Apparently something different is going on here. The speaker of (194) intends the expressions *the former world number one, 30* and *the Scot* both to refer to Andy Murray, but doesn't expect the hearer to figure out the referent from the description given in each new sentence. Rather, the speaker seems to be assuming that the hearer already knows who is being talked about – the same person as was being talked about earlier in the article – and is providing them with additional information to attach to that person (that he is the former world number one, thirty years old, Scottish, and so on).

This example illustrates that the speaker can use referring expressions not only to refer but also to provide additional information. This makes it harder to predict how they should appropriately be used. From a Relevance Theory perspective, calling someone *the former world number one* when you could call them *Andy Murray*, or *Murray*, or simply *he*, seems like a serious waste of effort if the only purpose is referring. However, if the purpose is to equip the hearer with new information, this might be a perfectly sensible way of doing so.

This situation obviously has points in common with the situation discussed in the preceding subsection. In the cases discussed there, the speaker provides additional information that is, strictly speaking, unnecessary for the successful identification of the referent, on the basis that they are unsure whether or not it actually was necessary (and figuring out whether it was necessary would itself be laborious). Here, again, the speaker is providing information that is unnecessary for the successful identification of the referent, but presumably might be useful to the hearer in some other capacity later on, and is therefore potentially worth providing.

Between these two kinds of usage, there's what we might think of as an intermediate case: where the speaker provides information that isn't entirely necessary for the successful identification of the referent, but might nevertheless help things along. The use of colour adjectives is one striking example. Colour is a particularly salient feature in the identification of objects, so providing information about the colour of a referent might be a helpful thing to do, purely in terms of enabling the hearer to locate the target referent within their field of vision. Rubio-Fernández (2016) shows that speakers are willing to use apparently redundant colour adjectives in order to help hearers identify the referent: for instance, they will refer to a figure as *the blue star* in a display in which there is only one star, particularly if it is a large display and all the other objects are the same non-blue colour. Of course, it is not entirely clear whether this reflects an awareness of the interests of the hearer or simply what is obvious to the speaker. By the same token, speakers are more inclined to use colour in discussing objects that are a non-standard colour (e.g. *the pink banana*), and they are more inclined to do so when talking about objects for which colour is an important property, such as clothing (*the yellow T-shirt* gets produced more often than *the yellow paperclip* in a comparable task).

We could think of the redundant use of colour as either being like the *former world number one, 30* case or like the *fat monster in a dark cap* case. That is to say, a speaker might use colour because they think this is useful information for the hearer – even if they don't need this to identify the referent, it might help them do so, or it might be useful in some other way at a future date. Or the speaker might use colour because it's part of how they themselves conceptualise the referent: they are surprised at an object being a non-standard colour, or the colour of the object makes it stand out in the display, or they think of the object in terms of colour as well as form for cultural reasons (as in the clothing case).

There is, however, a potential conflict between the speaker trying to provide useful extra information in this way and them trying to use an efficient referring expression. In an eye-tracking experiment, Sedivy et al. (1999) demonstrated that hearers are rapidly able to use contrastive adjectival information in order to resolve to a target referent. The crucial condition is one in which there are two objects that could reasonably be referred to as *tall*, for instance a jug and a glass, and a third object that contrasts in this respect with one of those items, such as a short glass. On hearing the word *tall*, hearers rapidly commence looking at the object which is contrastively tall – that is, the object that has a short counterpart in the display. The implication of this is that, when speakers use a redundant adjective, hearers might reasonably infer the presence or existence of a contrasting entity – if, for instance, we were to speak of an item in a display as *the blue star*, it could be taken to convey the existence of a non-blue star. In that respect, the use of additional colour modification might be misleading in some ways, even at the same time as being helpful in other ways.

In summary, there is abundant evidence that we use referring expressions to do more than just refer: however, when we do so, we potentially create a problem for the hearer to solve. Abstractly, this is a little like the case of markedness. When we describe something in more detail than we need to, there is a danger that we will cause our hearers to think that the simpler description actually wasn't appropriate in the circumstances. So, as cooperative speakers, we don't have entirely free rein: we need to know what our hearers expect, and provide them with information at a level of specificity that is tailored to their needs. The success of referential communication suggests that, in practice, we do this extremely well – however, theoretical accounts of what is going on have yet to capture the full complexity of this process.

5.4 Summary

Our language provides us with many ways of referring to an entity in discourse, ranging from full and relatively ambiguous expressions to far briefer but more ambiguous expressions such as pronouns. We draw on a wide range of knowledge about language and interaction when we interpret ambiguous referring expressions. We are also able to use complex processes of social negotiation to figure out which kind of referring expression to use, given the needs and expectations of our hearers. The process of referring appears to reflect Gricean principles of organisation – sometimes captured more neatly by Relevance Theory – but with some quirks that aren't fully understood by theorists. Nevertheless, there is a strong sense that the study of reference is potentially illuminating for our understanding not only of language but also of social interaction and perception more generally.

Exercises

Answers to the following are available at <edinburghuniversitypress. com/pragmatics>.

1. What are the possible consequences of using a pronoun instead of a name in the following utterances, in terms of being understood correctly?
    a. Jane met with Anne and awarded Anne/her a pay rise.
    b. Jane criticised Anne because Anne/she had refused to work late.
    c. Jane criticised Anne because Jane/she was difficult to please.
    d. Jane invited Anne because Anne/she was keen to talk to more people in the arts.
2. For each of the following potential Winograd schemas, which word(s) could you insert in the gap to make the pronoun refer to the subject of the first clause? Which word(s) would make the pronoun refer to the object of the first clause?
    a. The trophy would not fit in the suitcase because it was too _____.
    b. Paul tried to call George on the phone, but he wasn't _____.
    c. The delivery truck zoomed by the school bus because it was going so _____.
    d. Frank felt _____ when his longtime rival Bill announced that he was the winner of the competition.
3. In what way could we consider the referring expressions to be 'reduced' in the following utterances? Why is that appropriate, in each case?
    a. John, Mary and Esther were each interviewed for the job, but ultimately he was the one offered it.
    b. While we were in London, we went to the Palace, but Her Majesty was not in residence at the time.
    c. Professor Hawking was widely renowned as a cosmologist.

Discussion questions

1. Rubio-Fernández (2016) shows that speakers are, in some circumstances, more willing to use redundant colour modification in English than in Spanish. One relevant difference between these languages is that colour adjectives appear after the noun in Spanish – *the blue triangle* is expressed as *el triángulo azul*. Why might that make a difference to the speaker's preferences?

2.   Stewart Lee criticised the literary style of Dan Brown, author of *The Da Vinci Code*, as follows:

> Dan Brown writes sentences like 'The famous man looked at the red cup' . . . It's only to be hoped that Dan Brown never gets a job where he's required to break bad news. 'Doctor, is he going to be alright?' 'The 75-year-old man died a painful death on the large green table. It was sad'. (Stewart Lee, *Stewart Lee's Comedy Vehicle*, s1e1, 'Toilet Books')

Supposing this to be a fair criticism, what does this suggest about the purposes for which Dan Brown uses adjectival modification, and what is considered 'good literary style' in that respect?

6 Non-literal language

> I still light up like a candle burning when he calls me up
> I still melt down like a candle burning every time we touch
>
> (Macy Gray, *Still*)

In the previous chapters, we've considered various kinds of pragmatic meaning that arise in addition to the semantic, or literal, meaning of a particular utterance. However, in all these cases, that core, semantic meaning remains present, alongside the pragmatic enrichment. The speaker who says *Some elephants live in Africa* is still committed to the existence of elephants that live in Africa, even while they also suggest the existence of elephants that do not. Similarly, the speaker who says *Mary won again* is committed to the fact that Mary won this time, while indicating that she did so before; and the speaker who says *Pass me the tall glass* is committed to the presence of a tall glass, while hinting at the simultaneous presence of a short one.

In all these cases, we can try to explain the pragmatic meanings by appealing both to the content of what has explicitly been said, and to general principles about how cooperative communication works, as discussed back in Chapter 2. But in various other cases, utterances convey a pragmatic meaning which doesn't build upon the semantic 'literal' meaning, but instead contradicts it. These cases are much harder to explain systematically. Consider (195).

(195) Trigger: D'you find your way out of the maze alright, Dave?
Rodney: No, I'm still in there, Trig.

(John Sullivan, *Only Fools and Horses*, s7e6,
'Three Men, a Woman and a Baby')

Rodney's utterance in (195) is deliberately false, but it isn't intended to mislead the hearer: rather, the intention is to point out that the answer to Trigger's question is self-evident. Arguably it's uncooperative at some level, because it adopts an extremely literal interpretation of the question (cf. *Have you eaten?*). But in essence, (195) is an example of a perfectly functional and understandable kind of linguistic behaviour: the only oddity about it is that the speaker does not mean what he appears to be saying.

Cases such as (195) are traditionally identified as **irony**, which we can think of in terms of the speaker apparently meaning to convey the opposite of what is said (here, the speaker says *no* but means the hearer to understand it as *yes*). But various other figures of speech are similar in that they appear to admit two contradictory interpretations, one based on what is said and one corresponding to our best inference about what the speaker meant. **Metaphor** is another striking example of usage in which the intended meaning differs from what we might call the literal meaning of the utterance, as shown in (196). **Metonymy**, in which something is referred to by the name of one of its attributes or an associated expression, as in (197), is another such case. And **hyperbole** – dramatic overstatement, as in (198) – arguably differs from all these.

(196)   TUEs may have been the tip of an iceberg. (https://www.theguardian.com/sport/2018/mar/05/team-sky-dcms-report-bradley-wiggins)

(197)   White House denies John Kelly offered to resign. (https://www.ft.com/content/44a73ce6-0df4-11e8-8eb7-42f857ea9f09)

(198)   I took it along to a publisher ... he said ... 'This is the most boring story that has ever been written in the whole history of the universe'. And he's not a man who's given to superlatives. (Peter Cook, *Beyond the Fringe – The Miner*)

Taken separately, all these **figures of speech** – that is to say, distinct kinds of figurative language – represent a challenge for pragmatic theory, but taken together, we can see the full magnitude of the problem. From a Gricean point of view, we could argue that all these uses violate the maxim of Quality, and therefore invite the hearer to draw additional inferences about the speaker's intended meaning in order to account for why the speaker decided to utter the thing that they did. But this, in itself, isn't a very helpful observation. Importantly, it doesn't give us much of an indication as to the kind of inference that we ought to be drawing: all we know is that it must contradict what was literally said. To take a particularly striking illustration of this problem, consider an utterance like (199).

(199)   The Queen Mother was made of steel.

We can agree (dismissing some rather eccentric conspiracy theories) that (199) is not literally true, so we're invited to come up with some other kind of interpretation. The preferred option seems to be to treat the phrase *made of steel* as metaphorical, and infer that the speaker means to convey something to the effect that the Queen Mother was strong-willed. But (199) could just as easily be ironic, and have the intention of pointing out that the Queen Mother was, despite her lofty status, merely a human being and therefore subject to the same physical frailties as anyone else. Indeed, (199) could even be hyperbolic, alluding to the Queen Mother's hip replacement. So why is the metaphorical interpretation preferred – and, once we have settled on that, how do we know (even roughly) what the speaker actually meant by it?

In essence, then, the problem of how to understand figurative language is a big issue for pragmatics. At the same time, it's very typical of the kinds of issues that we've been talking about in this book. Notably, we all have access, as language users, to shared intuitions about what kinds of utterances would be appropriate for speakers to make, and what speakers mean when they make these utterances, but there are competing ideas about the processes that support these intuitions and interpretations. And at this level of description, some of the same general questions arise that we have already considered for other forms of pragmatic meaning. For instance, do we start from a literal interpretation and then adjust that, based on our understanding of how interactions work – or do we jump straight to a non-literal ('figurative') interpretation? Are there principled differences between types of meaning that have traditionally been regarded as distinct, such as metaphor and simile, or do they rely on the same mechanisms? And how do general principles of social cognition come into play – for instance, do conditions such as autism spectrum disorder influence the use and comprehension of figurative language, and if so, what could that tell us about the nature of the pragmatic processes involved?

It's also worth remarking on the similarity between this issue of figurative language interpretation and the issue of lexical disambiguation in general. When we interpret homonyms like *bank*, we have to choose between multiple different senses in which the speaker might mean this (here, 'financial institution' versus 'edge of a river'). This is often considered to be a matter of lexical semantics, although it's also clear that context plays a role in the interpretation that we ultimately draw.

Note on terminology

Homonymy refers to two words with different meanings having the same linguistic form (in spelling or pronunciation, or both). **Polysemy** refers to a single word having multiple related but distinct senses. In the discussion of metonymy in section 6.2.2, I'll compare metonymy to polysemy, as this seems the more appropriate analogy. However, the differences between homonymy and polysemy are not really important for the purposes of this chapter.

In much the same way, the interpretation of idioms such as *kick the bucket* involves choosing between multiple possible meanings, in this case one that is compositional and one that is holistic. Again, I'll consider this to be predominantly a semantic question and outside the scope of this volume. However, some of the issues raised in this chapter – for instance, the primacy of figurative versus literal interpretation, or the selection of an appropriate sense, in the case of metonymy – are conceptually related to these issues.

In this chapter, we will look at how studies of non-literal language have attempted to address these questions. First, focusing on irony, we look at the interplay between literal and figurative interpretations, and how various accounts have attempted to explain this process. Subsequently we'll look at the rather more complex case of metaphor, and see how that challenges our understanding of precisely what 'literal meaning' is. Finally, we'll look at the effects of social cognition, and in particular Theory of Mind, on various different forms of non-literal language, examining similarities and differences between them.

6.1 Are literal interpretations privileged?

One interpretation of the Gricean account of figurative language is to suppose that it calls for the literal meaning always to be accessed first. Once the hearer has arrived at an interpretation of this meaning, they can then evaluate whether it abides by the Gricean maxims or whether they need to perform additional pragmatic enrichments. In classic cases of irony, such as (195), for instance, the hearer can immediately tell that the utterance violates the maxim of Quality on its literal interpretation – perhaps in much the same way as *I haven't eaten* presumably does – and therefore that we cannot interpret the utterance literally, at least not while preserving the assumption that the speaker is broadly cooperative (without which we can't get anywhere).

Actually, calling this the 'Gricean' account is potentially a bit of a leap. Grice didn't present his account of pragmatic interpretation as a processing account: as argued by Noveck and Spotorno (2013), trying to describe it as one involves mixing up two levels of analysis. Grice's description of pragmatic interpretation is intended at a computational level, in the sense of Marr (1982), while the version of it presented above is an algorithmic one, describing a set of processes that could realise the computations that Grice describes. This is a potentially important distinction to make, because it suggests that evidence against this kind of literal-first account wouldn't necessarily constitute evidence against a Gricean view of pragmatics in general. Nevertheless, even with that concern in mind, it's useful to have this kind of literal-first account set out, so that we can contrast it with other possible explanations of what is going on.

One such alternative is offered by Gibbs (1994, 2002), and is a proposal he calls the **direct access** view, which he sets out in direct opposition to the literal-first account described above. He argues that hearers do not have to complete their analysis of the literal meaning of a linguistic expression before they have access to pragmatic information that is relevant to understanding the speaker's intended meaning. As a consequence, hearers are able to access non-literal meanings directly, at least when utterances are presented in realistic social contexts.

Giora (1997, 2002) offers another distinct view, arguing that neither the literal-first account nor direct access fully explains the patterns of interpretation for non-literal utterances. She proposes the **graded salience** account, on which salient meanings are processed first, regardless of whether these are traditionally classed as literal or figurative in a given case. Precisely how to quantify salience is left somewhat open in this account, but Giora (1997: 185) argues that it has to do with conventionality, familiarity, frequency and/or givenness in context. We can certainly recognise one meaning as more salient than another in a particular context. For instance, in the phrase *A man walks into a bar*, the salient interpretation of *bar* is 'venue for drinks' rather than 'long rigid object' (which presumably explains why it's possible to build a joke around the idea that *bar* might take on the latter, unexpected meaning).

To illustrate the subtleties of these two accounts, consider (200), an item discussed in detail by Gibbs (2002) which had originally been used in an earlier reading time study.

(200)   Gus just graduated from high school and he didn't know what to do with his life. One day he saw an ad about the Navy. It said that the Navy was not just a job, but an adventure. So Gus joined. Soon he was aboard a ship doing all sorts of boring things. One day as he was peeling potatoes, he said to his buddy, 'This sure is an exciting life'.

Experimental results suggest that ironies like Gus's utterance in (200) can be read just as quickly as the same words in contexts in which they are interpreted as true. If that's the case, it poses a particular challenge to the literal-first model, because under this model the reader must initially understand Gus's utterance literally and only later reanalyse it pragmatically as ironic – a process that we might assume takes effort and slows down reading.

The direct access and graded salience accounts tell slightly different stories about what is actually going on when we read (200). On the graded salience account, the rapidity with which a hearer can understand the ironic meaning of *This sure is an exciting life* reflects the salience of the ironic interpretation of these words: it's potentially relevant, for instance, that *this sure is* is a somewhat conventional ironic phrasing. By contrast, the direct access account holds that the context is key: the whole story told in (200) sets up a scenario in which there is a clear divergence between Gus's original expectations and the reality, and this creates a highly suitable environment for an ironic utterance like the one given. The reader knows this and is therefore ready to comprehend an utterance as ironic, if it's appropriate to do so. On this view, as Gibbs puts it, hearers 'may still need to draw complex inferences when understanding some ironic statements, but part of these inferences can occur before one actually encounters an ironic utterance' (2002: 462).

A possible compromise, summarised in Pexman (2008), is to try to build a model that takes into account all the various factors that are potentially relevant to understanding an utterance as literal or ironic, and considers those factors in parallel. Pexman sketches this out as a constraint satisfaction model that can be described by a connectionist network, following an approach that had previously been applied to various other kinds of ambiguity resolution. She argues that hearers consider a number of distinct cues when evaluating whether or not a speaker is being ironic, but individually these are not in any way necessary or sufficient conditions for irony: rather, the simultaneous presence of enough cues to irony will induce the hearer to interpret the utterance as ironic. The kinds of cues that Pexman has in mind include the words that are used and their relation to the circumstances in which they are being said – as captured by the direct access and graded salience accounts, respectively – but also things like the speaker's tone of voice, their facial expression, and what we know about their attitudes and beliefs. The most straightforward version of this model would involve the hearer taking each relevant piece of information as it becomes available – whether that's at the completion of the utterance, during the utterance, or even before it starts – and using that information to arrive at a probabilistic decision about whether or not the utterance is meant to be ironic.

The problem with this kind of account, as Pexman (2008) acknowledges, is that it is rather vague and permissive: we could accommodate all kinds of factors within that model, and we can have as many as we want. That makes the model hard to disprove with experimental evidence – if the model makes erroneous predictions, we could simply argue that it was set up incorrectly, or missed out some factors. At the same time, the ability of a model like this to include all kinds of factors is definitely a strength, in that it makes it possible to explore the usefulness of various different features of the interaction as predictors of irony.

For instance, one factor that fits naturally into that model is the hearer's awareness of whether the speaker is likely to be sincere in their literal meaning, or whether they might be disposed to be insincere, ironic or indeed unreliable. In both (201) and (202), ambiguously ironic statements are associated with clues to the speaker's unreliability, as far as literal meaning is concerned.

(201)   The headline asked 'Can Miami save itself?' For those readers too stupid to figure out the answer, there also was this helpful hint: 'A City Beset by Drugs and Violence'. The overall impression created by the cover was: 'Sure Miami can save itself! And some day trained sheep will pilot the Concorde!' (Dave Barry, *Can New York Save Itself?*)

(202)   Oh, life is a glorious cycle of song,
        A medley of extemporanea,
        And love is a thing that can never go wrong,
        And I am Marie of Roumania.

                                        (Dorothy Parker, *Comment*)

In (201), the author (a columnist for the *Miami Herald*) is discussing a then-recent headline in the Sunday magazine of the *New York Times*. *Sure Miami can save itself!* attracts an ironic interpretation on the understanding that the speaker is, or is pretending to be, 'too stupid' to figure out the correct answer to the headline question. In (202), the last line makes it clear that the whole verse is intended to be ironic, the message being that only someone mistaken enough to believe that last claim would believe the others. In both of these cases, hearers might also benefit from the overarching awareness that these authors are highly disposed to use irony to bring about their communicative effects.

Another feature that's arguably present in (201) is that the literal meaning of the speaker's utterance is ascribed to someone other than the actual speaker. However, in this case, the situation is a little over-complicated, because there are several different voices involved: the author of the article, the author of the *New York Times* headline, and the 'speaker' of the ironic utterance. A clearer case of a speaker dissociating themselves from the words they are uttering is (203), in which a female police officer takes exception to a male colleague's opinion on the effect of catcalling.

> (203) DS Boyle: I would have thought it were flattering.
>
> Sgt Dawkins: Of *course* it is, Boyle. There's nothing builds up a girl's self-esteem like having a human gorilla with a brain the size of a peanut inviting you to peel its banana.
>
> (Ben Elton, *The Thin Blue Line*, s2e5, 'Come on You Blues')

This kind of dissociation relates to a long-established observation about irony: namely that, in practice, irony doesn't merely convey the negation of what is literally stated, but also expresses a negative attitude towards the meaning that is literally stated, usually one that is sceptical or mocking. Importantly, this offers us a potential explanation for why a speaker should choose to use irony rather than simply directly saying what they mean: by using irony, they not only convey their meaning but also convey hostility towards its negation.

Using irony in this way obviously makes more sense, as an argumentative strategy, if the speaker is attacking a proposition that someone else has previously asserted or agreed with, as in (203). This is at the heart of Sperber and Wilson's (1981) echoic theory of verbal irony, in which irony specifically involves ascribing a thought to someone else and then expressing a negative attitude towards it (typically by asserting it in an obviously insincere way). And, to the extent that this is a solid generalisation about irony, it offers the hearer another cue to the potential presence of irony. We might think that a speaker who appears to be reiterating someone else's sentiment – which is explicitly the case in (203) – is rather more likely to have ironic intent than a speaker who asserts something new and distinctive. However, of course, this is a relatively weak cue: we don't assume that a speaker is being ironic every time they appear to be agreeing with someone else.

In summary, it appears that hearers don't always have to spend time processing the literal interpretation of an ironic utterance – under the right circumstances, it seems to be possible for the hearer directly to access the speaker's intended meaning. Speakers' utterances and general dispositions provide us with various indications of whether or not an ironic interpretation is likely to be appropriate, and it appears that we can use at least some of these indications early in processing. Other information about the interaction might also be in play, although precisely which factors are relevant and when they are relevant remains an open question. Ostensibly this idea of early non-literal interpretation runs counter to a Gricean account of pragmatics in this domain, but whether there is truly a conflict here depends on how we interpret that

Gricean account at a processing level. It also depends to some extent on how we understand literal meaning in the first place, a point we will discuss in more detail in the next section.

6.2 Metaphor and the modulation of concepts

Studies of metaphor have also addressed the question of whether literal meaning is accessed first, but this question turns out to be rather more complex for metaphor than it is for irony. Metaphor characteristically involves describing something with a word or phrase which is not literally applicable to it, as in (204) and (205).

(204) Your eyes are doves. (*Song of Solomon*, 1:15)

(205) Juliet is the sun. (William Shakespeare, *Romeo and Juliet*, Act II, scene ii)

More specifically, metaphors look like statements of class-inclusion: (204) identifies the addressee's eyes as belonging to the set of things that are doves, and (205) identifies Juliet with the sun. As with irony, there is a clear sense in which metaphors are not literally true. However, we do not take the speaker who produces a metaphor to be insincere or even uncooperative in the same way that the user of irony may appear to be. Instead, we might be inclined to defend the user of metaphor by arguing that they are conveying a particular meaning by saying something that is literally false but is true in some other sense (which we can't really say about irony).

To try to pin down what that involves, it is worth thinking about what it would mean for an ordinary class-inclusion statement to be true. Consider another potentially metaphorical example, (206).

(206) Love is a game for two players.

Under what circumstances could we say that *love is a game* is literally true? This is a deliberately complex example, not so much because philosophers have spent so much time debating the nature of love as because they have spent a great deal of time debating what constitutes a 'game'.

The work that's most closely associated with this debate is Wittgenstein (1953). He noted that we cannot identify a set of necessary and sufficient conditions that define whether or not something is a game. Rather, games are characterised by family resemblance, and arguably by a set of prototypical features: for instance, that they are fun, that they are governed by rules, that they are competitive, and so on. The crucial point is that none of these features are essential to something being a game (a world championship chess game might not be fun, children playing might not be governed by rules, solitaire is not competitive, etc.).

Given that there are no clear rules for what constitutes a 'game', it would be reasonable for the speaker of (206) to intend their utterance to be literally true: they might just mean that love has sufficient family resemblance to the concept 'game' to justify asserting its inclusion in that class. By contrast, we cannot possibly interpret Romeo's utterance (205) to be an attempt to convey literal truth. Even if Romeo isn't aware that the sun is a seething mass of fusing hydrogen nuclei, he is probably aware that it is a vast, distant, inanimate object. At the same time, he knows that Juliet is not inanimate, and he presumably doesn't mean to convey that she is either vast or distant. Instead, he means to convey that Juliet shares other properties with the sun – that she provides (in some sense) warmth, radiance and particularly light.

The crucial distinction between (205) and (206), then, is that the speaker making a class-inclusion assertion in (205) actually only means to convey that the individual being named has *some* of the essential properties of the class of entities to which she is said to belong, while discarding others from consideration, whereas the speaker of (206) doesn't discard properties in the same way.

Note on terminology

In studies of metaphor, the entity being described is variously called the **tenor**, **ground** or **target** of the metaphor, and the thing to which they are metaphorically compared is variously called the **vehicle**, **figure** or **source**. I think these terms are almost equally eccentric and unhelpful, so I will try to confine myself to using as few of them as possible, specifically **tenor** and **vehicle**.

Thus, the interpretation of a metaphor is not simply a matter of whether or not the metaphor vehicle receives its literal interpretation – in practice, part of its literal interpretation applies to the tenor, and part of it doesn't.

Two questions immediately arise from this. How do we establish which properties of the metaphor vehicle are actually relevant to the speaker's intended interpretation? And what happens to the properties that are and are not relevant, over the course of processing – how do we end up distinguishing them from one another in our mental representation?

The first question is not a straightforward one to answer, because in principle it seems that practically any component of meaning could be the basis for a figurative interpretation. For instance, although comparing someone to the sun, as in (205), wouldn't normally evoke the sun's status as a massive celestial body, that could be relevant in principle, as in (207).

(207)   Juliet is the sun; we all orbit around her.

One influential approach to this question is introduced by Glucksberg and Keysar (1990), and involves changing how we construe metaphor. They advance the view that, contrary to traditional analyses, metaphors like (204) and (205) are in fact class-inclusion assertions, just like (206) is (on the account given above). Glucksberg and Keysar argue that metaphors are not factually inaccurate as such – that is, the speaker doesn't violate Grice's maxim of Quality when they produce a metaphor. The crucial point is that the class of entities they are referring to, and asserting that the tenor of the metaphor belongs to, is not the class of entities that is usually referred to when we talk about that metaphor vehicle. To put it another way, the speaker of (205) isn't using the word *is* in an untruthful way – rather, what they're doing is using the phrase *the sun* in a non-standard way.

This turns out to have implications for how we identify the metaphorically relevant properties of the metaphor vehicle. Consider (208), which is one of the examples Glucksberg and Keysar (1990) consider in detail.

(208)   My job is a jail.

In the literal sense of *jail*, (208) can't be true. So in what sense could (208) be true? Glucksberg and Keysar (1990: 7) argue that *jail* is also a member of various superordinate categories, such as *punishments*, *multioccupant facilities* and *human-made structures*. It is also a member of a bunch of imaginable categories of things that don't have conventional names: for instance, the set of situations that share various undesirable properties such as being in a confined space that is difficult to escape from. Importantly, the speaker's job could also be a member of this kind of category.

The essence of Glucksberg and Keysar's idea is that, in using a metaphor like (208), we are evoking just this kind of ad hoc category, to which both the metaphor tenor and vehicle can simultaneously belong, and we are labelling that previously unnamed category with a label that is usually used to refer to a different category: specifically, the vehicle, in this case *jail*. As a consequence, the subset of the metaphor vehicle's properties that are relevant to the figurative interpretation of the utterance are just those which go towards making up the new ad hoc category. Precisely which properties these are depends on which properties are most obviously shareable between the metaphor tenor and vehicle. Thus, the utterance of (208) invites us to consider *jail* as being the label for (perhaps) a category of undesirable situations, to which category 'literally being in jail' belongs, and to understand the speaker as asserting that their job is another situation belonging to this broader category.

A slightly different account of metaphor interpretation is proposed by Carston (1996, 2002), working within a Relevance Theory framework. Carston argues that metaphor is merely a case of 'loose use', and the interpretation of a metaphorical expression such as (204) involves concept adjustment – either loosening (in which the concept actually communicated is more general than the underlying 'lexical concept') or narrowing (in which the concept communicated is more specific). From a Relevance Theory standpoint, these are local pragmatic processes, in the sense that they don't involve post-propositional reasoning of the classical Gricean kind. In this specific case, the meaning of *jail* is loosened in order to accommodate a broader range of entities than it normally would. As in Glucksberg and Keysar's (1990) account, this means that we can understand a metaphor like (208) as a straightforwardly true class-inclusion statement – it's just not a statement about *jail* in the normal sense of the word.

Studies addressing the second question raised in this section – how we process the parts of the metaphor vehicle meaning that are and are not relevant to the intended figurative meaning of the utterance – have gone some way towards supporting the class-inclusion account of metaphor. Glucksberg and Keysar's theory seems naturally to predict that the irrelevant aspects of meaning will be suppressed and the relevant aspects strengthened, in the hearer's mental representation. In order to study whether that is taking place, we need tools for establishing whether or not a given component of meaning is active in the hearer's mind at a specific moment in time, which takes us firmly into the realm of psycholinguistics.

Early attempts to study these metaphoric meanings psycholinguistically were made by Gernsbacher, Glucksberg and colleagues, in a series of papers from 1995 onwards. They presented participants with metaphorical materials (e.g. *That defence lawyer is a shark*) and asked them to perform truth-value judgements on sentences that either relate to an irrelevant aspect of the metaphor vehicle (*Sharks are good swimmers*) or relate to an aspect that is relevant to the figurative interpretation (*Sharks are tenacious*). Their participants were generally slower to judge the irrelevant sentences true and faster to judge the relevant sentences true (compared with how long each took when the same questions were asked without the metaphor having been presented). This suggests that, when a reader understands a metaphorical meaning, they do indeed suppress the irrelevant aspects of the literal meaning of the metaphor vehicle, while strengthening the relevant aspects of that meaning, making these parts of the meaning respectively less and more salient to them when they ultimately judge the sentences' truth-value. However, in this experiment, we only learn about the participants' understanding of metaphor after the fact – it doesn't tell us much about the process that delivers this eventual meaning, and therefore doesn't enable us fully to distinguish between the competing theories discussed above.

Later work has attempted to probe the time-course of metaphor processing rather more closely. For instance, Rubio-Fernández (2007) uses a lexical decision task under a cross-modal priming paradigm.

Methodology: lexical decision task, with priming

In a lexical decision task (LDT), participants are asked to judge whether or not a stimulus ('target') is a real word of their language, typically by pressing the appropriate key. The stimuli may be written or spoken. The real words are interspersed with other items, usually pseudowords (that is, strings of letters or speech sounds that could be words, according to the phonotactic rules of the language, but happen not to be words, such as *drun* in English). Experimenters measure the response times and error rates (the rate at which non-words are judged to be words, and vice versa).

The LDT is often used in conjunction with some form of **priming** task: that is to say, where the participant is provided with some additional material before the test stimulus that might influence their response to that stimulus. In a cross-modal priming paradigm, the prime is given in one medium (typically spoken) while the main task is performed in another medium (typically visual). Thus, in a cross-modally primed LDT, participants judge whether or not written stimuli are real words, while also hearing other words. Experimenters may also be interested in the effect of manipulating the **inter-stimulus interval (ISI)**: that is, in this case, the precise length of time that elapses between a prime word being heard and the next visual target being presented.

Research going back to Swinney (1979) has demonstrated that cross-modal priming can influence lexical decision. Among other things, if a written stimulus that is a real word is immediately preceded by a semantically related spoken word, participants will recognise it as a real word more quickly (on average) than if it is preceded by an unrelated spoken word. This is interpreted as evidence that the visual stimulus (target) is partially activated (primed) at the moment of lexical decision, and the faster lexical decision is referred to as a positive priming effect. Turning that around, faster lexical decision in a cross-modal priming task can be taken to constitute evidence that the spoken material has some kind of connection (for instance, a semantic association) to the visual target. Thus, we can use this paradigm to gain some insight into the interpretations that participants place on the spoken input.

In the critical items of Rubio-Fernández's (2007) experiment, participants listened to texts ending with class-inclusion metaphors (e.g. *John is a cactus*), and performed lexical judgements on words that were related either to the literal meaning of the metaphor vehicle (specifically, its superordinate category, in this case *plant*) or to its distinctive features that are relevant for the metaphorical interpretation (in this case, *spiky*). The baseline condition involved the same target words being presented after an entirely unrelated metaphorical text. When the target words were presented with a zero ISI – that is, immediately after the metaphorical prime – there was a positive priming effect for both the literal associates and the metaphorical associates. This also held at an ISI of 400 milliseconds. However, at an ISI of 1 second, there was a positive priming effect only for the metaphorical associate (*spiky*, in the above example) and not for the literal associate (*plant*).

The results of Rubio-Fernández's experiment suggest that there is initial activation of both parts of the metaphor vehicle's meaning that were tested – the one that was ultimately not relevant to the speaker's intended, figurative meaning, and the one that ultimately was relevant. However, the ultimately irrelevant meaning appears to be deactivated a little later in processing. In Glucksberg and Keysar's (1990) terms, this could correspond to the hearer comprehending the speaker's intended ad hoc superordinate category, and subsequently discarding the usual superordinate category for the metaphor vehicle – that is, continuing to think of a cactus as belonging to a category like 'things painful to the touch' and coming to forget its status as a member of the category 'plants'. Or, as Carston (1996, 2002) proposes, it could correspond to the hearer broadening the vehicle's category to include entities that don't usually belong to it – that is, reinterpreting *cactus* to mean something like 'an object that is painful to touch (and that might or might not be a plant)'.

6.2.1 Are metaphors (like) similes?

The idea that metaphors might be true class-inclusion assertions represents something of a break from the traditional analysis of metaphor. In classical rhetoric, and for much of the time since antiquity, metaphors have been regarded as implicit comparisons. From that perspective, we can see metaphor as a special case of simile, in which the speaker emphasises the similarity between tenor and vehicle even more intensely by saying that the tenor actually *is* the vehicle, rather than just being *like* the vehicle. Metaphors and similes certainly do a lot of the same work, rhetorically, and are both used to point to specific points in common between otherwise dissimilar entities. But under the kind of approach discussed in the previous subsection, in which metaphors are understood as literally true, the relationship between metaphors and similes becomes a little less clear. In particular, it gives us a different perspective on the issue of how metaphor and simile differ, and why (and under what circumstances) a speaker will choose to use one rather than the other.

Intuitively, there are several ways in which metaphor and simile differ. However, perhaps the most obvious difference is something that's tricky to explain for the theories discussed in the previous subsection, namely that metaphors and their corresponding similes seem to differ in whether or not they are perceived as literally true. For instance, (209) is not literally true, at first glance, whereas (210) might be.

(209)   Those kids are hyenas.
(210)   Those kids are like hyenas.

Under a traditional account, we could say that (209) is understood as an exaggeration of (210) for rhetorical effect, and the hearer is aware of this and would judge it not literally true. However, this explanation isn't really available to us under the Carston- or Glucksberg and Keysar-style accounts, in which *hyenas* receives a pragmatically adjusted meaning in (209) and thus makes the utterance true. If this is what's happening, why do we still have the intuition that this isn't like (210)? Presumably because we're aware that we're having to perform this pragmatic adjustment in a different way, or to a greater extent, than we do for (210). But this is a little surprising, particularly in the context of Carston's approach, for which metaphoric usage is nothing special – it's just like the other kinds of pragmatic adjustment that we perform all the time without really being aware of it. Therefore, we would need to argue that there is some kind of difference between how this adjustment happens in metaphors as opposed to similes, a point taken up by Carston and Wearing (2011) which we will return to below.

An easier difference to explain is the widely shared intuition that simile is more permissive than metaphor, in the sense that similes can be judged appropriate or acceptable where the corresponding metaphor is not. This is presumably because the kind of category assignment suggested by metaphor requires a high degree of conceptual overlap between the tenor and the vehicle, whereas simile only requires that the entities being compared are alike in some identifiable respect. Consequently, similes like (211) are felicitous when the corresponding metaphors might be odd, as seen in (212).

> (211)   Laila Ali is like her father.
> (212)   ?? Laila Ali is her father.

In some sense, similes are more defensible than metaphors because pretty much everything is like pretty much anything else in at least some identifiable respect. Even the most inappropriate simile could therefore be defended by a sufficiently imaginative speaker finding the appropriate point of comparison, as illustrated by the following example (paraphrased from *Monty Python's Flying Circus*). It's not clear that the corresponding metaphor could be rescued in the same kind of way.[1]

> (213)   Your Majesty is like a stream of bat's piss. I mean, you shine out like a shaft of gold when all around is dark.

Still another argument against reducing similes to metaphors is that similes can sometimes be seen to contrast directly with metaphors. There's general agreement (at least since Ortony 1979) that metaphors are more forceful or direct than their corresponding similes. Presumably this is for the same kind of reason just discussed: the felicitous use of a metaphor requires a stronger or more wide-ranging set of similarities between the tenor and vehicle than is the case for the corresponding simile.

The use of simile may also have pragmatic effects that would not arise in the same way from the use of metaphor. This could help us explain why an utterance like (214) seems to be at least infelicitous, if not outright false, given that we know that (215) is true.

> (214)   Dolphins are like mammals.
> (215)   Dolphins are mammals.

One explanation for this is that (214) gives rise to an implicature: the speaker who says (214) could instead have said (215), which would have been briefer and presumably easier to process, as well as conveying a stronger meaning than (214). In fact, if we understand (215) to be literally true, we could argue that it's more informative than (214) in a traditional Gricean sense, on the grounds that (215) asserts that dolphins share all the properties common to all mammals, whereas (214) merely points out some kind of likeness between dolphins and mammals, which (as argued above) could be quite tenuous in practice. Consequently, the specific implicature arising from (214) is a quantity implicature that (215) is not true: as this implicature is false, (214) is infelicitous.

Of course, even if we agree that (214) conveys the negation of (215), this doesn't have to be as a result of an implicature. It could be an entailment: perhaps to say that something is *like* something is necessarily to say that it is *not* that thing. If this is an entailment, then the generalisation is that similes entail the falsity of their corresponding metaphors. This is a point of view that has often been assumed in the literature, although there is some recent experimental evidence against it and in favour of the implicature account of the interpretation of *like* (Rubio-Fernández et al. 2016).

This point is worth dwelling on for a moment because, at least from a Relevance Theory perspective, it challenges one idea about how to explain the differences between metaphors and similes. For Relevance Theory, word meanings are locally pragmatically adjusted as a result of context being taken into account. That's true for both metaphors and similes, as it is for any kind of language use – but as discussed above, this raises the problem of why the latter are perceived as literally true while the former are not. Taking this perspective, Carston and Wearing (2011) argue that there must be a difference between the ways in which a metaphor vehicle and the corresponding simile 'vehicle' are pragmatically adjusted. Specifically, they discuss (216) and (217).

(216) Mr Smith is a mouse.
(217) Mr Smith is like a mouse.

In understanding (216), according to Relevance Theory, we interpret *mouse* as meaning 'member of the broader class of entities that are quiet, unassertive, weak, etc.': following Carston's notation, let's call that meaning MOUSE*. Carston and Wearing argue that we cannot interpret *mouse* as MOUSE* in (217), because 'Mr Smith is not *like* that thing, he is a member of that category' (2011: 296; their emphasis). If they're right, there must be a fundamental difference between how the metaphor (216) and the simile (217) are understood.

However, if Rubio-Fernández et al. (2016) are right, Carston and Wearing's (2011) argument falls down: we can perfectly well interpret *mouse* as MOUSE* in (217), because it's true to say that Mr Smith is a

MOUSE* and also true to say that he is like a MOUSE*. On this view, it's still possible that the pragmatic adjustment of the 'vehicle' in a simile is just the same as the pragmatic adjustment undergone by the corresponding word in a metaphor. In fact, in this case, interpreting *mouse* as MOUSE* in (217) would be quite sensible: while Mr Smith may resemble an actual mouse in some respects, he is probably even more similar to the other human members of the class MOUSE*.

In short, there's broad agreement about the main points of difference between metaphor and simile in terms of their communicative effects, but there is still an ongoing debate about what interpretation processes are responsible for those differences. The idea that metaphors are literally true assertions involving pragmatic adjustment is a helpful one in some respects, but also rules out one obvious type of explanation for the differences between metaphor and simile, namely that metaphors aren't really true but appropriate similes are. Instead, it suggests a view in which the difference between metaphor and simile has more to do with the strength of the meaning and the closeness of the comparison being expressed.

6.2.2 Metaphor, metonymy and hyperbole

Metonymy and hyperbole are also traditionally distinguished as separate figures of speech, but they have a certain amount in common with metaphor. Both involve asserting something that is, at first glance, not literally true, but like metaphor – and unlike irony – the speaker's intended meaning is related in some fairly transparent way to the meaning that they appear to be expressing. Indeed, we could consider the traditional account of metaphor to be one that treats it as a hyperbolic simile, in which *like* is exaggerated to *is*. The speaker's motivation for using metonymy or hyperbole is not always easy to understand, but researchers have made more progress in establishing how the hearer recovers the speaker's intended meaning.

In the case of metonymy, it may be worth distinguishing conventional from less conventional forms. Compare (218) and (219).

(218)   Anne enjoys reading Dickens.
(219)   The ham sandwich is at the table by the window.

(218) exhibits a producer-for-product metonymy, which is so conventional that it could pass completely unremarked: we can use the name of an author to refer to their works. In the same spirit, when we refer to a *fake Picasso*, we are talking about an artwork rather than a person who pretends to be the artist. By contrast, (219) uses a form of metonymy in

which a person is identified by the food they have ordered, which may be conventional in the restaurant business but is somewhat less clear (although comprehensible) to the non-specialist hearer.

Particularly in the case of conventional forms, the challenge of identifying what the speaker means is very similar to the challenge of disambiguating polysemous words in general (for instance, understanding whether *wood* refers to a substance or to an area containing trees). Schumacher (in press) discusses the following set of examples.

(220)   The newspaper was in shreds after the kitten played with it.
(221)   The newspaper was boring and full of typographical errors.
(222)   The newspaper burned down in 1892 and was never rebuilt.
(223)   The newspaper fired the editor.

We can fairly straightforwardly understand *the newspaper* as referring to a physical artefact in (220), a written document in (221), a physical location of an institution in (222) and an institution as an organisational unit in (223). These senses are related in that we understand the broad notion of a *newspaper* as typically referring to an organisation, existing in some physical location, which aggregates written material and potentially publishes it on paper. The relevant sense for each sentence is determined by the context, in that only one of these sentences is plausible for each of those possible senses: a kitten can, for instance, shred a physical item made of paper, but probably not a whole building, and certainly not an abstract concept.

By the same token, conventional metonymies offer us potential interpretations that will enable us to make sense of sentences like (218). In that case, there is only one conventional interpretation that does the job, which is the one in which the name of the author is being used for their work. In (224), we would need more context to resolve the ambiguity, as the name might refer to the author or his work.

(224)   Anne admires Dickens.

In this case, it could be argued that the name *Dickens* is simply represented in our mental lexicon as polysemous, meaning either the author or his work. Frisson and Pickering (2007) investigated this by testing participants' abilities to access the latter interpretation with an unfamiliar author's name (*My great-grandmother often read Needham*). They showed that participants were slower to process the unfamiliar metonym than a familiar one (. . . *Dickens*), but this slowdown could be prevented if the prior context made it clear that *Needham* was the name of an author (*My great-grandmother had all the novels by Needham in her library*). This suggests that we might have an abstract understanding of the possibility of producer-for-product metonymy, and that we activate that understanding whenever we encounter the name of a potential producer.

What does metonymy have to do with hyperbole? As noted above, both are a little like metaphor in that they are traditionally thought of as being literally untrue but in some sense pointing in the direction of truth (unlike irony, which traditionally points in the opposite direction). But both metonymy and hyperbole have been argued to be easier to process than metaphor. In the case of hyperbole, for instance, Deamer et al. (2010) showed that the italicised portion of (225) – interpretable as hyperbolic – is read faster than the italicised portion of (226), which comprises the same words but attracts a metaphoric interpretation.

(225)   The backyard definitely needed pruning. *It was a forest.*

(226)   Sam always got lost. The university was enormous. *It was a forest.*

It's difficult to construct experimental materials involving figurative language, particularly when we're considering multiple different kinds of figurative language, that are properly controlled in all relevant ways – for instance, with respect to their comprehensibility. There's a danger that when we attempt to construct novel metaphors, we end up with materials that don't achieve the communicative effects that we intend. However, to the extent that we can rely on the experimental findings so far, they invite us to wonder what it is about metonymy and hyperbole that might make them simpler to understand than metaphor. One idea about this, going back to Gibbs (1994), is that metaphor involves a cross-domain comparison, in which an entity from one domain is related to an entity from another domain, whereas both metonymy and hyperbole involve within-domain comparison. In both metonymy and hyperbole, the intended figurative meaning is directly linked to the semantic meaning of the material that was uttered: in metonymy, a referring expression is used to denote some entity that is not the usual referent for that expression but is closely related to it, while in hyperbole, an expression denoting an extreme point on a scale (e.g. *millions, freezing, starving*) is used to refer to some less extreme point on the same scale (e.g. *hundreds, cold, hungry*). By contrast, the hearer interpreting a metaphor doesn't have the advantage of being able to search in this confined space of meanings to find the one that the speaker intended: they may have to go a lot further afield and try to construct an understanding that makes sense of the utterance, although by going through this elaborate reasoning process they may be able to experience particularly strong, vivid or novel communicative effects.

We can interpret this idea quite nicely from a Relevance Theory standpoint. On this view, metonymy and hyperbole, like metaphor, are instances of 'loose use', and call for pragmatic adjustment of the meanings of words in order to be properly understood. But in the cases of metonymy and hyperbole, the kind of pragmatic adjustment that is necessary is rather modest: we simply need to accept a related word as the name for an entity, or accept an expression for an extreme scale-point as the name for a less extreme one. In the case of metaphor, as discussed earlier, the pragmatic adjustment is considerably greater, and presumably much more effortful. However, as is characteristic of Relevance Theory, that greater effort meets with greater reward, in the case of a felicitous use of metaphor: it brings about a potentially powerful cross-domain comparison that represents a new way of thinking about an entity. Thus, the extra effort achieves greater cognitive effects, in just the way that Relevance Theory argues is characteristic of language interpretation across the board.

6.3 Social cognition and non-literal understanding

One of the defining characteristics of autism spectrum disorder (ASD) is a difficulty in social communication, and one of the stereotypical manifestations of this is a difficulty in understanding non-literal language. This has been argued to stem from a general inability to represent a speaker's intention. As Happé puts it, under this assumption, 'communication should break down most noticeably where the speaker's attitude must be taken into account in modifying the literal meaning of the utterance' (1993: 103).

The ability to represent another person's mental state is sometimes termed **Theory of Mind** (ToM). This includes the ability to ascribe beliefs, desires and intentions to another person, even when those are different from our own (or from observable reality). In normal development this ability emerges gradually, and can be explored experimentally through the use of classic 'false-belief' tasks.

Methodology: false-belief tasks
False-belief tasks are those in which the participant is tested on their ability to understand that someone else can have an erroneous belief. The classic example is the Sally-Anne task, developed by Baron-Cohen et al. (1985) based on earlier work by Wimmer and Perner (1983). The story introduces two characters, Sally and Anne. Sally then hides a marble in a basket, and leaves the scene. Anne takes the marble out of the basket and puts it in a box. Sally then returns to the scene: the test question is 'Where will Sally look for her marble?'

In order to answer this question correctly ('The basket'), participants must appreciate that their own knowledge of the scene – specifically, that the marble is now in the box – is not shared by Sally, who erroneously believes that the marble is still in the basket. That is, they must appreciate that Sally holds a false belief about the location of the marble and will act accordingly.

Participants are recorded as passing or failing the task according to whether or not they gave the correct answer. A limitation of this method is that it involves the recording of a single data point per participant, and it would be possible to pass the task half of the time by guessing, or to fail the task as a consequence of not paying attention at some point in the story.

The results of false-belief tasks indicate that, in typical development, children are able to attribute false belief around the age of four (Wellman et al. 2001), although it has been argued that this ability can in fact be detected in younger children given the right experimental conditions (Scott and Baillargeon 2017).

Intuitively, we could expect Theory of Mind to play a considerable role in the understanding of irony, where there is a complete mismatch between what the speaker seems to be saying and what they actually mean to convey. However, the importance of Theory of Mind to other forms of non-literal language is not so clear. Happé (1993) proposed that different figures of speech impose different ToM demands. Specifically, she argues that similes do not require ToM, as they can be treated just like literal comparisons. Metaphor, however, requires (first-order) ToM, as 'the propositional form of the utterance is a more or less loose interpretation of the speaker's thought' (ibid.: 104). And irony requires second-order ToM: that is to say, the hearer needs to be able to recognise that the speaker is themselves attributing a thought to someone else. In assuming this, Happé is following the Sperber and Wilson (1981) approach to irony, discussed in section 6.1: that is, she assumes that the speaker is not only asserting something at variance with what they believe, but also that they are doing so because someone else believes this assertion, and the speaker wishes to call attention to that.

Happé (1993) tested the role of Theory of Mind in figurative language comprehension in a series of experiments involving participants with ASD. The participants were divided into three groups (each of six participants) according to whether they possessed second-order ToM, first-order ToM only or no ToM, in a pre-test involving false belief and deception tasks that were not linguistic in character. One experiment was a sentence completion task, in which participants were asked to choose one option from a list to complete a sentence, either as a metaphor or as a simile; a second experiment tested metaphor and irony by presenting a story containing a metaphorical and an ironic remark and asking participants to choose between two possible interpretations for each remark.

The results of Happé's study provided partial support for the theoretical claims about the necessity of ToM. The participants with no ToM struggled with metaphor but had partial success with simile; the participants with first-order ToM managed both simile and metaphor but had difficulties with irony; and the participants with second-order ToM could comprehend all three figures of speech. However, the results were not as clear-cut as might have been predicted: only the participants with second-order ToM performed perfectly in any condition, and more advanced ToM capabilities appeared to confer an advantage in figurative language comprehension across the board, whether or not they were predicted to be necessary in a given case.

A partial explanation of Happé's pattern of results is that general language abilities, as well as ToM, might play a role in the comprehension of figurative language. Norbury (2005) tested children with ASD and showed that the children's language ability (as measured by a series of standard tests) was a better predictor of their metaphor comprehension than (non-linguistic) ToM ability. However, ToM ability remained a significant predictor of metaphor comprehension. Moreover, as Rundblad and Annaz (2010) point out, one of the tests of language ability used by Norbury included figurative expressions, so the assessments of ToM and language ability might not have been independent. Rundblad and Annaz (2010) tested children with ASD on their comprehension of metaphor and metonymy and found that they had significantly more difficulty with metaphor than would be predicted based on their language abilities alone; by contrast, their understanding of metonymy was at the level expected given their overall language level.

On the available evidence, it seems that people with ASD do tend to have difficulties with the comprehension of figurative language, and that this is most evident in the case of irony. Metaphors pose less of a problem, and metonymies perhaps less still. There is relatively little work attempting to compare a wide range of figures of speech in this respect (although MacKay and Shaw (2004) compare six types of figurative meaning, including hyperbole but unfortunately not including metaphor).

Theory of Mind thus appears somewhat relevant as an explanation of the issues with figurative language comprehension experienced by people with ASD. This in turn supports the idea that ToM is implicated in figurative language use in general. However, there are several complications. For one thing, we can't easily rule out the possibility that ToM deficits only indirectly cause delays in the understanding of figurative language. ASD is associated with delays in language acquisition (perhaps connected to the deficit in ToM), which in turn could result in poorer performance on difficult language comprehension tasks, such as those involving figurative language – but that doesn't itself prove that ToM is directly involved in figurative language comprehension.

Moreover, as discussed above, the experimental record suggests that ToM ability is not always a necessary or sufficient condition for the correct understanding of figurative language. And from a theoretical standpoint, this is hardly surprising: as we've already seen in this chapter, not only do different figures of speech vary in how conceptually complex they are (as discussed in section 6.2.2), but there are many different accounts of how they should be understood, which even differ on whether they are truly figurative at all (section 6.2). It is not obvious why a limited capability for ToM should necessarily impair an individual's ability to form and label the kinds of categories posited by Glucksberg and Keysar (1990), for instance: so, on their account, ToM might not be essential to the comprehension of metaphor. Nor it is obvious why an individual with ASD should necessarily have difficulty with the kind of local pragmatic adjustment of meaning that is posited by Relevance Theory.

In summary, if we fully understood the mechanisms underlying the comprehension of figurative language, we could make good progress in clarifying the pragmatic profile of individuals with ASD. By the same token, if we had a clear understanding of the pragmatic profile of individuals with ASD, we could considerably advance our understanding of the mechanisms used in the comprehension of figurative language. However, at present, the best we can achieve seems to be gradual progress on these two questions in parallel.

6.4 Summary

Studying non-literal language offers us useful insights into the pragmatic processes involved in language comprehension. Figurative interpretations do not tend to proceed via an initial stage of literal interpretation, which appears to rule out the most obvious Gricean account of these meanings – although in fact it's not clear that Grice himself was committed to any such predictions about processing. The evidence appears to point to the existence of some more direct means of accessing the speaker's intended meaning, which might, for example, involve treating a wide range of contextual factors as probabilistic cues to the speaker's intention. At the same time, many categories of ostensibly figurative meanings, including metaphor, metonymy and hyperbole, can plausibly be argued to be literal meanings that have undergone some kind of local pragmatic modulation. There is also evidence that general abilities in social cognition are relevant for the understanding of at least some kinds of non-literal language, but precisely how these capabilities figure in the process of interpretation remains an open question.

Exercises

Answers to the following are available at <edinburghuniversitypress. com/pragmatics>.

1. What kinds of non-literal interpretations are evoked by the following utterances?
    a. He's a whirlwind of activity.
    b. It's like fire and ice, and I feel my role in the band is to be kind of the middle of that, kind of like lukewarm water. (*This Is Spinal Tap*)
    c. If I have to attend that class, I'll die of boredom.
    d. You're not going to die.
2. In the following metaphors, which properties of the vehicle are attributed to the tenor? Which are not?
    a. Jane is a bulldozer.
    b. This place is a pigsty.
    c. Jake's eyes are limpid pools.
3. How might the speaker indicate that the following utterances are intended ironically?
    a. That's a good idea.
    b. I'd love to be there.
    c. What a surprise.

Discussion questions

1. Mixed metaphors are those in which there is inconsistency at the literal level, as in the following examples.
    a. If you spill the beans, it will open up a can of worms.
    b. The sacred cows have come home to roost.
    c. I smell a rat, and I want to nip it in the bud.

To the extent that these bring about unintended and odd communicative effects, what does that suggest about the limitations on constructing extended metaphors? And what does it suggest about the activation of literal meaning when we process metaphors?

2. The term 'dead metaphor' is sometimes used to describe phrases which were originally metaphorical in meaning but have become conventionalised, to the extent that language users aren't aware that they were originally metaphors. For instance, *time is running out* started as a metaphor identifying time with the sand in an hourglass. How could we tell, for instance by using experimental methods discussed in this chapter, whether a given expression is still understood as a metaphor or has become a 'dead metaphor'?

Note

1. In terms of Glucksberg and Keysar's (1990) account, accepting this as a metaphor would amount to accepting the term *stream of bat's piss* as an expression to denote the entire set of things that 'shine out like a shaft of gold when all around is dark'. Presumably, for one reason or another, this expression isn't generally considered a good one with which to refer to this whole category of entities.

7 Arranging information in coherent discourse

Clerk of the Court: Call Mrs Fiona Lewis.

Mrs Lewis: *(taking Bible)* I swear to tell the truth, the whole truth and nothing but the truth. So anyway, I said to her, I said, they can't afford that on what he earns, I mean for a start the feathers get up your nose, I ask you, four and six a pound, and him with a wooden leg? I don't know how she puts up with it ... (...)

Judge: Mr Bartlett, I fail to see the relevance of your last witness.

(Graham Chapman, John Cleese, Terry Gilliam, Eric Idle,
Terry Jones and Michael Palin, *Monty Python's Flying Circus*,
s1e3, 'How to Recognise Different Types of Trees from Quite a
Long Way Away')

As discussed in Chapter 2, a cooperative speaker, by definition, has to say things that are relevant to the current discourse purpose. Grice articulated this idea through the maxim of relation, which he initially stated simply as 'be relevant', noting as he did so that 'its formulation conceals a number of problems that exercise me a good deal' (1989: 27). In developing Relevance Theory, Sperber and Wilson argued that a fully articulated notion of relevance is in fact the essential feature of a working theory of communication. They argue that 'utterances raise expectations of relevance ... because the search for relevance is a basic feature of human cognition, which communicators may exploit' (Wilson and Sperber 2004: 250–1).

We've already seen some examples of how this can play out in a conversational exchange. Consider Grice's (1975: 32) example of an apparent relation violation, repeated in (227).

(227)   A: I am out of petrol.
        B: There is a garage around the corner.

B's utterance appears to be only very loosely semantically connected to A's, but in practice we immediately realise that there is more going on here. A is presenting information with a particular agenda in mind – they presumably want B to help them address the problem of their being out of petrol – and B's utterance consequently is understood as being somehow germane to that point. As a consequence, B is understood to be conveying that (as far as they know) the garage is open and sells petrol. These are not part of what B literally says: instead, they are pragmatic enrichments arising from the assumption that their utterance is relevant to A's needs.

In a similar spirit, we generally expect a cooperative speaker to make certain specific discourse moves in response to specific prompts. If there's a question, for instance, we expect them to answer it (unless they can't, or there is some good reason not to). In cases such as this – which we will discuss in more detail in Chapter 8 – there are quite strong constraints on what a cooperative speaker can do when they start their conversational turn.

However, in a lot of cases, the speaker isn't under any very tight constraint as to what they can say or do at a given point. Perhaps the previous utterance was made by another speaker, but didn't mandate any specific kind of reply. Or perhaps they themselves produced the previous utterance – that is to say, they are continuing their own conversational turn. However, even in circumstances such as this, we still expect a cooperative speaker to be coherent, in the sense that their utterance should relate in some discernible way to what has gone before. One reason this is important is that the expectation of coherence makes various kinds of pragmatic inference available. In the following sections, we'll look at two major aspects of this, and their consequences for pragmatics: how we package information as 'given' or 'new' in discourse, and what kinds of conceptual relations can exist between what is newly uttered and what has already been established.

7.1 Information structure

Back in section 3.1.2, we saw an example in which *and* invites the interpretation 'and then' – that is, when a hearer naturally infers that the events described in two conjoined clauses occurred in the order in which they are mentioned. This seems to relate to our expectations about the manner in which information is presented – doing so in chronological sequence is perhaps more 'orderly', in a Gricean sense. Of course, this enriched interpretation of *and* is not obligatory: we can use *and* to conjoin timeless truths, or events that happened in the opposite order to that (potentially) implicated, as in (228) and (229) respectively.

(228)   There are eight protons in an oxygen atom and six protons in a carbon atom.

(229)   Nicola Sanders won the silver medal in the 2007 world championship 400m, and Christine Ohuruogu won the gold.

Given that a single clause expresses a single thought, there's not much scope for the content within a clause to be 'orderly' in quite the same kind of way. Nevertheless, it turns out that we do have expectations about how information is going to be presented within a single clause. As in the case of presupposition, this has a lot to do with how we understand the information, rather than about the order of events in the real world, or any such notion.

7.1.1 Components of clausal meaning

It's traditionally acknowledged that, within a clause, we can distinguish 'what is being talked about' from 'what is being said about it'.

Note on terminology
Various different traditions of analysis refer to these components of meaning in different ways. 'What is being talked about' is variously called the **topic** or the **theme**, and 'what is being said about it' is called the **comment, focus** or **rheme**. Here I will stick to the terms **topic** and **focus**.

As a generalisation, the subjects of ordinary sentences of English tend to serve as topics, whether the sentences are active or passive: for instance, *Mary* is the topic of (230) and *the letter* is the topic of (231).

(230)   Mary forged the letter.
(231)   The letter was forged by Mary.

Alongside this, there are also grammatical devices in English (as in other languages) that seem to serve the function of marking topichood. The construction *as for* in (232) and (233) is one such example: it makes *the letter* the topic of the sentence each time, whether or not that would otherwise be the case. In each example, we would be justified in saying that this is a sentence about the letter.

(232)   As for the letter, Mary forged it.
(233)   As for the letter, it was forged by Mary.

Given that the core meanings of (230)–(233) are all essentially the same, it is natural to wonder what a speaker would mean to convey by uttering one of these variants – and in particular, what extra effects we get in return for the additional cost that is presumably incurred when we utter a more complex or verbose variant such as (231), (232) or (233).

A relevant observation here is that topic and focus differ in how they are related to the preceding discourse (which is part of the motivation for attempting to distinguish them in the first place). Given that we expect a cooperative speaker to address the current discourse purpose, we expect their choice of topic to be connected to what has gone before. Consequently, a speaker might choose to promote a particular entity to the topic position in order to reinforce the relation between what they are saying and what is already established in the discourse.

In cases such as (232) and (233), the speaker goes out of their way to promote *the letter* unambiguously to the topic position. Correspondingly, it would be odd for them to utter either of these sentences in a context in which the letter is not already somewhat salient in the discourse, or at least familiar to the hearer. The effect of using *as for* here resembles the 'bookkeeping' function of one category of presupposition triggers (as discussed in section 4.3.3) – the speaker seems intent upon 'collecting' the letter from somewhere in the previous discourse and bringing it back to be discussed further.

We can further illustrate the role of topichood by looking at the contrast between definite and indefinite noun phrases. There's a striking difference in acceptability between (234) and (235).

(234)   As for the barman, he was half-asleep.
(235)   ?? As for a barman, he was half-asleep.

The awkwardness of (235) suggests that we have difficulty in promoting the indefinite NP *a barman* to topic position: that is, that there is some kind of clash between indefiniteness and topichood. As a general observation, the use of the indefinite is a strong signal that the referent in question is **discourse-new**. When we mention that same referent again, we are pretty much obliged to use a definite reference (e.g. *the barman*). We can see this in (236) – here, the repeated use of *a barman* is infelicitous, at least if we are trying to refer to the same person already mentioned.

(236)   The club employed four waiting staff and a barman. ?? A barman was half-asleep.

We can use definite NPs to refer to things that are **discourse-old**, and we can also use them to refer to things that are **hearer-old**: that is, things that are already mutually known to exist (*the Pope, the President of the United States, the force of gravity*, and so on). And we can use definite NPs for things that are **inferable** – that is, things that might reasonably also be presumed to exist, granted the existence of things that we know about. If we speak of *a house*, we can immediately start talking about *the front door*, as that is an inferable feature of the house. Notably, we can promote things that are inferable based on the current discourse into topic position, but that doesn't necessarily apply to hearer-old material that hasn't been mentioned in the current discourse: compare (237), featuring the inferable *students*, and (238), featuring the hearer-old *Pope*.

(237) The university strike is upsetting for the staff. As for the students, they have mixed views.

(238) The university strike is upsetting for the staff. ?? As for the Pope, he has not yet stated his position on the issue.

7.1.2 Inferring a Question Under Discussion from information structure

How we package information within a clause can have immediate pragmatic consequences, just at a propositional level. Consider the following pair of examples, discussed by Onea (in press): an ordinary unmarked statement and the corresponding 'it-cleft' sentence.

(239) Donald lied at the debate.

(240) It was Donald who lied at the debate.

Both of these entail that Donald lied at the debate. Both also convey that 'someone lied at the debate' – which is entailed by the fact that Donald lied at the debate, although it has also been argued to be a presupposition of (240) (a point discussed by Horn (1981) which we will return to shortly). And both could be argued to convey that no one other than Donald lied at the debate: that is, an **exhaustivity inference**. However, there is a widespread intuition that this exhaustivity is conveyed to a much greater extent by (240) than it is by (239). Correspondingly, (241) seems to be felicitous, whereas (242) is awkward in much the same way that (243) is, both verging on being self-contradictory.

(241) Donald lied at the debate. Hillary did too.

(242) ?? It was Donald who lied at the debate. Hillary did too.

(243) ?? Only Donald lied at the debate. Hillary did too.

Promoting a referent to topic position using the *as for* construction seems to have a similar effect, but in the opposite direction. The speaker of (244) seems to be almost entirely noncommittal on the question of whether or not anyone other than Donald lied at the debate.

(244) As for Donald, he lied at the debate.

The use of a passive also appears to make a difference to the kind of exhaustivity inference that is available. It is tempting to think that *Hillary* can be interpreted exhaustively in (245) and *Donald* can be interpreted exhaustively in (246): that is to say, (245) tends to convey that Donald continually interrupted Hillary and no one else, while (246) tends to convey that Hillary was continually interrupted by Donald and no one else.

(245)   Donald continually interrupted Hillary.
(246)   Hillary was continually interrupted by Donald.

How can we explain these patterns pragmatically? Well, we've already seen at least one example of an exhaustivity inference arising under the general heading of quantity implicature. The setup was as follows.

(247)   A: Did you meet her parents?
        B: I met her mother.

In this exchange, B's reference to *her mother* is interpreted exhaustively, relative to the set of individuals that are currently of interest (*her parents*) – that is, it is interpreted roughly as though B had actually said *Only her mother*. This is a classic quantity implicature, but it also relies on relevance, as quantity implicatures usually do: given A's question, it would not only have been more informative for B to answer with respect to both parents (as it always would be), but it would have been more relevant in the current conversational context for B to have done so.

The striking difference between (247) and the other examples that we have been discussing in this subsection is that, in (247), there is an explicit question, and that creates a very clear expectation as to how much information the next speaker is expected to provide. Elsewhere, we have just been judging individual utterances taken out of context. However, even without an explicit question, we can nevertheless understand pairs of utterances like (239) and (240), or (245) and (246), as answering subtly different questions. Even in the absence of a clear, explicit question, we could expect this difference to have consequences for the pragmatic interpretation of these utterances.

We touched on this idea already in Chapter 4, where the notion of Question Under Discussion (QUD) was introduced, as conceived by Roberts (1996). On a QUD view, we can see every utterance as offering a full or partial answer to some question that needs answering at that moment in the discourse. That question can be explicit, as it is in (247), but it doesn't have to be. In section 4.4, we briefly looked at how the QUD approach offers insights into presupposition, following Simons et al.'s (2010) idea that material that does not address the QUD is not affected by operators such as negation.

To flesh out the idea of how the QUD might bear upon the pragmatic interpretation of an utterance, let's revisit (240).

(240)   It was Donald who lied at the debate.

This appears to be a reasonable answer to a question such as (248) or (249), but is somewhat odd as a response to (250).

(248)   Who lied at the debate?
(249)   Who was it who lied at the debate?
(250)   What did Donald do?

Now, the speaker of (240) asserts that Donald lied at the debate, and it obviously follows from that that there exists someone who lied at the debate. However, the general point that someone lied at the debate seems to be taken for granted by the speaker of (240) – it doesn't look like something that they're introducing to the discourse for the first time. To be more precise, it behaves somewhat like a presupposition: if we negate (240), or modify it with a modal, or make it a question, or make it the antecedent of a conditional – as in (251)–(254) respectively – the fact that someone lied at the debate still seems to be assumed.

(251)   It wasn't Donald who lied at the debate.
(252)   Perhaps it was Donald who lied at the debate.
(253)   Was it Donald who lied at the debate?
(254)   If it was Donald who lied at the debate, the fact-checkers will have a field day.

If we consider (251), it seems that the same kind of QUD is likely to be in play as it was for the positive version of the utterance, (240). Again, (251) seems like a reasonable response to (248) or (249), but is much less satisfactory as an answer to (250). So we can make two observations about (251): that the QUD is probably something like (248) or (249), and that it conveys the meaning that 'somebody lied at the debate', which projects from under the scope of negation.

For Simons et al. (2010), these two observations are connected. Both of the questions that seem appropriate here also assume that someone lied at the debate, and the issue that arises is merely 'who?' Consequently, the fact that someone lied at the debate is not relevant to answering the QUD, when (251) (or (240)) is uttered: instead, it's understood to be background content, already assumed by speaker and hearer.

In summary, it looks as though the form of words used in (251) – and in (240) – signals that the QUD is something of the nature of (248) or (249), rather than something like (250). The projection behaviour demonstrated by (251) is consistent with this, under Simons et al.'s (2010) analysis.

Moreover, if (240) is an attempt to answer the question of who lied at the debate, we would be entitled to think that it might be intended as an exhaustive answer to that question. That is to say, we would expect the speaker to respond by listing all the people who lied at the debate, rather than just giving an example of a person who did so. Thus, we're back in the standard quantity implicature scenario, where naming one person as a liar is naturally understood as implicating that (as far as the speaker knows) no one else lied.

How does (244), repeated below, differ from the *It was Donald who . . .* version in (240)?

(244)   As for Donald, he lied at the debate.

Here, the form of the utterance sends a very different signal about what kind of question is being answered. Specifically, this would be an odd response to anything like (255), but a perfectly reasonable one to a question like (256).

(255)   Who lied at the debate?
(256)   What about Donald?

Just like (240), (244) commits the speaker to the claim that Donald lied at the debate, and hence to the claim that someone lied at the debate, but this time, this latter meaning doesn't seem to be presupposed in any sense. For instance, if we negate the sentence, we obtain (257), which wouldn't convey that someone lied at the debate – which suggests that the meaning that 'someone lied at the debate' isn't presuppositional in (244).

(257)   As for Donald, he didn't lie at the debate.

Another pragmatic difference is that, if we interpret (244) as an answer to a question like (256), we have no reason to expect the speaker to provide an exhaustive list of the people who lied at the debate. Whether or not someone else lied at the debate isn't relevant to answering (256): the question is merely about what Donald did. If this is the QUD, we shouldn't draw an exhaustivity inference from the utterance of (244).

We might expect passives to have a similar effect. (258) is a reasonable response to (256), whereas (259) would be a poor answer to that question.

(258)   Donald continually interrupted Hillary.
(259)   Hillary was continually interrupted by Donald.

Under the assumption that the QUD is something like (256), we should expect (258) to be potentially exhaustive with respect to 'Hillary' – if Donald continually interrupted anyone else, that might also be worthy of mention – while this should not apply to (259). However, (259) would be a good answer to the corresponding question *What about Hillary?*, in which case we should expect it to be exhaustive with respect to 'Donald', for the same reason.

However, those assumptions about the likely QUDs in these cases are probably not very safe. Compared with the *as for* and *it was* constructions, (258) and (259) don't offer very specific indications of what kind of QUD is likely to be in effect. Both would be perfectly good answers to a question such as (260), for instance – the only difference being that the speaker has chosen to make one or other participant the central figure in their answer.

(260)   What happened in the debate?

And it's also possible that the QUD is something more specific than (260), but still not something that supports the kind of exhaustivity inference described above. (258) would be a perfectly sensible answer to (261), just as (259) would to (262), for instance – and if those are the QUDs, we should expect *Donald* to be interpreted exhaustively in (258) and *Hillary* to be interpreted exhaustively in (259).

(261)   Who continually interrupted Hillary?
(262)   Who was continually interrupted by Donald?

So, determining which pragmatic interpretation is actually appropriate in a case like this is a complex matter: even if it is predictably mediated by the QUD, that doesn't help us all that much. We cannot take a simple declarative utterance like (258), or even a passive like (259), and read off the QUD with much confidence – although it might still be useful for us to note that some of the possible QUDs are presumably much more likely than others, given the utterance.

We may have to weigh up various competing considerations in order to arrive at a best guess about what the speaker takes the current QUD to be, and therefore how we should shape our pragmatic interpretation of their utterance. As we've seen in the above examples, syntax is one relevant factor in helping us determine the likely QUD, but it is not the only relevant factor. For instance, another way of influencing the pragmatic interpretation of an utterance is to change its intonation pattern. The speaker can mark part of the sentence as focused by placing stress on it (typically through higher pitch and louder amplitude). This kind of focus is often represented in the literature by the use of capital letters, which would enable us to distinguish (263) and (264).

(263)   DONALD continually interrupted Hillary.
(264)   Donald continually interrupted HILLARY.

As its name suggests, focal stress indicates that something is to be interpreted as the focus of the sentence – that is to say, the new material, rather than the topic. Consequently, changing the position of focal stress can change the hearer's understanding about which part of the sentence is supposed to be new information, which in turn bears upon their understanding of what the QUD is likely to be. In (263), what is new is the identity of the person who interrupted Hillary, rather than the fact that someone did so. Similarly, what's new in (264) is the identity of the person who Donald continually interrupted, rather than the fact that he continually interrupted someone.

In these cases, we can go a bit further, and say that the fact of someone having continually interrupted Hillary is part of the background of (263), and the fact of someone having been continually interrupted by Donald is part of the background of (264). Again, that background information behaves rather like a presupposition: for instance, when we negate these sentences, while keeping the focus the same, those background meanings survive, as illustrated by (265) and (266).

(265)   DONALD didn't continually interrupt Hillary.
(266)   Donald didn't continually interrupt HILLARY.

As a consequence of this focus structure, on hearing (263) (or (265)) out of the blue, we might reasonably infer that it is occurring in a context in which it is already mutually known that someone interrupted Hillary, and that the QUD is likely to concern who that was. Again, this would invite us to infer that (263) was supposed to constitute an exhaustive answer to the question, and convey that no one else continually interrupted Hillary. ((265) obviously doesn't constitute an exhaustive answer, because it leave the presupposition standing without giving us any information about who the interrupter actually was.) By the same token, the utterance of (264) would invite us to infer that the speaker meant to answer a QUD about who it was that Donald continually interrupted, and thus invite us to draw the exhaustivity inference that Donald didn't continually interrupt anyone other than Hillary.

Overall, then, we can partially explain how the speaker chooses to structure the information in semantically equivalent utterances by understanding those utterances to be answering different questions.

Those questions might be explicit in the preceding context, or purely implicit. It certainly appears that some constructions, such as it-clefts and presentational constructions using *as for* . . ., as well as specific intonation patterns, can give us a very strong sense that a particular question is under discussion. By virtue of this, we are sometimes able to enrich the speaker's meaning with an additional pragmatic interpretation, corresponding to the one that we would have if the signalled QUD had actually been uttered. Typically, this assumption about the QUD enables us to treat an utterance as giving an exhaustive answer, which is something we can potentially arrive at using the standard mechanisms for quantity implicature.

7.1.3 Isomorphism: another case of QUD influence?

In the previous subsection, we discussed a set of cases where the Question Under Discussion makes a difference to the pragmatic interpretation of an utterance. In this section, we look at a slightly different case in which the QUD might be implicated in the disambiguation of utterances which have two possible semantic interpretations. These are utterances featuring a quantifier and negation, as in (267) and (268).

(267)   All of the toys are not in the boxes.
(268)   Some of the toys are not in the boxes.

The most obvious reading of (267) is one in which it asserts that the location of 'all of the toys' is 'not in the boxes' – that is, that none of the toys are in the boxes. However, (267) is widely agreed to admit another possible interpretation, in which it merely denies that all of the toys are in the boxes – thus making it equivalent to asserting that not all of the toys are in the boxes. Likewise, (268) has an obvious reading in which it asserts that the location of 'some of the toys' is 'not in the boxes' – that is, that not all of the toys are in the boxes – and a less obvious reading in which it denies that some of the toys are in the boxes (thus asserting that none of the toys are in the boxes).

There's a broad consensus in the literature that, for each of these sentences, what I've described as the obvious reading is indeed somehow preferred in interpretation. Musolino et al. (2000) attribute this to what they call **isomorphism** – that is, the idea that the semantic scope relations in the sentence should agree with the syntactic scope relations. Syntactically, the quantifier takes scope over the negation in both (267) and (268) – more precisely, it c-commands the negation – and in the preferred interpretations of (267) and (268), the quantifier takes semantic scope over the negation in the same way, hence predicating the property of being 'not in the boxes' to 'all of the toys' and 'some of the toys' respectively. We might think of isomorphism as a specific case of the more general principle 'be orderly' – it seems to be preferable for speakers to encode their meanings in a way that makes the semantic relations obvious in the syntax.

Musolino et al. (2000) demonstrated, using a truth-value judgement (TVJ) task, that young English-speaking children (aged around five) had access to the isomorphic but not the non-isomorphic readings of sentences of this type, which they attributed to the child's grammar not yet having grown to incorporate the potential for non-isomorphic readings. However, subsequent work by Musolino and Lidz (2006) demonstrated that children (aged five) could interpret sentences non-isomorphically given appropriate contextual support.

To see what 'appropriate contextual support' means, let's look a little more closely at these two studies. In both cases, children were presented with a scenario in which three individuals each attempted to perform two actions. For instance, there are three horses, and they like to jump over things. In Musolino et al.'s (2000) Experiment 2, all of the horses consider jumping over a barn, but they all decide that it's too high; two of them then jump over a fence instead, but the third decides not to. A puppet then describes what has happened, and the child participant is asked whether what the puppet said was correct. Under this condition, Musolino et al.'s participants endorse (269) but don't agree that (270) is true – which suggests that they are restricted to isomorphic interpretations of these utterances.

(269)   Every horse didn't jump over the barn.
(270)   Every horse didn't jump over the fence.

In Musolino and Lidz (2006), the horses all jump over a log, but only two of them subsequently jump over a fence. Children participating in their experiment were willing to agree that (271) was a true description of this, even though this requires a non-isomorphic interpretation in the second clause.

(271)   Every horse jumped over the log but every horse didn't jump over the fence.

Apparently, the context for this utterance, even though it doesn't seem to be all that different from that in the Musolino et al. (2000) study, is sufficient to make the non-isomorphic interpretation available, even for young children.

Gualmini et al. (2008) aim to explain this contrast by appeal to the idea of QUD. Specifically, they argue that isomorphic interpretations are preferred only when these provide a better answer to the current QUD, which they argue is the case for the materials used by Musolino et al. (2000). By contrast, in Musolino and Lidz (2006), the answer (271) suggests that the QUD is something like (272).

(272)   What did every horse jump over?

If this is the question, we can understand (271) as saying that *the log* is part of the answer, and *the fence* is not part of the answer. But we can understand that without having to interpret the second clause of (271) in the informationally stronger isomorphic way: the non-isomorphic interpretation will already give us the relevant information.

If this is along the right lines, the same argument applies to the cases discussed at the beginning of this subsection. Consider (267), repeated below.

(267)   All of the toys are not in the boxes.

This could stand as an answer (or partial answer) to either (273) or (274).

(273)   Where are the toys?
(274)   Are all of the toys in the boxes?

If the QUD is something like (273), then interpreting (267) isomorphically will make it a better answer, because it commits the speaker to a claim about the location of every one of the toys (for each one, that it is not in the boxes). By contrast, the non-isomorphic interpretation merely asserts that at least one of the toys is not in the boxes (because it denies that all of them are in the boxes). On the other hand, if the QUD is something like (274), either the isomorphic or the non-isomorphic interpretation of (267) is good enough: both would entail that the answer to (274) is 'no'.

This kind of explanation is potentially quite appealing, intuitively, in that – as adults – we probably think that the non-isomorphic reading of a sentence like (267) is much more readily available if the current question (whether explicit or implied) is a yes/no question like (274) than if it is a general information-seeking question like (273). Indeed, if we were told that the intended meaning of (267) was 'it is not the case that all of the toys are in the boxes', we might infer that the QUD was something like (274), presumably because we think that the speaker's choice of utterance makes more sense in this scenario.

Nevertheless, it's not entirely obvious why the non-isomorphic reading is better in such a case: as noted above, either reading would still answer this question successfully, so we still seem to lack a pragmatic explanation as to why the straightforward isomorphic interpretation is suddenly less favourable. Cummins and Katsos (2013) discuss one possible explanation for this – namely that the choice of reading is, in effect, structurally primed by the QUD – but the issue remains open.

7.2 Discourse relations

In the previous section, we looked at some of the factors that bear upon how a cooperative speaker should structure information within an utterance. As mentioned at the beginning of the chapter, this is not the only constraint that bears upon a speaker's communicative choices: it is also important to consider how a speaker's utterances relate to what else is going on in the discourse. Chapter 8 will discuss one major aspect of this, namely the question of what kind of discourse move a cooperative speaker should make when they take their turn, given the immediate needs of the situation.

Before turning to that question, let's look at the situation in which a speaker is continuing their own conversational turn: that is, when they are producing several distinct utterances in sequence. We still expect a cooperative speaker to abide by certain obligations when they are doing this, for instance with respect to relevance, but it is not always easy to identify precisely what these obligations are. Nevertheless, we can recognise when a speaker is producing cooperative, coherent utterances in a prolonged conversational turn, and when they are not (as in the example at the beginning of this chapter).

As argued particularly by Relevance Theorists, hearers appear to be geared up to attempt to find relevance in what speakers say. However, as applied to continuing discourse, this can occasionally lead to odd interpretations, as in the following much-quoted examples, allegedly from parish newsletters.

(275) Don't let worry kill you – let the church help.

(276) At the evening service tonight, the sermon topic will be 'What is Hell?' Come early and listen to our choir practice.

(276) The sermon this morning: 'Jesus Walks on the Water'. The sermon tonight: 'Searching for Jesus'.

In these examples, the hearer infers a relation between two parts of the discourse – let's call them **discourse units** – which is (presumably) not the relation that the speaker intended to convey. And this calls our attention to two questions of general pragmatic interest: what kinds of relations can exist between discourse units? And how do hearers infer which relation is intended in a particular case?

7.2.1 Possible discourse relations

In some cases, describing the relation between two units of text as a 'discourse relation' can seem a little grandiose. Consider a simple narrative, or a set of directions, or a recipe. What we mean by a text like this being coherent may simply be that all the relevant events or necessary steps are listed, and that they are listed in the order in which they take place, or are supposed to take place. If we had to describe that kind of coherence in terms of discourse relations, the best we could do might be to say that the consecutive units of text are related in that each one continues the narrative which was taking place in the previous unit.

However, chronologically ordered narrative is not the only kind of coherent discourse. Narratives don't have to take place in strict chronological order to be coherent, so there is more to narration than just continuing the story from the previous unit of text. But, more importantly, there are many other relations that can hold between units of discourse, which aren't analysable as narrative continuations: and these relations can be more complex, and can apply more broadly, not just to consecutive discourse units.

There are many different approaches to describing the ways in which discourse units can be related to one another. These approaches tend to share the overarching assumption that it is useful to think of discourse as having some form of complex structure. However, the precise way in which theories try to capture that structure varies considerably, as we shall see. This reflects not only differences of opinion as to how specific relationships should be described, but also differences in theoretical focus and practical aims, and differences in the kinds of materials that are used to inform the theories.

Given that, in practice, there is no definitively correct answer to the question of how to describe discourse relations, why should we care about the work done so far? There are a couple of good reasons to be interested in the progress made on the topic. One reason, initially advanced by Hobbs (1985) and developed by Kehler (2002), is that discourse relations are a reflection of the cognitive principles that we apply when we try to make sense of the world. On this view, understanding what discourse relations are possible tells us something about the organisation of the human cognitive system. A more immediately practical consideration is that discourse relations are also of considerable importance for computational approaches to the processing of natural language, where it is important to be able to describe precisely how units of discourse fit together in terms of their meaning, as this is crucial to understanding the speaker's broader communicative intention.

Just to illustrate these ideas, consider what we can learn from a straightforward (and theoretically fairly uncontroversial) example like (278).

   (278) John can unlock the safe. He knows the combination.

It seems intuitive to interpret the second sentence of (278) as an explanation of the first sentence. The fact that we can do this underscores the (admittedly rather obvious) point that humans are capable of representing the relationship between facts and their explanations. However, the readiness with which we draw the conclusion that this is an explanation suggests something rather stronger about our cognition, namely that we're fairly proactively engaged in the search for possible explanations – they are something that we expect to encounter. Also, in order to interpret the second sentence of (278) as an explanation, we need to infer (or perhaps accommodate) something else based upon the utterance of (278), namely that the safe has a combination lock. This is something that a computational system might also be able to infer based upon the utterance of (278), but only under the assumption that the relationship between the sentences of (278) was one involving explanation. Thus, being able to identify the discourse relation that is in effect opens up an additional source of information about things in the world based on utterances about them.

To illustrate the variety of approaches taken to the classification of discourse relations, let's briefly consider some examples of the systems that have been proposed.

Rhetorical Structure Theory

Mann and Thompson's (1988) Rhetorical Structure Theory (RST) posits a set of relations that can hold between the **nucleus** and the **satellite**, these being two non-overlapping spans of text.

Note on terminology

In describing these relations, RST makes a choice about which of the two spans of text is to be called the nucleus and which is to be called the satellite. There are guiding principles to which way round this labelling should apply. Mann and Thompson (1988: 266) argue that the label 'nucleus' is applied to the member of the pair that tends to be independent of the other, more essential to the writer's purpose, and less available for substitution. For instance, one link between portions of text is between a claim and the evidence for it: Mann and Thompson argue that the claim is more central to the writer's purpose, that the provision of evidence is likely to be a non sequitur unless there is a claim being supported by it, and that one piece of evidence could be substituted by another without changing the discourse effects much, whereas changing the claim would be a more fundamental alteration. Thus, in describing the relation between claim and evidence, they would take the claim to be the nucleus and the evidence to be the satellite.

Mann and Thompson's (1988) paper sets out twenty-three such relations, under twelve broader headings. They select the relations that 'have proven most useful for the analysis of the data . . . examined' (ibid.: 249), focusing on written monologue. Each relation definition consists of four particulars (ibid.: 245): constraints on the nucleus, constraints on the satellite, constraints on the combination of nucleus and satellite, and the effect that the relation has.

As an illustration, we can think of (278) as an example of Mann and Thompson's Condition relation, in which 'realization of the situation presented in [the nucleus] depends on realization of that presented in [the satellite]' (ibid.: 276). Here the first sentence is the nucleus and the second the satellite. The intended effect, according to their analysis, is to cause the reader to recognise the dependency between the two sentences.

To take a more complex example, another of the headings in the RST scheme is 'Antithesis/Concession', which comprises just those two rhetorical relations. They share the property that both intend to cause the hearer (reader) to have positive regard for the nucleus, but they are distinguished by how they achieve that. In Antithesis, the material in the nucleus and satellite is presented as the same in many respects but differing in some, and the effect is to draw the hearer's attention to the impossibility of having positive regard for both the nucleus and satellite, thereby increasing their positive regard for the nucleus. In Concession, the speaker (writer) is claiming that the material in the satellite is in fact compatible with the material in the nucleus, despite first appearances, and aims to increase the hearer's (reader's) positive regard for the nucleus by pointing out this lack of incompatibility.

To unpack this a little further, let's look at a couple of specific examples. Mann and Thompson cite (279), from a discussion of the chemical dioxin in *Scientific American*, as an example of a Concession relation, noting that the word *although* frequently (but not obligatorily) signals this relation.

(279)   Although it is toxic to certain animals, evidence is lacking that it has any serious long-term effect on human beings.

Here, the first clause is the satellite, and the second clause the nucleus. The speaker aims to encourage the hearer to believe the claim in the nucleus, by conceding that another piece of evidence might seem to militate against that claim, but affirming that there is in fact no contradiction in holding both things true at once.

Mann and Thompson's first example of Antithesis can be paraphrased slightly as (280).

> (280)   The sight of hundreds of people queueing for a job indicates that unemployment is caused by lack of opportunity, not laziness.

Here, the first clause is the nucleus and the satellite consists of the word *laziness* (which is presumably elliptical for *the sight . . . indicates that unemployment is caused by laziness*). By contrasting that with an alternative explanation, and emphasising their incompatibility, the speaker intends to influence the hearer towards believing the claim in the nucleus.

The notion of antithesis is not a new one: it's a familiar idea from classical rhetoric, dating back to Aristotle. However, the use to which the term is being put here is slightly different from and more specific than that used in the rhetorical tradition. In that tradition, antithesis involves the presentation of contrasting ideas, but doesn't necessarily involve one being presented merely to increase the hearer's belief in the other. Dickens's famous line (281) would count as a use of antithesis in this sense, but doesn't fit Mann and Thompson's criteria.

> (281)   It was the best of times, it was the worst of times.

As noted above, Mann and Thompson (1988) don't claim that the list of discourse relations that they propose is definitive. However, the chief point in its favour is that it offers excellent coverage, despite all the relations being narrowly and positively defined. That is to say, there is no guarantee that any of these relations will hold between two meaningful units of a text: it would be quite possible for none of them to be applicable, in a given instance. Nevertheless, virtually every text analysed by Mann and Thompson prior to the publication of their article turned out to have a thorough and plausible RST analysis – and those that did not were precisely the kinds of texts that we wouldn't expect to exhibit rich internal structure of this kind (such as statements of law, contracts, and some forms of poetry). In that sense, the presence of RST relations does seem to reflect the presence of textual coherence in some intuitive sense.

Reese et al.'s (2007) elementary discourse units in SDRT

A different approach to the classification of discourse relations is proposed by Reese et al. (2007), working within a different framework, the Segmented Discourse Representation Theory (SDRT) of Asher and

Lascarides (2003). Reese et al.'s work was conducted within a project that aimed to explore the interaction between discourse structure and the interpretation of anaphora, a point we'll discuss in more detail in section 7.2.3.

Terminologically, there are dissimilarities between Reese et al.'s account and that of Mann and Thompson (1988): Reese et al. call the basic units of meaning that are being connected **elementary discourse units** (EDUs). But there are also more substantial architectural differences. An important point is that the set of relations is structured differently: they distinguish coordinating and subordinating relations (which we'll come back to in section 7.2.2), and orthogonally to this they distinguish **veridical** from **nonveridical** relations. Veridical relations are those which entail the content of both their EDU arguments, whereas for nonveridical relations at least one of the EDUs is not entailed.

To illustrate what they mean by this, compare (282), which is one of Reese et al.'s examples of the (veridical) Background relation, and (283), which is one of their examples of the (nonveridical) Attribution relation.

(282)   Also, about 585 workers were laid off at a stamping plant near Detroit. That plant normally employs 2,800 hourly workers.
(283)   The union said the size of the adjustments was inadequate.

In (282), the second EDU (the second sentence) provides background information to the first. This relation is veridical because the speaker is committed to both sentences being true. By contrast, in (283), the second EDU comprises the words *the size of the adjustments was inadequate*, and this material is related to the content of the first EDU *The union said* in the respect that that sentiment is attributed to the union. However, the speaker of (283) isn't committed to the factuality of the second EDU in itself – they're merely committed to the fact that the union said this – which implies that the relation present in (283) is a nonveridical one. This makes intuitive sense, because when we attribute a claim to someone else, we are naturally disclaiming the responsibility of committing to it ourselves.

The Penn Discourse TreeBank (PDTB)

Still another distinct kind of approach to discourse relations is exemplified by the annotation of the Penn Discourse TreeBank (PDTB). This focuses on discourse connectives, such as *so, therefore, because, then*, and many others besides, which take units of discourse as their arguments and encode relations between them. The project involved annotating a large corpus, the WSJ corpus in the Penn TreeBank, with these discourse connectives and their arguments.

To take one of the examples from Webber et al. (2006), (284) contains two discourse connectives in the same sentence, *but* and *instead*, but these two connectives select different pairs of arguments.

(284)   Buyers can look forward to double-digit annual returns if they are right. But they will have disappointing returns or even losses if interest rates rise instead.

Specifically, on Webber et al.'s analysis, the *but*-relation holds between the content of the first sentence and the (rest of the) content of the second sentence. We can think of it as expressing a contrast of sorts between the two possible scenarios that are described by these sentences. At the same time, the *instead*-relation holds between *they are right* and *interest rates rise*: it expresses an incompatibility between these two possibilities.

Challenges in achieving consensus

Given the variety of systems for classifying discourse relations – the three systems described above, and many others besides – how can we tell which is the most appropriate to use? For practical purposes, such as automatic annotation of text, it seems that there is no general answer to that question: the appropriate system to choose depends upon the aims of the researcher. For instance, the PDTB focuses upon explicit discourse connectives: this is because the original aim of the enterprise was precisely to shed light on the relation between those connectives and their arguments – that is, to establish how we can tell which portions of the text are actually related by those connectives, which (as the example above suggests) turns out to be surprisingly complex. On the other hand, if we're interested in the understanding of discourse more generally, we wouldn't want to restrict our attention to cases involving explicit connectives (although of course we would want our system to be able to deal with them appropriately) – we would need to consider how to treat discourse relations that are only implicitly signalled.

However, our interest in choosing an appropriate system for classifying discourse relations is not merely informed by a wish to develop better systems for text annotation or understanding. As noted at the beginning of this subsection, we're also interested in the question of what kinds of discourse relations are mentally represented by human language users, as part of our linguistic competence. In fact, as far as this book is concerned, that is our higher priority. Of course, given that humans are extremely adept at understanding connected discourse, we would expect that a suitably human-like system would do an excellent job of understanding texts. Optimistically, we might hope that classification schemes will therefore tend to converge upon the same systems that humans are actually using, and hence that a 'meta-analysis' of the research in this area might give us some insight into human capabilities in this domain.

As a recent example of this approach, Jasinskaja and Karagjosova (2015) attempt to build a 'consensus list' of discourse relations, synthesising ideas from various different research programmes. Their list ultimately comprises the following categories: Elaboration, Explanation, Parallel, Contrast, Narration and Result. In certain respects, this looks quite promising: for instance, as they note, the first two of these categories are usually subordinating and the latter four coordinating, respecting a fundamental distinction posited by Asher and Lascarides (2003), which we will discuss in more detail in the following subsection. However, in other respects, there are potential problems. For instance, Kehler (2002) argues that there are fundamentally three kinds of ways in which things can be related (drawing on ideas originally due to David Hume): resemblance, cause–effect and contiguity (this last category corresponding to Narration relations). But Jasinskaja and Karagjosova's (2015) categories can't be nested within Kehler's system, because Contrast relations are sometimes resemblance and sometimes cause–effect, in Kehler's terms. So the patterns emerging in the literature conflict, at least to some extent, with well-established philosophical views on how discourse relations should be itemised.

Should we, then, be led by the data-driven models, and ignore a priori views about how human cognition is likely to represent discourse relations? We could take this view, but it would be risky, for instance because the nature of the 'discovery procedure' for discourse relations is potentially controversial. As noted earlier, Mann and Thompson (1988) select their set of discourse relations on the basis of having annotated a lot of data and thereby formed an opinion about the kinds of relations that emerge within that data. But, as Knott and Dale (1994) observe, in order to claim at the same time that these discourse relations have anything to do with textual coherence, we actually need to impose additional constraints on the system, limiting the kinds of discourse relations that we can posit. They illustrate this with (285).

(285)   John broke his leg. I like plums.

Our intuition is that (285) is incoherent, and we would like our system to reflect that incoherence by not identifying the two sentences as being linked by any sort of discourse relation. However, following Mann and Thompson's (1988) principles, there's nothing to stop us positing a new discourse relation, such as *inform-accident-and-mention-fruit*, that would hold between the two sentences. Indeed, there's nothing wrong with introducing that kind of discourse relation, if it would give us a system that was more useful for some practical purpose (if, for instance, there turns out to be an epidemic of accident-informing and fruit-mentioning in some corpus, and we want our system to be able to deal with that). But in this case it would be a mistake to think that the discourse relation had anything to do with human intuitions about textual coherence, or to imagine that it pointed the way towards a deeper understanding of human cognition.

7.2.2 Disambiguating the intended discourse relation

Whichever set of discourse relations we take to exist, the question arises of how we identify them in practice, when we interpret a speaker's utterances. Within an approach like that of Webber et al. (2006), this part is relatively straightforward – we understand that a *because*-relation is in effect whenever we hear the word *because*, and the challenge is to pick out the discourse units that are related by that relation. But in the case of other proposed sets of discourse relations, such as those laid out by Mann and Thompson (1988) and Reese et al. (2007), this is not straightforward at all, because the discourse relations are not typically signalled directly by the words that are used. Rather, they have to be inferred by the hearer.

In some of the proposed cases, this inference depends largely on real-world knowledge. To see this, let's look at another example drawn from Mann and Thompson (1988), which I'll abbreviate somewhat as (286). In their schema, this is categorised as an instance of the Evidence relation: the first sentence is the nucleus, the second sentence is the satellite, and the relation is that the satellite induces the hearer to believe in the material in the nucleus by providing evidence for it.

(286)   The program really works. It gave me the right result in minutes.

Importantly, this classification relies on the assumption that we can recognise that the second sentence constitutes evidence for the first. This draws upon real-world knowledge about what it would mean, in practice, for a program to work. We can compare this with (287), which follows a similar pattern, both in form and content.

(287)   The program opened with a single click. It gave me the right result in minutes.

Here, we can't infer any causal connection between the meanings of these two sentences, because the speaker is recounting two independent experiences that they had with the program. That doesn't mean that (287) is incoherent – it just seems to exhibit a simpler discourse relation, perhaps Narration, in which the second sentence continues the story being told in the first sentence about how good the program is. Much like in the case of the Winograd schemas, discussed back in section 5.1, we are making use of rich non-linguistic knowledge in order to understand the discourse relations that the speaker is trying to convey here.

At the same time, there are also purely linguistic features that are relevant to helping us understand what relation is being conveyed. Even if we aren't adopting a coding scheme in which each explicit discourse connective encodes a different relation, the presence of these connectives is obviously relevant to our interpretation. For instance, (288) appears to convey a relation involving contrast, which in this case is presumably strongly cued by the presence of the word *but*. In this context, other options such as *yet, however, on the other hand, still, nevertheless* would probably have brought about much the same effect.

> (288)   The program is relatively inexpensive. But it gave me the right result in minutes.

Intonation is another potentially relevant feature, although it's hard to do justice to the full range of effects that can be achieved. To take a very simple example, Weber et al. (2006) studied the effect of intonation in an eye-tracking study, using spoken stimuli like (289). (Their study was conducted in German, but the same effects are presumed to hold in other languages.)

> (289)   Click on the purple scissors. Now click on the red scissors.

Weber et al. (2006) manipulated the intonation pattern in the second sentence of these stimuli, sometimes placing a high (L+H*) pitch accent on the adjective, in this case *red*. In the first sentence, there was always a high (H*) pitch accent on the noun, here *scissors*. When the adjective received a pitch accent, participants were more likely to look at the red scissors in the display even before the noun was uttered: when it did not, they were more likely to look at another red object. Weber et al. (2006) argue that this shows an early effect of contrast – the presence of the high pitch accent cues the hearer to think that the object about to be referred to stands in a colour-contrasting relation to the object that has already been mentioned.

Although this is not really the point of Weber et al.'s demonstration, we could at a pinch argue that the use of intonation in this case introduces a new discourse relation into something that was otherwise purely narrative (requesting two distinct and unrelated objects in sequence). In

SDRT terms, this would stand in parallel to the Narration relation. A similar pattern seems to emerge in more intentionally contrastive discourse: for instance, the proverb (290) is usually produced with (sometimes quite exaggerated) pitch accents on *morning* and *warning*.

(290)   Red sky at night, shepherd's delight; red sky in the morning, shepherd's warning.

Another potential signal that a discourse relation should be inferred is clausal adjacency. The quote at the beginning of this chapter especially strikingly violates this expectation: although the speaker places disparate ideas in the same sentence, they defy any kind of unification by the hearer. (291), frequently misattributed to Groucho Marx, relies on a similar effect – the hearer is invited to infer some relation between the two statements, due to their proximity and the repetition of the word *flies*, and is consequently misled into thinking that they are parallel or contrastive.

(291)   Time flies like an arrow. Fruit flies like a banana.

Similarly, the *Two Ronnies* sketch 'Crossed Lines', written by David Renwick, works on the basis that the audience – overhearing two people talking, but not to each other, on the phone – will spontaneously infer discourse relations between the adjacent turns, even though they are not actually part of the same conversation. In the following excerpt, during which RC is talking about his supermarket shopping and RB about a friend's recent liaison, RC's turns are interpretable as Elaboration, Explanation and two Narration continuations of RB's contribution.

(292)   RB: Did you say her parents were in oil?
        RC: Yes, they're pilchards.
        RB: She sounds a right little raver. I don't know how she had the energy.
        RC: She said the milkman hadn't been round yet.
        RB: Ah, well, that would explain it, of course, yes. What did you do?
        RC: I had to get sterilised.
        RB: Good God.
        RC: To be on the safe side, I'll put them in the fridge when I get back.

Although adjacency is highly relevant to establishing which discourse relations are intended, other higher-level structural factors are also relevant. As mentioned in section 7.2.1, Reese et al.'s (2007) taxonomy distinguishes between subordinating and coordinating discourse relations, a distinction inherited from Asher's (1993) work introducing

Segmented Discourse Representation Theory. This is one way of getting at the idea that discourse segments, of the kind that can enter into discourse relations, also have a hierarchical structure, much like syntax (although not necessarily corresponding with the syntactic structure of a given sentence). As discussed by Asher and Vieu (2005), there are good reasons to suppose that some discourse relations (such as Elaboration) are **subordinating**, in the sense that they place one discourse unit below the other in a tree structure, while other discourse relations (such as Narration) are **coordinating**, in the sense that they place one discourse unit beside the other in the tree.

Part of the motivation for this distinction is a proposal due to Polanyi (1988) called the **Right Frontier Constraint** – the idea that certain kinds of information can only 'attach' to the rightmost edge of the discourse tree. As applied to discourse relations, this theory predicts that new material can only enter into relations with discourse units that are on the right edge of the tree. Taken in conjunction with the idea that some discourse relations are coordinating and others subordinating, this seems to offer an attractive account of many patterns in discourse. Asher and Vieu (2005) show this with respect to the following materials.

(293)   (a) John had a great evening last night.
        (b) He had a great meal.
        (c) He ate salmon.
        (d) He devoured lots of cheese.
        (e) He then won a dancing competition.
        (f) ? Then he had a great dessert.
        (f_0) # It was a beautiful pink.
        (f_{00}) John had lots of fun.

(293a–e) represents a coherent discourse. However, it doesn't seem to be possible to continue this discourse coherently with (f) or (f_0), while it is possible to continue it with (f_{00}). For Asher and Vieu (2005), this is because of the discourse relations that (f), (f_0) and (f_{00}) could enter into with the previous discourse segments. Specifically, (f) appears to continue the narration from (d), while (f_0) represents an elaboration of (c), and neither of these options is apparently allowed; (f_{00}), however, which is presumably a continuation of (a) or (e), is fine. In summary, it appears that the next discourse element introduced after (e) is allowed to enter into a discourse relation with (a) or (e), but not with (c) or (d). Also, the fact that (e) was acceptable in the first place – and assuming that this is a narrative continuation of (b), because it's presumably something that happened after the meal rather than as part of it – suggests that, after (d) is uttered, the next discourse element is allowed to attach to (b).

If we assume that Elaboration is subordinating and Narration is coordinating, these observations fit nicely with the Right Frontier Constraint. (b) is an Elaboration of (a); (c) is an Elaboration of (b). After (a), (b) and (c) have been uttered, the discourse tree has no branches, and everything is on the right edge: the next discourse unit could legitimately enter into relations with (a), (b) or (c). In fact, (d) is a Narration continuation of (c), so it enters into a coordination relation with (c) – making it also subordinate to (b) – at which point the tree is as shown in Figure 7.1.

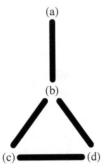

Figure 7.1 Discourse structure for (293a–d).

After (d) attaches in this way, (c) is no longer on the right edge of the tree, so nothing further can readily attach to it – hence, by this stage, it's too late to produce something that is an Elaboration upon (c), such as (f_0). (e) is still fine, because it is going to stand in a Narration relation to (b), which is on the right edge. The Narration relation is coordinating, and places (e) alongside (b) in a subordinate relation to (a). After (e) is added to the discourse model, it will be as shown in Figure 7.2.

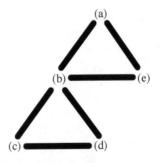

Figure 7.2 Discourse structure for (293a–e).

At this stage, the right frontier consists only of (a) and (e). Although (d) appears to be on the right edge of the graph, it is subordinate to a node (b) which is not. According to the Right Frontier Constraint, then, it shouldn't be possible to continue this discourse by adding something that is supposed to stand in a discourse relation to (d) – which offers a possible account of why (f) is problematic. But it is fine to attach something which will stand in a discourse relation either to (a) or to (e), which is why (f_{00}) is OK.

If we are implicitly aware of these kinds of mechanisms and rules for building discourse structure, we are correspondingly constrained in the way that we interpret a new unit of discourse when we first encounter it. Assuming, in the spirit of Grice's Cooperative Principle, that it is a coherent contribution towards achieving the current discourse purpose, there are likely to be only a few ways in which we can connect it to the preceding discourse, while drawing upon a finite set of possible discourse relations and obeying the Right Frontier Constraint. We do not have to consider how the new material could relate to just any of the units of discourse that have gone before, but only how it could relate to the handful that remain open for attachment. Taken in conjunction with all the other possible cues to the type of discourse relation that is indicated – the lexical and prosodic considerations, as well as our real-world knowledge – structural factors of this kind could be something that makes the task of understanding coherent discourse somewhat easier for the hearer than it initially appears to be.

7.2.3 Discourse relations and other ambiguities: the case of pronouns

In the examples discussed in this chapter, the hearer has to understand what discourse relation is in effect in order to understand precisely what the speaker means to convey. However, at the same time, the hearer has to disambiguate various other aspects of the speaker's utterance, as we have discussed elsewhere in this book.

Sometimes, understanding the discourse relation seems to interact with other disambiguation tasks. One striking example of this is the case of pronoun resolution, discussed back in Chapter 5. In some cases, such as (294), we can resolve the pronoun *she* just on semantic grounds (it presumably refers to Jane rather than Bill); but in other cases, such as (295) and (296), ambiguity arises, because multiple different potential referents satisfy the semantic requirements of the pronoun (either Mary or Jane could be referred to as *she*).

(294)   Bill invited Jane to the dinner because she was successful.
(295)   Mary invited Jane to the dinner because she was successful.
(296)   Mary invited Jane to the dinner because she wanted to look generous.

In practice, the ambiguity in (295) seems easy to resolve: drawing upon our real-world knowledge, we might assume that 'Jane being successful' is a better explanation for Mary inviting Jane to the dinner than 'Mary being successful' would have been. The preference is reversed in (296), and again we can explain this in terms of our real-world knowledge (specifically, that inviting someone, rather than being invited by someone, is something that makes a person look generous).

In both of these cases, our inference about what the pronoun means is underpinned by an assumption about the discourse relations: we are looking for an interpretation of the pronoun that makes the *because*-clause an explanation of the initial clause. This is a perfectly reasonable assumption, as this is what *because* means – it signals to us that the clauses are connected by the kind of discourse relation (whatever we choose to call it) that makes the upcoming material an explanation of the preceding material.

However, discourse relations are not always explicitly signalled, and when they are not, we have to infer the intended discourse relation while also interpreting ambiguous units of language such as pronouns. Consider (297).

(297)   John fired Bill from the company. He swore at Mary.

There are several possible interpretations of this utterance. One is that John fired Bill from the company because Bill swore at Mary, in which case the second sentence serves as an explanation of the first. A second possibility is that John fired Bill from the company and as a consequence of this Bill swore at Mary, in which case the second sentence describes a result of the action of the first sentence. A third possibility is that John fired Bill from the company and then John swore at Mary, in which case the second sentence seems just to continue the chronological narrative of the first sentence.

A speaker could make (297) less ambiguous by explicitly conjoining the sentences, in which case they would choose an appropriate strategy for the interpretation that they intended to convey. If the speaker wanted to convey the first of those three interpretations, they might use *because*; for the second, they might use *so*; for the third, they might use *then*. But (297) is a perfectly legitimate sequence in its own right, and the speaker might simply assume that the hearer can apprehend their intended meaning without this additional help.

So what about the interpretation of the pronoun *he* in (297)? The subjecthood and parallelism preferences seem to suggest that it should refer to John; the recency preference suggests that it should refer to Bill. But if we take *he* to be John, then we're forced to adopt the third of those possible interpretations of the utterance, even if one of the other interpretations might seem more likely. The point is that, in cases like these, choosing an interpretation for the pronoun constrains the possible discourse relations that could be in effect – and, by the same token, making a decision about which discourse relation is in effect constrains our interpretation of the pronoun.

This complexity makes it even harder to tease apart the factors that might be influencing pronoun interpretation. Kehler (2002) argues that there is a systematic confound in the literature on pronominal bias (at least up to that point): the kinds of discourse that appear to show a subject bias are those which exhibit narrative continuation relations. If we were to study pronouns using materials like (297), where the description of the firing event may favour a causal interpretation and the resolution of *he* to Bill, we'd probably find very little evidence for a subject bias (or indeed for parallelism); whereas if we were to use materials like (298), we'd find a lot of evidence. But this might have more to do with the relation between the two sentences – event and explanation in (297), consecutive events in (298) – than any general preference about how hearers interpret pronouns.

(298)   John fired Bill from the company. He hired a new employee from the agency.

In short, when we're studying pronouns, we might still want to bear in mind the complexity of discourse relations. And even compared with the resolution of pronouns, the identification of discourse relations is a challenging task: we are not merely choosing between a couple of possible referents that a pronoun might denote, but potentially between a large set of possible discourse relations that a speaker means to convey. Indeed, as discussed earlier, we don't even know how many possible discourse relations there are. Nevertheless, some progress has been made on this task: researchers have convincingly argued for the relevance of various factors that guide the hearer towards the appropriate interpretation. The successful recognition of discourse relations is yet another facet of the incredibly complex challenge of language understanding that hearers nevertheless manage to meet so effortlessly in everyday communication.

7.3 Summary

Speakers convey and hearers recover additional information in discourse as a result of the shared expectation that speakers will be coherent. Within a clause, speakers can arrange information in various different ways, thus enabling the hearer to understand what the speaker takes to be their new contribution to the discourse – the (perhaps implicit) question that they are answering, or the information they are treating as new rather than given. This has rich pragmatic effects, for instance in the way it allows the hearer to derive specific exhaustivity inferences. Between discourse units, there are many potential relations that can hold, and the speaker has a great deal of freedom in how they continue their own discourse turn: but their choice isn't entirely free, in that there are constraints on how they can add information to the existing discourse while still maintaining coherence. Knowledge of these constraints helps a hearer to understand the nature of a speaker's intended contribution, and a general appreciation of which discourse relations are likely to be involved may also help the hearer disambiguate other aspects of the speaker's meaning, such as the interpretation of pronouns.

Exercises

Answers to the following are available at <edinburghuniversitypress. com/pragmatics>.

1. Assuming that the following utterances occur at the beginning of a discourse, which referents are discourse-new, discourse-old, hearer-old and inferable?
    a. The tallest man in the world saved the lives of two dolphins by extracting shards of plastic from their stomachs.
    b. The annual ceremony in which all the swans on the River Thames are counted is called 'swan-upping'.
    c. The first rule of Fight Club is: you do not talk about Fight Club.
2. Which explicit connectives could be added to link the following pairs of sentences? What interpretations would they give rise to?
    a. I arrived at the party late. She didn't want to talk to me.
    b. It's brilliant. It's very expensive.
    c. You've convinced me. I'll buy it.
3. What discourse relations would arise for each of the possible interpretations of the pronouns in the following utterances?
    a. Artists dislike critics. They're motivated by envy.
    b. Bob encouraged Mike. He was a good manager.

c. Rebecca hadn't dared say anything to Monica. She was a bag of nerves.

Discussion questions

1. Taking an example like *Donald continually interrupted Hillary*, how many different stress patterns are there for this utterance that would lead to different pragmatic interpretations? Are these clearly distinguished from one another? Is there any limit to how many different interpretations we can convey, as speakers?
2. How should speakers decide whether or not to use an explicit connective in order to indicate their intended discourse relation? What are the implications of this, as far as the Gricean maxim of Quantity is concerned?

8 Speech acts

> Wouldn't it be pleasant if we tried a little courtesy, instead of shooting each other over trivial provocations? Wouldn't it be wonderful if, when we irritated each other, we said 'Sorry!' and then shot each other? At least it would be a start.
>
> (Dave Barry, *Kill 'em with Kindness*)

Most of the book so far has focused on how we tell other people things – or, to dress that up in slightly more technical language, how speakers convey and hearers recover propositional meanings, particularly when these involve appreciable pragmatic enrichment. In the case of implicature, this involves propositional meaning that is additional to that which is semantically encoded. For presupposition, it involves meaning (often propositional, although it may also be about the existence of certain entities) that is logically necessary to the meaning that is semantically encoded. In the case of reference, we discussed how hearers understand which entities populate the propositions that the speaker conveys. In the case of non-literal language, we were examining how hearers reinterpret the (typically propositional) meaning-bearing utterances that the speaker produces, in order to draw from them the completely different propositions that are what the speaker actually intends to convey. And in the case of coherence, we were predominantly exploring how items of propositional content are themselves related to one another.

However, in practice, we can do many more things with language than merely communicating propositional content. We can use language to perform a remarkable array of social actions – to ask questions, issue commands, greet people, thank them, apologise, and so on – including many actions that rely on enormously elaborate shared social institutions (e.g. declaring two people to be married, sentencing someone for a crime, naming a ship, and so on). The term **speech act** is often used when we are discussing an utterance in terms of the social action that it is used to perform.

In one construal of pragmatics, speech acts are the epitome of the discipline: they represent the very essence of language in use. However, as noted way back in Chapter 1, the focus in this book is on the processes by which we understand meaning that goes beyond what is literally said. From this point of view, it would appear that there's a limited amount that we can say about an example like (299): we can point out that the hearer needs to appeal to the context of utterance in order to resolve the pronoun *you*, but apart from that, what is going on in this utterance is fairly easy to determine.

(299)   I now pronounce you husband and wife.

Nevertheless, examples like (299) are interesting in one particular respect, namely their status as **performative** utterances – those which appear to bring about the action that they describe – and as these are highly relevant to the historical development of approaches to speech acts, I'll discuss them further in section 8.1.

A more general issue of pragmatic interest, in the sense meant here, is that it is very frequently not obvious (on first inspection) what kind of speech act is being performed. Consider (300)–(302).

(300)   Pass the salt.
(301)   Could you pass the salt?
(302)   I'd be grateful if you would pass the salt.

These examples appear to perform similar social actions, aiming to bring about the same outcome, but they use quite different linguistic means to do that. In fact, they involve different **sentence types**: (300) is **imperative**, (301) **interrogative** and (302) **declarative**.

Note on terminology

I'll use **sentence type** in this chapter to refer to the syntactic form of the sentence being uttered, and specifically its status as imperative, interrogative or declarative. We could think of these as the sentence types that traditionally correspond to orders, questions and statements respectively – however, orders, questions and statements are not sentence types, they are speech acts. The whole point of the discussion here will be to emphasise that there is not a straightforward correspondence between sentence type and speech act.

By contrast, (303)–(305) involve the same sentence type (interrogative), yet appear to be performing very different kinds of social actions.

(303)   Would you tell me the time?
(304)   Would the receptionist not tell you the time?
(305)   Would you look at the time?

The question of how we figure out the intended speech act from the available information is a classically pragmatic one. As the above examples suggest, it is another issue that is difficult to explain straightforwardly, even though hearers can seemingly do this without difficulty in practice. And as the above examples also indicate, the most obvious explanation – that the speech act is syntactically specified by the speaker, through their use of an appropriate sentence type – isn't going to suffice. We'll consider this problem in more detail in section 8.2.

A question that naturally follows from that is: what kinds of speech acts are there? Much as in the case of discourse relations, as discussed in section 7.2.1, the kind of analysis that we might wish to pursue depends on our theoretical aims. Nevertheless, it's potentially instructive to look at some of the taxonomies that have been pursued, and how they can be used and (to some extent) validated. We'll consider this in section 8.3.

It's also worth remarking at this stage that, although most of the earlier chapters in this book have dealt with statements (that is, utterances that convey information), much of what has been said applies to various other categories of speech act as well. For instance, we've already seen that questions can have presuppositions, as in (306).

(306)   When did you start contradicting people?

Similarly, we can construe (307) as an offer, but it still conveys an implicature, in that *some* is naturally interpreted as *not all*, and this bears upon what the speaker is understood to be offering.

(307)   You can have some of the ice cream.

And we can use metaphors and metonymies in all sorts of speech acts. Irony can also feature – (308) might be heard from someone who has performed a service for another person and conspicuously not been thanked for it.

(308)   Don't mention it.

In practice, implicature, presupposition and non-literal language are always with us, whatever kind of speech act we are performing. So rather than trying to extend the earlier discussions of those topics to the case of speech acts in general, this chapter takes a more general approach, and discusses the points of pragmatic interest specifically connected with how utterances are used to perform speech acts and how we understand those speech acts.

8.1 Performatives and illocutionary force

Austin identifies a class of ordinary and uncontroversial utterances that share three properties: 'they fall into no hitherto recognized *grammatical* category save that of "statement"', 'they do not "describe" or "report" or constate anything at all, are not "true or false"', and 'the uttering of the sentence is, or is a part of, the doing of an action' (1962: 4–5; emphasis in original). The examples that he gives include (309)–(311).

(309) I name this ship the *Queen Elizabeth*.
(310) I give and bequeath my watch to my brother.
(311) I bet you sixpence it will rain tomorrow.

Austin drew attention to these examples initially as a rebuttal to the then-prevalent philosophical viewpoint that all statements must be verifiable in order to be meaningful (a view associated with positivism). He asserts that utterances of this type – which he terms **performatives** – cannot properly be regarded as true or false, because they do not serve merely to state a fact, but to perform a social action. That is, on Austin's view, the speaker of (309) is not asserting that they are naming the ship, they are in fact naming the ship (or at least trying to), by uttering those words.

As Austin also notes, the utterance of a performative doesn't necessarily bring about the social action that is potentially associated with it. Other things may have to be done to achieve the effect, and importantly, various social conditions already have to be in place. In the case of (309), the speaker has to be duly appointed as the person who is to name the ship, and they have to utter these words in the context of a ship-naming ceremony for them to have any effect. (Even if you're the properly appointed person, practising saying these words in front of a mirror wouldn't have the effect of naming the ship.) In the case of (310), which would normally occur in the context of a will, the speaker (testator) must be of sound mind and not acting under coercion in order for their words to achieve a legally binding effect, and the fact of the speaker committing to these words must also be witnessed in the appropriate way. In the case of (311), there are no obvious conditions binding upon the speaker – other than, perhaps, the usual requirement that they should be sincere in their utterance – but the bet is not effective unless it is accepted by the hearer. The conditions that have to be satisfied in order for a performative utterance to be effective are customarily referred to as **felicity conditions**: we can describe a performative utterance as being made **felicitously**, in which case it will be effective, or **infelicitously**, in which case it will not be effective.

Typically, we can identify performatives by the verb that is used, which names the action that is being performed as a consequence of the utterance. *Promise, name, bet, declare, apologise* and *resign* are among a large number of potentially performative verbs in English. Performative verbs can, however, easily be used in utterances that are not performative. As a generalisation, performative utterances use the verb in the first person: thus, for instance, (312) reports on a promise being made but doesn't serve to make one.

(312)   John promises to be there early tomorrow.

They also have present time reference: (313) and (314) don't perform the action of naming, for instance. If the ship had not been named immediately prior to either of these utterances, it would remain unnamed immediately after them.

(313)   Yesterday I named this ship the *Queen Elizabeth*.
(314)   Tomorrow I will name this ship the *Queen Elizabeth*.

In the same spirit, it also doesn't seem to be possible to make a performative utterance conditional upon something else happening, in order for it to take effect. Should the speaker of (315) subsequently be found guilty, they will not be deemed to have resigned automatically as a consequence of having previously uttered these words.

(315)   If I am found guilty, I will resign.

A useful diagnostic for performativity is whether the utterance licenses the insertion of the word *hereby*. This word makes it explicit that the utterance is intended to be performative. According to this diagnostic, *welcome*, in (316), is performative, whereas *criticise* or *impress*, in (317) and (318), are not. We can certainly criticise or impress people with our words, but not just by affirming that that's what we're trying to do.

(316)   I hereby welcome our distinguished guests.
(317)   * I hereby criticise our distinguished guests.
(318)   * I hereby impress our distinguished guests.

Explicit performatives are essentially fairly easy to identify. However, it rapidly becomes clear (by about page 33 of Austin (1962), in fact) that much of what we say about performatives is true of a much broader class of utterances – and then the problem of identifying the speaker's intention becomes a lot more acute. For instance, (319) appears to perform a social action – greeting – by virtue of being uttered, and it has felicity conditions (for instance, it appears to require that this action of greeting hasn't already taken place in the interaction), but it doesn't satisfy the above criteria for being regarded as performative.

(319)   Hello.

Moreover, as shown by cases like (320) and (321), we often seem to be able to achieve the same effect either with an explicit performative or by some other means – (320) is performative, according to the above criteria, but (321) is not.

(320)   I order you to get out.
(321)   Get out!

Indeed, even when performative verbs are being used, whether or not the utterance is a true performative doesn't necessarily make a big difference to its interpretation. (322) is a non-performative version of (323) – *be delighted* is not a performative verb, and it doesn't seem to be very natural to insert *hereby* anywhere in (322) – yet the effect is much the same. Importantly, the felicity conditions for (322) appear to be the same as those for (323).

(322)   I am delighted to declare this supermarket open.
(323)   I declare this supermarket open.

It's therefore useful to introduce a more general way of describing the kinds of effects that utterances can bring about, that will encompass both performative and non-performative utterances. Austin (1962: 98) labelled this kind of social effect the **illocutionary** effect or force of the utterance. He introduced a three-way distinction, which has persisted in the literature: we can also describe utterances at a **locutionary** and at a **perlocutionary** level. The locutionary act of performing an utterance is simply the fact of these words having been said: for instance, (324) describes the locutionary effect of (323). The illocutionary act is the speech act performed: thus, (325) describes the illocutionary effect of (323).

(324)   Someone said 'I declare this supermarket open'.
(325)   Someone declared the supermarket open.

Perlocutionary effects are those which arise as a consequence of the corresponding locutionary or illocutionary act but which we can talk about without making reference to those other levels. For instance, the intended perlocutionary effect of (321) is to make the addressee leave, which is not something that can be achieved by any kind of purely illocutionary force. Indeed, compelling or persuading someone to adopt a course of action doesn't seem to be possible within the realms of illocutionary force – just by uttering words, a speaker can't make the hearer do things – and nor is convincing someone of a fact (* *I hereby force you to* . . ./ *convince you that* . . .). However, any or all of these might be effects that a speaker ultimately intends to bring about as a consequence of having uttered the words that they did, in which case they are perlocutionary effects.

The idea of distinguishing locution, illocution and perlocution has persisted in the literature since Austin's work. Much of the time, however, locution is uncontroversial and not especially interesting, and perlocution involves a lot of processes that are usually considered to fall outside the scope of linguistics. The principal focus of much of the linguistically oriented work on speech acts has therefore been the recognition, and classification, of illocutionary force. That's also going to be the main point of interest in this chapter.

One important idea initiated by Austin's work, then, is that we can study utterances in terms of the social actions that speakers perform by uttering them. In doing so, it makes much less sense to fixate upon the question of what it would mean for an utterance to be true or false, and more sense to enquire into the circumstances under which it can appropriately be used. From the hearer's point of view, focusing on speech acts moves us away from the issue of what the speaker means to convey, in terms of the information about the world that they transmit, and towards the issue of what the speaker means to do, in terms of the social actions that they are attempting to perform. However, some of the crucial issues that arise have parallels to issues we've already discussed when we were talking just about conveying information. Above all, there is a lack of a one-to-one mapping between utterance and action. The same utterance can be used, under different circumstances, to perform many different actions, and different utterances can be used to perform the same actions. The goal of a pragmatic analysis of speech acts is to understand how hearers manage to resolve this complexity and correctly understand the speaker's intention.

8.2 Direct and indirect speech acts

As discussed in the previous section, it is usually straightforward – at least in principle – to identify an utterance as performative, and in that case we can easily read off what kind of action the speaker is performing. If they say *I apologise*, they are apologising; if they say *I resign*, they are resigning. If they say *I promise*, things are a little less straightforward, because the utterance might have the character of what we would normally call a promise, as in (326), or it might be something more like a threat, as in (327). But in either case, the speaker appears to have done a rather similar thing, in terms of the commitment that they have undertaken to bring about a specific state of affairs.

(326) I promise that I will pay for this.

(327) I promise that you will pay for this.

For non-performatives, the most obvious indication of what kind of speech act is being performed might be the sentence type that is used. Several major sentence types are distinguished in many languages, including English, notably including the declarative, interrogative and imperative. Stereotypically, declaratives are used to make statements, interrogatives to ask questions, and imperatives to issue commands or requests, as illustrated by (328)–(330) respectively. They are syntactically distinct, with the interrogative having an auxiliary verb (or copula) first, and the imperative not having an overt subject.

(328) The window is open.

(329) Is the window open?

(330) Open the window.

However, as we've already seen, there are numerous exceptions to any rule that tries to associate sentence type directly with speech act. For instance, utterances beginning with the words *Could you* . . ., which have the syntactic form of questions, often seem to be most naturally understood as requests, as in (331).

(331) Could you tell me the time?

Similarly, utterances of the declarative sentence type which make certain kinds of statements about the speaker's wishes and preferences, such as (332), also tend to be interpreted as requests.

(332) I'd be grateful if you could tell me the time.

And, of course, there are more kinds of speech acts in play than just statements, questions and orders/requests. We've already discussed how performative utterances can be used to promise, apologise and bet, among much else. But we can do these actions with various different utterances, including utterances that make use of different sentence types. For instance, (333)–(335) are declaratives that achieve these three respective effects.

(333) If you take me back, I will never lie to you again.

(334) I'm sorry.

(335) Ten quid says she doesn't show up.

And (336) and (337) are formally imperatives, but seem to achieve almost identical illocutionary effects to (333) and (334) respectively.

(336)   Take me back and I'll never lie to you again.
(337)   Forgive me.

Consequently, in practice, we are faced with a significant challenge in trying to determine the speech act type based on the syntactic form of the utterance. The following subsections discuss a couple of the broad trends in thought about how we do this.

8.2.1 Literal Force

The overall picture sketched above is one in which sentence type may contribute to helping us identify the speaker's intended illocutionary act, but it nevertheless leaves a lot of different possibilities open. Opinion has varied as to how important sentence type really is to speech act recognition. On a traditional view, it's uniquely central to the process. One way of expressing that idea is through what Gazdar (1981) called the Literal Force Hypothesis (Levinson (1983) refers to it as the Literal Meaning Hypothesis), which suggests that every utterance has a literal illocutionary force which can be read off its surface form. We can then distinguish **direct speech acts**, which are those in which the actual illocutionary force matches this syntactically driven expectation, and **indirect speech acts**, which are those in which it does not.

If we assume the Literal Force Hypothesis, the challenge as far as pragmatics is concerned is how we go about recovering the meaning of indirect speech acts. Gordon and Lakoff (1971) and Searle (1975a) made good progress in establishing how this might happen. Let's consider (338), a classic example of an indirect speech act: a question, in terms of its literal force, that is naturally (and seemingly effortlessly) understood as a request, at least in its most common context of utterance.

(338)   Could you pass the salt?

The first observation we can make about (338), following Gordon and Lakoff (1971), is that it's obviously deficient as an information-seeking question, because – in its normal context of utterance – it's asking for information that is already evident to the speaker. The speaker of (338) can typically assume that the hearer is in fact able to pass the salt, and therefore they shouldn't need to ask whether this is possible. This is also obvious to the hearer. As a consequence, the hearer can immediately be aware that the literal interpretation is not the one that the speaker actually means to communicate. To borrow some terminology from much later work in Relevance Theory, we can see this as a case in which the utterance – on its literal interpretation – does not satisfy the hearer's expectations of relevance. The hearer therefore undertakes a pragmatic enrichment process in which they attempt to derive an interpretation of the utterance that would satisfy their thirst for relevance (and thereby explain why the speaker chose to say this thing in the first place). However, by itself, this doesn't quite explain why the enrichment that the hearer ends up with is the precise one in which (338) is actually a request.

Searle (1975a) goes into a little more detail about the way we might reason about (338). On his view, the speaker who asks (338) can initially be treated as though they are genuinely asking the question that they appear to be asking. However, the hearer is entitled to wonder why the piece of information that the speaker appears to be seeking should be relevant to the speaker's needs. As a consequence, the hearer starts to reason abductively about the best explanation for why a cooperative speaker should wish to establish, and draw the hearer's attention to, the fact that the hearer is able to pass the salt. Given that someone's capability to perform an action is a logical prerequisite for them doing it, one reason why we might be interested in someone's capability to pass the salt is that we want them to do it. Hence, a plausible explanation for why the speaker has uttered (338) is that they want the hearer to pass them the salt. Having established that, the hearer can respond *yes* and wait for the actual request, or – being more proactive in their cooperation – they can respond directly by performing the action that they infer the speaker wants them to. Our intuition is that this latter kind of response, which doesn't require the speaker of (338) to have to go on and produce a direct request, is the most cooperative behaviour that a hearer can perform in response to this utterance.

These accounts suggest a general kind of recipe for the interpretation of speech acts which involves the hearer reasoning in quite some detail about the speaker's motivations for uttering the words that they did. We can think of the speaker's utterance as constituting part of a plan that they have constructed in order to bring about some social result. Then, understanding precisely what the speaker wants to achieve by a particular utterance is a matter of understanding (to some extent) the broader social plan that the speaker is trying to execute.

The ideas of Searle and others about the interpretation of indirect speech acts have informed one of the major approaches to the topic in the subsequent literature, which Jurafsky (2004) calls the plan-inference model. This is situated within the broader tradition of artificial intelligence (AI) modelling based upon beliefs, desires and intentions (BDI).

Within this approach, models of the production of speech acts involve taking the speaker's (or conversational agent's) overarching plan for the discourse (for instance, to find out a particular fact) and breaking it down into subtasks. These subtasks can then be performed by the appropriate use of speech acts (for instance, asking yes–no questions). Conversely, models of the interpretation of speech acts consider the subtask that the speaker is performing by the use of each utterance and attempt to figure out from that what the speaker's overarching plan is likely to be. This corresponds to the idea that, by figuring out what a speaker is actually trying to do in the discourse as a whole, we can (if we care to be cooperative) help them achieve that aim without them having to execute all the subtasks that they have identified as necessary.

From the plan-based point of view, we can unpack (338) as follows. The speaker wishes to obtain the salt, and formulates a plan for getting it, which involves causing someone else to pass it to them. The speaker breaks this down into two tasks: establishing that a specific other person is able to do this, and requesting that they do it. They then perform this first task by uttering (338). The hearer recognises this as the first step in a plan by which the speaker wishes to obtain the salt, and, being cooperative, passes the salt to the speaker.

(338) exemplifies one way of requesting something, which is asking whether the hearer is able to provide it. There are various other categories of indirect request, which we can accommodate within the plan-based approach in much the same way. Jurafsky (2004) identifies three further broad categories: mentioning the speaker's wish (as in (339)), mentioning the hearer doing the action (as in (340)), and questioning the speaker's permission to receive the results of the action. The last in particular sounds rather arcane, but makes perfectly good sense when we see it in practice, as for example in (341).

(339)   I'd like some salt.
(340)   Will you pass the salt?
(341)   May I have the salt?

Importantly, from a plan-based perspective, the hearer is expected to understand each of these utterances, whichever is chosen, as a step in a plan to bring about the situation in which the speaker has the salt. And we start that reasoning process by first understanding the literal force of the utterance, and trying to come up with an explanation of why the speaker might have wanted to perform the speech act that the utterance is literally associated with.

But what if we don't assume the Literal Force Hypothesis? Suppose that there isn't a literal force associated with all – or for that matter, any

– utterance. Could we still understand speakers' illocutionary intentions, and if so, how?

8.2.2 Problems with Literal Force

In fact, both Gazdar (1981) and Levinson (1983) are very sceptical about the idea of literal force being attached to utterances. Part of Levinson's argument, rather like his later argument for default implicatures (discussed in Chapter 2), is that proceeding via literal force and plan-based reasoning would be inefficient in practice, given that many (perhaps even most) speech acts are indirect. For instance, he notes that imperatives are seldom used to issue requests or commands. It seems peremptory and impolite to utter (342) as a request, for instance: imperatives are much more socially acceptable when they relate to something that the hearer might actually want to do, as in (343), in which case they are more likely to be interpreted as offers than as orders.

(342)   Pass the salt.
(343)   Help yourself to a drink.

In Levinson's view, the relation between the sentence type of an utterance and its actual illocutionary force is so inconsistent and tenuous that it is difficult to establish what 'literal force' could possibly be associated with each of these sentence types. It's also difficult to know what the literal force could be for various other utterances, such as *yeah*, which can have numerous different discourse functions. And in addition to this, there are cases in which an utterance behaves syntactically as though it 'directly' possessed its indirect force. For instance, consider (344).

(344)   I would (hereby) like to declare this supermarket open.

It seems to be somewhat acceptable to insert *hereby* into this utterance, as in practice it is understood to be performative. But in literal force terms, the performative interpretation of (344) is indirect: (344) is underlyingly a purely declarative statement about the speaker's preference, which wouldn't normally license the insertion of *hereby*, as shown by (345) and (346). Put differently, the presence of the words *would like to*, which (assuming the Literal Force Hypothesis) turn the utterance from one that is literally performative to one that is literally merely declarative, don't seem to influence either our interpretation of the utterance or our view on whether the insertion of *hereby* is acceptable.

(345)   * I hereby like chocolate.
(346)   * I hereby want to visit Paris.

Another point against the plan-based model is that it is not clear that there is any stage of processing at which the hearer has access to the literal force and not to the indirect force of the utterance. Jurafsky (2004) compares this to the case of figurative language, for which the so-called literal interpretation does not always appear to be accessed first (see Chapter 6). On hearing the words *Could you . . .* or *Would you . . .*, we might reasonably infer that we are listening to a request (or perhaps an offer), even before we have heard the rest of the utterance, which presumably will have the syntactic form of an interrogative. Yet the Literal Force Hypothesis seems to commit us to having to understand the whole utterance as a question first, before we can entertain alternative possibilities.

A further challenge for plan-based accounts is the speed and apparent ease with which we understand indirect speech acts. On an account like that of Gordon and Lakoff (1971) or Searle (1975a), we use elaborate post-propositional reasoning to reconstruct the speaker's intention, going through a number of complex reasoning steps, after first having understood the full literal import of the utterance. We do this even in cases where the indirect interpretation is thoroughly conventional, as it seems to be for *Could you . . .* utterances. We're not conscious of performing this kind of reasoning – although that in itself is not necessarily a problem for the theory, because the kind of reasoning that is posited could take place without conscious awareness. But more problematically, judging by the very small gaps between conversational turns (see for instance Stivers et al. 2009), this process takes place remarkably quickly. Indeed, given that it takes the speaker some time to plan an utterance at all, it seems clear that speakers must generally know what they're going to start saying before the preceding turn has even finished. It's difficult to reconcile this with the assumption that we typically have to perform elaborate reasoning, after someone has finished talking, in order to understand what it was they wanted in the first place (and therefore how it would be cooperative for us to respond to them).

None of these arguments are intended to deny that syntactic factors are often relevant to the illocutionary force conveyed by an utterance, but they do point towards a view in which other factors are also in play, and in which reasoning about illocution is gradual and incremental rather than being purely post-propositional. The following subsection discusses the major trend in this line of thinking.

8.2.3 Cue-based approaches

A broad class of alternative approaches to the plan-based reasoning discussed in section 8.2.1 are what have been termed cue-based approaches to speech act recognition. The idea is that, rather than starting with assumptions about literal meaning and drawing further inferences about what the speaker is actually trying to achieve, we can draw upon a wide range of cues to the speaker's intention. Our task is simply to decide which interpretation is preferable based on all the relevant factors. From this point of view, there is really no such thing as a 'direct' or 'indirect' speech act (although I will continue to refer to them as such for consistency with the preceding subsections).

We've already discussed one example of how a lexical cue might interact with a syntactic cue. Utterances beginning *Could you* ..., like the one repeated below as (347), seem naturally to be interpreted as requests. The syntax could certainly be relevant – maybe utterances beginning with auxiliaries are quite likely to be requests – but the choice of word also seems likely to be relevant (*Could* is more likely to preface a request than *Have* is, for instance).

   (347)   Could you pass the salt?

Given a list of possible speech acts (a point we'll come back to in section 8.3), it would be reasonably straightforward to create a computational model which integrates this probabilistic information in some way, and can thus answer questions like 'Given that this utterance has the sentence-type "interrogative" and begins with the words "Could you", what kind of speech act is it likely to be?' We could train that model to learn the associations between features of utterances and the speech acts that they are likely to realise, by exposing it to an annotated corpus of utterances, which identifies the speech act that is being performed in each case.

This type of computational approach has turned out to be useful in the building of artificial dialogue systems that can interact in some sensible way with humans. We need a system of this kind to be able to recognise what kind of social action the human conversational partner is attempting to perform by using the utterance that they do. We'll discuss that line of research a little more in the following section. At the same time, the cue-based account is interesting from a linguistic point of view: could it be that we humans also use this kind of technique to identify speech acts in normal conversation? Such an approach would presumably solve the problem of how we identify conventional but 'non-literal' speech acts so quickly and effortlessly, although it might be a poor substitute for reasoning about speakers' goals and preferences in more complex social interactions.

Whether we want to build better dialogue systems or to understand human speech act recognition, the natural question that arises from the cue-based account is which factors actually serve as cues. It's fairly uncontroversial that lexical and syntactic factors are likely to be relevant, and there are numerous other cases where these seem to contribute to the recognition of a particular speech act. Just to take a few examples, the use of the word *sorry* makes an utterance more likely to be an apology; the addition of *right* at the end of the utterance makes it more likely to be a check-question (an utterance that seeks confirmation of something from the hearer); the use of *sure* might make an utterance more likely to be an acceptance.

But, of course, there are many other factors that might influence how we perceive an utterance's illocutionary force. Prosody is one major factor. Perhaps the most famous example of prosody being relevant to speech act recognition is the observation that questions tend to have rising intonation. Sag and Liberman (1975) showed this for yes–no questions in American English. Moreover, so-called 'upspeak' (first discussed by Lakoff 1975) – in which declarative sentences exhibit a late rise in intonation – is sometimes thought to indicate that the speaker is asking a check-question (Labov and Fanshel 1977), although actually its precise illocutionary effect is not yet fully understood (Warren 2016): for instance, it may signal more generally that the speaker wishes to elicit some kind of response from the hearer.

We can even see the effect of prosody on the illocutionary interpretation of a single word. Curl and Bell (2001) examined the use of the utterance *yeah* in the Switchboard corpus, an utterance which they argued to have three distinct functions – as an agreement, as an affirmative answer, and as a **backchannel** (essentially confirming that the hearer is paying attention, but not intending to interrupt the speaker's ongoing turn). They documented a systematic difference between the intonation contours used to perform agreements with *yeah* (high falls) and those used to produce backchannels (level or low falls), which is presumably something hearers could use to distinguish these two kinds of speech acts.

In short, prosody is a potentially powerful cue to the identity of the speech act that a speaker intends to perform. Moreover, there is a lot still to understand about it: the above examples all rely on relatively simple prosodic features, but the intonation contour as a whole exhibits great complexity and potentially offers enormously rich information about the speaker's intention (see for instance Rangarajan Sridhar et al. 2009).

Going beyond the content of the utterance itself, another category of potential information about the speech act that a speaker is performing is provided by the context of utterance. Way back in the discussion of implicature in Chapter 3, we noted that we have a strong expectation that, if a question has just been asked, a cooperative speaker will attempt to answer it. This accounts for the interpretation of B's utterance in (348) as potentially not only relevant but also an attempt to answer A's question in the negative.

(348) A: Is John a good teacher?
B: Whoa, look at the time.

At the level of speech acts, we can view this as a pair of acts, Question and Answer, that tend to occur sequentially. We have a strong expectation that, after having encountered the first one of these in a dialogue (for instance, because we've uttered it), we will now encounter the other (for instance, because our cooperative hearer will provide it). In fact, that expectation is so strong that, assuming that the next speaker is cooperative, their failure to utter anything at all can still be interpreted as pragmatically meaningful: it suggests that they are either unwilling or unable to answer the question.

Schegloff and Sacks (1973) term utterances of this type **adjacency pairs**, and they suggest that there are several such pairs that we can describe at the speech act level. Potential examples include Greeting–Greeting, Call–Response, Inform–Acknowledge and Offer–Response (where in this case we mean 'response' to consist of either acceptance or rejection). Importantly, competent language users are implicitly aware of the existence of adjacency pairs, and can consequently make additional assumptions about how they should interpret ambiguous utterances, and how their own ambiguous utterances are likely to be interpreted.

To illustrate this, let's return to the examples from Gisladottir et al. (2012) that were introduced early in Chapter 1 and revisited briefly in Chapter 2.

(349) A: How are you going to pay for the ticket?
B: I have a credit card.
(350) A: I can lend you money for the ticket.
B: I have a credit card.
(351) A: I don't have any money to pay for the ticket.
B: I have a credit card.

B's utterance, *I have a credit card*, attracts three different interpretations in these three discourse environments. We can think of them as being different speech acts: in (349), B directly answers A's question, in (350) they decline an offer, and in (351) they issue a (pre-)offer. Given that the words used are precisely the same, that they are in the same syntactic combination, and that they don't appear to require different intonation contours, it seems clear that the difference in interpretation can't stem purely from the utterance itself, but relies upon context. Invoking the notion of adjacency pairs gives us one idea of how this might play out:

- In (349), A produces the first unit of an adjacency pair (a question), creating the strong expectation that B should complete the pair by producing an answer. B's utterance is indeed interpretable as an answer, so the hearer naturally concludes that that's what it is.
- In (350), A produces the first unit of a different adjacency pair, an offer, so the expectation arises that B's utterance will be either an acceptance or a rejection of that offer. Presumably we have to reason a little about the meaning of B's utterance in order to figure out which of these is more likely, but by appeal to the adjacency pair we have already narrowed this down to two possibilities.
- In (351), we can perhaps interpret A's utterance as (at least implicitly) a request of some kind, which would again suggest that B's utterance should express whether they will fulfil or not fulfil that request. Based on its content, we are subsequently able to understand B's utterance as fulfilling the request.

Adjacency pairs are not the only feature of dialogue organisation that are potentially relevant to the interpretation of speech acts. Nor are they exceptionless, in terms of the relationship between the two turns: it's possible to insert a sub-sequence into an adjacency pair, as in the following example.

(352)   A: Will you come to the party?
        B: When is it?
        A: Saturday night.
        B: Sorry, I'll be out of town.

In (352), B's second turn is an indirect answer to A's first turn. In between, B has initiated a question–answer sequence in search of more information. Once that is resolved, the conversation is back to the situation it was in before B's utterance – A's invitation is hanging, and there's a strong expectation that a cooperative B will respond to it in some way.

Among other things, what (352) illustrates is that the kind of expectation or dependency between turns that is captured by adjacency pairs can also arise between non-consecutive turns in a dialogue. It wouldn't be absurd to think that the speech act performed at one time might have a direct effect on what speech act is most likely to be happening two, three or even more turns downstream. Flipping that around, the speech act being performed at one turn might be seen as a function of the speech acts that were being performed in the several preceding turns. This is something we can model reasonably straightforwardly within a cue-based account.

Cue-based approaches have come to predominate over plan-based approaches in much of the computational work that aims to build artificial dialogue systems. The cue-based approach offers an enormously powerful and flexible method for recognising speech acts, because in principle it can take into account so many distinct factors that might be relevant to the task. We can try to identify these factors individually – syntax, lexical choice, prosody, turn adjacencies, higher-level dialogue considerations – and incorporate them into a model, which can learn the associations between each of these factors and the speech act being performed, through exposure to a large set of annotated training data. A sufficiently detailed and well-trained model will offer a reasonable approximation to human behaviour in terms of speech act recognition. However, it is not clear whether that means that these are the mechanisms that humans use – and it seems unlikely that we could manage to be as accurate as we are in recognising illocutionary force without using any kind of plan-based reasoning.

8.3 Possible speech acts

In section 8.2, I discussed approaches to speech act recognition while trying to remain agnostic on the question of which speech acts potentially exist. However, even then it was impossible to avoid introducing a couple of distinctions that aren't intuitively obvious. For instance, at least three kinds of questions were quietly distinguished: yes–no questions, such as (353), which were the focus of Sag and Liberman's (1975) work on prosody; check-questions, such as (354), which were identified by Labov and Fanshel (1977) and which are potentially signalled by adding *right* at the end of a sentence; and questions in the broader sense of utterances that enter into adjacency pairs with answers. (353) and (354) also belong to this broader category, but so do wh-questions, such as (355).

    (353)   Does this bus go to the zoo?
    (354)   This bus goes to the zoo, right?
    (355)   Where does this bus go?

At one level of description, all these kinds of questions share the classic property of aiming to elicit information from the hearer. But at another level of description they aim to elicit different kinds of behaviour from the hearer. (353) requires only a *yes* or *no* answer, and indeed a more detailed answer would be unnecessary and might be considered unco-operative. (354) doesn't even seem to require that level of verbosity – replying *mhm* would be adequate and indeed polite, nodding would also suffice, and even silence might potentially be interpreted as confir-mation of the speaker's assumption. (355) invites an open-ended answer. To the extent that these three classes of question bring about different kinds of social behaviour in a cooperative hearer, we have a case for regarding them as different speech acts.

The question of how many distinct speech acts exist is one that goes back a long way. Even in Austin's (1962) original work on performatives, the precise relationship between the verb and the speech act is not always clear. For instance, although each verb could be said to name the action that it performs, it's not clear whether these are necessarily different actions: does the speaker who *affirms* something perform a different action from the speaker who *declares*, or *asserts*, or *avers* it? Is the speaker who *asks* doing something different from the speaker who *enquires*? Thus, even for the limited case of explicit performa-tives, it's not straightforward to map out the space of possible social actions and determine how many can be distinguished. And having done that, we would still be left with the problem of how to classify all the social actions that are potentially achieved through the use of non-performative utterances, and which might not happen to correspond with specific performative verbs in a given language.

Within the tradition of linguistic work on speech acts, perhaps the most influential taxonomy is the one due to Searle (1975b). He proposes that speech acts can be sorted into five broad classes. **Assertives** commit the speaker to the truth of a statement; **directives** induce the hearer to perform an action; **commissives** commit the speaker to a future action; **expressives** convey the speaker's feelings about a state of affairs; and **declarations** (which include Austin's performatives) change the state of the world to make it conform with their asserted content.

In his approach, Searle rejects not only the taxonomy that Austin (1962) tentatively suggested, but also the assumption that 'any two non-synonymous verbs must mark different illocutionary acts' (Searle 1975b: 9). He argues that this idea leads us to the error of thinking that the classification of the verbs of one language (in this case, English) into different illocutionary categories, which was part of Austin's project, represents a classification of speech acts in general. Searle goes on to argue that, taking illocutionary force as the basis for categorising lan-guage use, it is unsurprising that there are so few categories, as this reflects the few things that we do with language: 'we tell people how we are, we try to get them to do things, we commit ourselves to doing things, we express our feelings and attitudes and we bring about changes through our utterances' (ibid.: 23).

By contrast, computational approaches to dialogue understanding have tended to adopt a much larger set of possible speech acts. One widely used coding scheme is Dialog Act Markup in Several Layers (DAMSL). As set out by Core and Allen (1997) – with the promise of future development – DAMSL distinguishes forward- and backward-looking functions, the former comprising ten types of act (including for instance Assert, Offer and Commit) and the latter thirteen types (including Accept, Acknowledge and Answer). In DAMSL, utterances can be annotated with multiple functions: for instance, per Core and Allen (1997), check-questions are to be labelled as both Asserts and Info-Requests, and replies to them are both Asserts and Accepts (or Rejects).

Generally, the level of granularity required in a speech act annotation system will depend on the purpose of the annotation. In artificial dialogue systems, it's often appropriate to adopt a much finer level of detail still. For instance, Paek and Horvitz (2000) discuss their implementation of a robot receptionist. One of the requirements for this system is that it should be able to identify when a user is requesting it to perform a specific task that is within its competence. However, an additional complication is added by the limited accuracy of the speech recognition system itself. Paek and Horvitz specifically note an example in which the system understands the utterance (356) as (357).

(356)   Hi, I'm here to visit Fred Smith. Can you contact him?
(357)   I am here to visit Fred Smith way you contact in.

As rendered by the speech recognition software, (357) has lost many of the features that represent cues to the status of (356) as a request. (Of course, (356) itself was only an indirect request, so a plan-based system working on a perfect transcription of (356) would still be obliged to infer that the speaker's intention in asking whether the receptionist can contact Fred Smith is to get to the receptionist actually to do so.) Yet, even given (357) as the input to its reasoning about the speaker's intention, the system correctly identifies that the speaker's most likely goal is 'Visitation', and by activating a template for responses it is able to react appropriately by uttering (358) and performing the action it names.

(358)   I will call Fred Smith for you right away.

How does this work? Crucially, the system is selecting among an array of possible interpretations for the incoming utterance, but these possible interpretations are distinguished at a very fine level of detail. This makes sense because it is only possible for the system to respond appropriately to a relatively small, finite set of possible requests. For instance, there may only be a couple of things that it can do with respect to Fred Smith – calling him being one of them – in which case even being able to recognise the words *Fred Smith* substantially narrows down the possible speech acts that the speaker could be performing, as far as the system is concerned. Perhaps the words *visit Fred Smith* are sufficient by themselves to force the system to the conclusion that the speaker is trying to visit Fred Smith.

In essence, it would make sense for a system like this to distinguish between speech acts that we would normally think of as being essentially the same – between VISIT-FRED-SMITH and VISIT-JOHN-BROWN, for example. (We do not need to retain the traditional demarcation between the speech act and its semantic content, as Thomson (2010: 10) characterises it.) The system wouldn't derive any advantage from being able to recognise the utterance as a request, because that level of specificity is not sufficient to tell it how to respond – and in any case, perhaps virtually everything that it is able to deal with is a request. And it would be even less helpful for the system to be able to identify the utterance as a directive, in Searle's (1975b) sense, because all the utterances it deals with are directives.

The possible trade-off is that the system is likely to be confused by utterances that would be unproblematic for a human listener. I conjectured above that, whenever it hears the words *visit Fred Smith*, it concludes that the speaker is trying to visit Fred Smith. But, of course, the speaker isn't bound by the limitations of the system: they might be trying to perform various other actions. It's easy to see how a speaker might utter (359) and the system, failing to apprehend the actual point of their utterance, would respond inappropriately by calling Fred Smith, without realising that there was anything wrong in doing so.

(359)　　On what day is it possible to visit Fred Smith?

In a case like this, the human receptionist has an advantage over the automated system. However, it could be argued that this is a question of scope: the engineers designing an automated dialogue system have to make a choice about how wide its coverage will be, and it would be excessive to attempt to equip the system with the capability to have conversations that are far removed from its functions.

Why might it be advantageous for humans to use the more abstract categories of speech act that the likes of Searle (1975b) have posited, even though automated systems can get by without them? Part of the reason is connected to the breadth of scope of human communication. Automated dialogue systems have predominantly been designed for relatively specific tasks – being a receptionist at one building, providing tourist information about a city, or holding a conversation about a fairly narrow topic – whereas the human capacity for dialogue is not restricted in this way. In order to extend coverage to the full breadth of human dialogue, an automated system of the Paek and Horvitz (2000) type would need to be able to recognise and distinguish many thousands of distinct speech acts. The resulting system would not only be very complex, but would require a vast amount of training data in order to identify the cues that pick out each speech act.

Another limitation of such a system is that it would fail to generalise spontaneously to novel speech acts: for instance, if the company hires a new employee named Cheryl Anderson, a new set of utterances such as (360) become possible, to perform the newly created speech act VISIT-CHERYL-ANDERSON. A human receptionist would immediately recognise this as analogous to the well-established (356), just taking a different individual as its argument: however, a simple cue-based model would have to learn the relevant associations anew.

(360)   Hi, I'm here to visit Cheryl Anderson. Can you contact her?

The possibility of generalisation, in various ways, is an important advantage that emerges from having fewer distinct categories in the system. Take the case of adjacency pairs. The observation that questions are usually followed by answers is a useful one, in that it helps us identify ambiguous utterances as answers, as discussed earlier. However, it's only useful to the extent that utterances occur that are identifiable as questions, which requires us to have a category of thing called 'question' in our system. If we classified these utterances into an even larger category instead, such as Searle's directives, the generalisation that utterances of this category are followed by answers would no longer hold. But if we classified them into smaller and more precise categories – for argument's sake, 'questions about people', 'questions about places', 'questions about things', etc. – we would again lose the generalisation that all questions tended to be followed by answers: we would have to learn this pattern separately for each of the categories we actually used.

In some sense, the purpose of speech acts is to 'factorise' dialogue. That is to say, rather than thinking of dialogue as comprising sequences of arbitrarily distinct utterances – where there are billions of possibilities about what might go into an utterance – we can think of it as comprising sequences of speech acts, each of which is drawn from only a small selection of possible types. We can then identify patterns in the occurrence of speech acts that simply wouldn't be evident in the mass of utterances. However, whether it's useful to us to spot these patterns rather depends on what we propose to do with that information. For us as hearers, some of these patterns are useful in the disambiguation of utterances, as in the case of adjacency pairs. It's also possible that similar patterns might be helpful to us in production – for instance, knowing what general kind of response is appropriate might help us in the early stages of planning the utterance.

By contrast, for simple dialogue systems in constrained domains, being able to identify patterns in speech acts might not be helpful in the same way. In the case of the robot receptionist, identifying the human's utterance as a request doesn't usefully narrow down the space of possible responses, because essentially all the useful actions that it can perform at all are responses to requests. Traum (1999) discusses this issue, and concludes that what we can think of as speech acts (or, in the terminology of the computational literature, 'dialogue act types') are potentially useful as an intermediate step in communication planning, but that this is much more relevant to larger systems designed to offer much wider coverage of communicative domains. Relatively constrained artificial dialogue systems can manage perfectly well without a notion of speech acts. Humans, presumably, are adapted to deal with an exceptionally broad range of communicative domains, and need to make use of speech acts in order to deal with that.

8.4 Summary

Language can be used to perform a range of social functions, from greeting, questioning, thanking and apologising, through to complex and culturally specific actions such as naming, marrying, sentencing, and so on. The use of speech acts poses a particular pragmatic challenge, in that the relation between the form of words used and the action being performed (or illocutionary force of the utterance) is often subtle, inconsistent and context-dependent. As for other pragmatic enrichments, such as implicature, there are competing accounts of how this takes place: these prominently include a plan-based account in which we reason about how to enrich the apparent illocutionary force of the utterance in order to make sense of the speaker's aims, and a cue-based account which aims to reconstruct the speaker's intention more directly based upon all available sources of information. Both approaches are relevant not only to our understanding of human interaction but also to the development of artificial dialogue systems. The question of which speech acts should be included in the system can be approached with reference to ideas about what actions can be performed through the use of language. However, the set of speech acts used in a model tends to vary according to its specific needs, and the needs of an artificial dialogue system can diverge considerably from what is likely to be going on in human psychology.

Exercises

Answers to the following are available at <edinburghuniversitypress. com/pragmatics>.

1. Which of the following utterances are typically used to perform indirect speech acts?
   a. Please shut the door.
   b. Please could you shut the door.
   c. I'd really like a cup of tea.
   d. I'd really like to finish the job.
2. What kind of act – locutionary, illocutionary or perlocutionary – is being <u>described</u> by each of the following utterances?
   a. Jane promised to come to the party.
   b. Jane said that she would come to the party.
   c. Jane convinced me to come to the party.
   d. Jane pretended that she would come to the party.
3. On a cue-based account, which features of the following utterances are likely to be helpful in identifying them as the speech acts that they are? Which features would be unhelpful?
   a. Tell me straight away if it happens again, eh?
   b. I would like to invite you to justify this absurd decision.
   c. You'll come to dinner, won't you?

Discussion questions

1. Could we learn anything about the range of possible illocutionary acts by studying the performative verbs that are made available in different languages? What would be the limitations of that exercise?
2. Some researchers have considered the possibility of applying the notion of adjacency pairs to social interactions that don't involve the use of words. What kinds of interactions could usefully be analysed in terms of adjacency pairs?

References

Abrusán, M. and Szendrői, K. (2013). Experimenting with the King of France: topics, verifiability, and definite descriptions. *Semantics and Pragmatics*, 6(10), 1–43.

Abusch, D. (2002). Lexical alternatives as a source of pragmatic presuppositions. In B. Jackson (ed.), *Proceedings of Semantics and Linguistic Theory (SALT)* 12. Ithaca, NY: Cornell University. 1–19.

Abusch, D. (2010). Presupposition triggering from alternatives. *Journal of Semantics*, 27(1), 37–80.

Altmann, G. T. M., and Kamide, Y. (1999). Incremental interpretation at verbs: restricting the domain of subsequent reference. *Cognition*, 73(3), 247–64.

Anderson, A., Garrod, S., and Sanford, A. I. (1983). The accessibility of pronominal antecedents as a function of episode shifts in narrative text. *Quarterly Journal of Experimental Psychology*, 35, 427–40.

Ariel, M. (2010). *Defining Pragmatics*. Cambridge: Cambridge University Press.

Asher, N. (1993). *Reference to Abstract Objects in Discourse*. Dordrecht: Kluwer.

Asher, N., and Lascarides, A. (2003). *Logics of Conversation*. Cambridge: Cambridge University Press.

Asher, N., and Vieu, L. (2005). Subordinating and coordinating discourse relations. *Lingua*, 115(4), 591–610.

Austin, J. L. (1962). *How to Do Things with Words*. Oxford: Clarendon Press.

Bach, K. (2006). Impliciture vs. explicature: what's the difference? Granada workshop on 'Explicit Communication', in honor of Robyn Carston. Retrieved from <http://userwww.sfsu.edu/kbach/Bach.ImplExpl.pdf> (last accessed 16 July 2018).

Bach, K., and Harnish, R. M. (1979). *Linguistic Communication and Speech Acts*. Cambridge, MA: MIT Press.

Bar-Hillel, Y. (1971). *Pragmatics of Natural Languages*. Dordrecht: D. Reidel.

Baron-Cohen, S., Leslie, A. M., and Frith, U. (1985). Does the autistic child have a 'theory of mind'? *Cognition*, 21(1), 37–46.

Bergen, L., and Grodner, D. J. (2012). Speaker knowledge influences the comprehension of pragmatic inferences. *Journal of Experimental Psychology: Learning, Memory, and Cognition*, 38(5), 1450–60.

Boland, J. E., Tanenhaus, M. K., and Garnsey, S. M. (1990). Evidence for the immediate use of verb control information in sentence processing. *Journal of Memory and Language*, 29, 413–32.

Bott, L., and Noveck, I. A. (2004). Some utterances are underinformative: the onset and time course of scalar inferences. *Journal of Memory and Language*, 51(3), 437–57.

Breheny, R. (in press). Scalar implicatures in a Gricean cognitive system. To appear in C. Cummins and N. Katsos (eds), *Oxford Handbook of Experimental Semantics and Pragmatics*. Oxford: Oxford University Press.

Breheny, R., Katsos, N., and Williams, J. N. (2006). Are generalised scalar implicatures generated by default? An on-line investigation into the role of context in generating pragmatic inferences. *Cognition*, 100(3), 434–63.

Brennan, S. E., and Clark, H. H. (1996). Conceptual pacts and lexical choice in conversation. *Journal of Experimental Psychology: Learning, Memory and Cognition*, 22(6), 1482–93.

Carroll, J. M. (1980). Naming and describing in social communication. *Language and Speech*, 23, 309–22.

Carston, R. (1996). Enrichment and loosening: complementary processes in deriving the proposition expressed? *UCL Working Papers in Linguistics*, 8, 205–32.

Carston, R. (2002). *Thoughts and Utterances: The Pragmatics of Explicit Communication*. Oxford: Blackwell.

Carston, R., and Wearing, C. (2011). Metaphor, hyperbole and simile: a pragmatic approach. *Language and Cognition*, 3–2, 283–312.

Chafe, W. L. (1976). Givenness, contrastiveness, definiteness, subjects, topics, and point of view. In C. N. Li (ed.), *Subject and Topic*. New York: Academic Press. 25–56.

Chemla, E., and Bott, L. (2013). Processing presuppositions: dynamic semantics vs pragmatic enrichment. *Language and Cognitive Processes*, 38(3), 241–60.

Chierchia, G., Fox, D., and Spector, B. (2012). The grammatical view of scalar implicatures and the relationship between semantics and pragmatics. In P. Portner, C. Maienborn, and K. von Heusinger (eds), *Semantics: An International Handbook of Natural Language Meaning*. Berlin: Mouton de Gruyter. 2297–332.

Chomsky, N. (1965). *Aspects of the Theory of Syntax*. Cambridge, MA: MIT Press.

Clark, H. H., and Marshall, C. (1981). Definite reference and mutual knowledge. In A. K. Joshi, B. L. Webber, and I. A. Sag (eds), *Elements of Discourse Understanding*. Cambridge: Cambridge University Press. 10–63.

Clark, H. H., and Wilkes-Gibbs, D. (1986). Referring as a collaborative process. *Cognition*, 22, 1–39.

Clifton, C. (2013). Situational context affects definiteness preferences: accommodation of presuppositions. *Journal of Experimental Psychology: Learning, Memory, and Cognition*, 39(2), 487–501.

Cooper, R. M. (1974). The control of eye fixation by the meaning of spoken language: a new methodology for the real-time investigation of speech perception, memory, and language processing. *Cognitive Psychology*, 6(1), 84–107.

Core, M. G., and Allen, J. F. (1997). Coding dialogs with the DAMSL annotation scheme. *Working Notes of the AAAI Fall Symposium on Communicative Action in Humans and Machines*, Cambridge, MA. 28–35.

Crawley, R. A., Stevenson, R. J., and Kleinman, D. (1990). The use of heuristic strategies in the interpretation of pronouns. *Journal of Psycholinguistic Research*, 19, 245–64.

Crinean, M., and Garnham, A. (2006). Implicit causality, implicit consequentiality and semantic roles. *Language and Cognitive Processes*, 21, 636–48.

Cummins, C., Amaral, P., and Katsos, N. (2013). Backgrounding and accommodation of presupposition: an experimental approach. In E. Chemla, V. Homer, and G. Winterstein (eds), *Proceedings of Sinn und Bedeutung 17*. 201–18.

Cummins, C., and Katsos, N. (2013). Empirical and theoretical evidence for a model of quantifier production. In F. Liedtke and C. Schulze (eds), *Beyond Words: Content, Context, and Inference*. Berlin: De Gruyter Mouton. 253–82.

Curl, T. S., and Bell, A. (2001). Yeah, yeah, yeah: prosodic differences of pragmatic functions. Ms.

Deamer, F., Breheny, R., and Pouscoulous, N. (2010). A contrastive look at the processing of metaphor and hyperbole. *UCL Working Papers in Linguistics*, 22, 1–16.

Degen, J., and Franke, M. (2012). Optimal reasoning about referential expressions. In S. Brown-Schmidt, J. Ginzburg, and S. Larsson (eds), *Proceedings of the 16th Workshop on the Semantics and Pragmatics of Dialogue*. 2–11.

Doran, R., Baker, R. E., McNabb, Y., Larson, M., and Ward, G. (2009). On the non-unified nature of scalar implicature: an empirical investigation. *International Review of Pragmatics*, 1, 211–48.

Frege, G. (1892). On sense and reference. In P. Geach and M. Black (eds), *Translations from the Philosophical Writings of Gottlob Frege*. Oxford: Blackwell. 56–78.

Frisson, S., and Pickering, M. J. (2007). The processing of familiar and novel senses of a word: why reading Dickens is easy but reading Needham can be hard. *Language and Cognitive Processes*, 22(4), 595–613.

Garvey, C., and Caramazza, A. (1974). Implicit causality in verbs. *Linguistic Inquiry*, 5, 459–64.

Gazdar, G. (1981). Speech act assignment. In A. Joshi, B. Webber, and I. Sag (eds), *Elements of Discourse Understanding*. Cambridge: Cambridge University Press.

Geis, M. L., and Zwicky, A. M. (1971). On invited inferences. *Linguistic Inquiry*, 2, 561–6.

Geurts, B. (2010). *Quantity Implicatures*. Cambridge: Cambridge University Press.

Geurts, B., and Pouscoulous, N. (2009). Embedded implicatures?!? *Semantics and Pragmatics*, 2(4), 1–34.

Gibbs, R. W. (1994). *The Poetics of Mind: Figurative Thought, Language and Understanding*. Cambridge: Cambridge University Press.

Gibbs, R. W. (2002). A new look at literal meaning in understanding what is said and implicated. *Journal of Pragmatics*, 34(4), 457–86.

Giora, R. (1997). Understanding figurative and literal language: the graded salience hypothesis. *Cognitive Linguistics*, 8(3), 183–206.

Giora, R. (2002). Literal vs. figurative language: different or equal? *Journal of Pragmatics*, 34(4), 487–506.

Gisladottir, R. S., Chwilla, D., Schriefers, H., and Levinson, S. C. (2012). Speech act recognition in conversation: experimental evidence. In N. Miyake, D. Peebles, and R. P. Cooper (eds), *Proceedings of the 34th Annual Meeting of the Cognitive Science Society (CogSci 2012)*. Austin, TX: Cognitive Science Society. 1596–601.

Glanzberg, M. (2005). Presuppositions, truth values and expressing propositions. In G. Preyer and G. Peter (eds), *Contextualism in Philosophy: Knowledge, Meaning, and Truth*. Oxford: Oxford University Press. 349–96.

Glucksberg, S., and Keysar, B. (1990). Understanding metaphorical comparisons: beyond similarity. *Psychological Review*, 97, 3–18.

Gordon, D., and Lakoff, G. (1971). Conversational postulates. *CLS-71*. University of Chicago. 200–13.

Gordon, P. C., Grosz, B. J., and Gilliom, L. A. (1993). Pronouns, names, and the centering of attention in discourse. *Cognitive Science*, 17, 311–47.

Grice, H. P. (1975). Logic and conversation. In P. Cole and J. Morgan (eds), *Syntax and Semantics III: Speech Acts*. New York: Academic Press. 183–98.

Grice, H. P. (1989). *Studies in the Way of Words*. Cambridge, MA: Harvard University Press.

Gualmini, A., Hulsey, S., Hacquard, V., and Fox, D. (2008). The question–answer requirement for scope assignment. *Natural Language Semantics*, 16, 205–37.

Happé, F. G. (1993). Communicative competence and theory of mind in autism: a test of relevance theory. *Cognition*, 48(2), 101–19.

Hartshorne, J. K., Snedeker, J., Azar, S. Y.-M. L., and Kim, A. E. (2015). The neural computation of scalar implicature. *Language, Cognition and Neuroscience*, 30(5), 620–34.

Hauser, M., Chomsky, N., and Fitch, W. T. (2002). The faculty of language: what is it, who has it, and how did it evolve? *Science*, 298, 1569–79.

Hazlett, A. (2010). The myth of factive verbs. *Philosophy and Phenomenological Research*, 80, 497–522.

Hobbs, J. R. (1985). On the coherence and structure of discourse. Technical report CSLI-85-37, Center for the Study of Language and Information, Stanford University.

Holtgraves, T. (in press). Politeness. To appear in C. Cummins and N. Katsos (eds), *Oxford Handbook of Experimental Semantics and Pragmatics*. Oxford: Oxford University Press.

Horn, L. R. (1972). On the semantic properties of logical operators in English. PhD thesis, University of California, Los Angeles. Distributed by Indiana University Linguistics Club.

Horn, L. R. (1981). Exhaustiveness and the semantics of clefts. In V. A. Burke and J. Pustejovsky (eds), *Proceedings of the 11th Annual Meeting of the North East Linguistic Society*. Amherst, MA: University of Massachusetts. 108–31.

Horn, L. R. (1984). Toward a new taxonomy for pragmatic inference: Q-based and R-based implicature. In D. Schiffrin (ed.), *Meaning, Form, and Use in Context: Linguistic Applications*. Washington, DC: Georgetown University Press. 11–42.

Huang, Y. T., and Snedeker, J. (2009). On-line interpretation of scalar quantifiers: insight into the semantics–pragmatics interface. *Cognitive Psychology*, 58(3), 376–415.

Hurford, J. (2007). *The Origins of Meaning*. Oxford: Oxford University Press.

Hymes, D. H. (1966). Two types of linguistic relativity. In W. Bright (ed.), *Sociolinguistics*. The Hague: Mouton. 114–58.

Jasinskaja, K., and Karagjosova, E. (2015). Rhetorical relations. Ms.

Jayez, J., Mongelli, V., Reboul, A., and van der Henst, J.-B. (2015). Weak and strong triggers. In F. Schwarz (ed.), *Experimental Perspectives on Presuppositions*. Cham: Springer International Publishing. 173–94.

Jurafsky, D. (2004). Pragmatics and computational linguistics. In G. Ward and L. R. Horn (eds), *Handbook of Pragmatics*. Oxford: Blackwell.

Kameyama, M. (1996). Indefeasible semantics and defeasible pragmatics. In Makoto Kanazawa, C. Piñon, and Henriëtte de Swart (eds), *Quantifiers, Deduction, and Context*. Stanford, CA: CSLI. 111–38.

Katsos, N., and Bishop, D. V. M. (2011). Pragmatic tolerance: implications for the acquisition of informativeness and implicature. *Cognition*, 120(1), 67–81.

Kehler, A. (2002). *Coherence, Reference, and the Theory of Grammar*. Stanford, CA: CSLI.

Kehler, A., Kertz, L., Rohde, H., and Elman, J. L. (2008). Coherence and coreference revisited. *Journal of Semantics*, 25, 1–44.

Keysar, B., Barr, D. J., Balin, J. A., and Brauner, J. S. (2000). Taking perspective in conversation: the role of mutual knowledge in comprehension. *Psychological Science*, 11, 32–8.

Keysar, B., Barr, D. J., and Horton, W. S. (1998). The egocentric basis of language use: insights from a processing approach. *Current Directions in Psychological Science*, 7, 46–50.

Kim, C. S. (2008). Processing presupposition: verifying sentences with 'only'. *Proceedings of the 31st Penn Linguistics Colloquium. University of Pennsylvania Working Papers in Linguistics*, 14(1), article 17.

Klinedinst, N. (2012). THCSP. Ms., UCL.

Knott, A., and Dale, R. (1994). Using linguistic phenomena to motivate a set of coherence relations. *Discourse Processes*, 18(1), 35–62.

Krauss, R. M., and Weinheimer, S. (1964). Changes in reference phrases as a function of frequency of usage in social interaction: a preliminary study. *Psychonomic Science*, 1, 113–14.

Labov, W., and Fanshel, D. (1977). *Therapeutic Discourse*. New York: Academic Press.

Lakoff, R. T. (1975). *Language and Woman's Place*. Cambridge: Cambridge University Press.

Lasersohn, P. (1993). Existence presuppositions and background knowledge. *Journal of Semantics*, 10(2), 113–22.

Levesque, H. J. (2014). On our best behavior. *Artificial Intelligence*, 212, 27–35.

Levinson, S. C. (1983). *Pragmatics*. Cambridge: Cambridge University Press.

Levinson, S. C. (1995). Interactional biases in human thinking. In E. Goody (ed.), *Social Intelligence and Interaction*. Cambridge: Cambridge University Press. 221–60.

Levinson, S. C. (2000). *Presumptive Meanings*. Cambridge, MA: MIT Press.

McCawley, J. (1978). Conversational implicature and the lexicon. In P. Cole (ed.), *Syntax and Semantics 9: Pragmatics*. New York: Academic Press.

MacKay, G., and Shaw, A. (2004). A comparative study of figurative language in children with autistic spectrum disorders. *Child Language Teaching and Therapy*, 20, 13–32.

Mann, W. C., and Thompson, S. A. (1988). Rhetorical Structure Theory: toward a functional theory of text organization. *Text – Interdisciplinary Journal for the Study of Discourse*, 8, 243–81.

Marr, D. (1982). *Vision: A Computational Investigation into the Human Representation and Processing of Visual Information*. New York: W. H. Freeman.

Mill, J. S. (1867). *An Examination of Sir William Hamilton's Philosophy*. London: Longmans.

Musolino, J., Crain, S., and Thornton, R. (2000). Navigating negative quantificational space. *Linguistics*, 38, 1–32.

Musolino, J., and Lidz, J. (2006). Why children aren't universally successful with quantification. *Linguistics*, 44, 817–52.

Norbury, C. F. (2005). The relationship between theory of mind and metaphor: evidence from children with language impairment and autistic spectrum disorder. *British Journal of Developmental Psychology*, 23, 383–99.

Noveck, I. A., and Posada, A. (2003). Characterizing the time course of an implicature: an evoked potentials study. *Brain and Language*, 85(2), 203–10.

Noveck, I. A., and Spotorno, N. (2013). Narrowing. In L. Goldstein (ed.), *Brevity*. Oxford: Oxford University Press. 280–96.

Onea, E. (in press). Exhaustivity in *it*-clefts. To appear in C. Cummins and N. Katsos (eds), *Oxford Handbook of Experimental Semantics and Pragmatics*. Oxford: Oxford University Press.

Ortony, A. (1979). Beyond literal similarity. *Psychological Review*, 86(3), 161–80.

Paek, T., and Horvitz, E. (2000). Conversation as action under uncertainty. In *Proceedings of the 16th Conference on Uncertainty in Artificial Intelligence*. San Francisco: Morgan Kaufmann. 455–64.

Pexman, P. M. (2008). It's fascinating research: the cognition of verbal irony. *Current Directions in Psychological Science*, 17(4), 286–90.

Pickering, M. J., and Majid, A. (2007). What are implicit causality and implicit consequentiality? *Language and Cognitive Processes*, 22, 780–8.

Polanyi, L. (1988). A formal model of the structure of discourse. *Journal of Pragmatics*, 12, 601–38.

Politzer-Ahles, S., and Fiorentino, R. (2013). The realization of scalar inferences: context sensitivity without processing cost. *PLoS ONE*, 8(5), e63943.

Potts, C. (2012). Conventional implicature and expressive content. In C. Maienborn, K. von Heusinger, and P. Portner (eds), *Semantics: An International Handbook of Natural Language Meaning*, vol. 3. Berlin: Mouton de Gruyter. 2516–36.

Rangarajan Sridhar, V. K., Bangalore, S., and Narayanan, S. (2009). Combining lexical, syntactic and prosodic cues for improved online dialog act tagging. *Computer Speech and Language*, 23, 407–22.

Recanati, F. (1995). The alleged priority of literal interpretation. *Cognitive Science*, 19, 207–32.

Reese, B., Hunter, J., Asher, N., Denis, P., and Baldridge, J. (2007). *Reference Manual for the Analysis and Annotation of Rhetorical Structure (version 1.0)*. Technical report, University of Texas at Austin.

Roberts, C. (1996). Information structure in discourse. Towards an integrated formal theory of pragmatics. J.-H. Yoon and A. Kathol (eds), *Ohio State University Working Papers in Linguistics*, 49, 91–136.

Romoli, J., Sudo, Y., and Snedeker, J. (2011). An experimental investigation of presupposition projection in conditional sentences. In N. Ashton, A. Chereches, and D. Lutz (eds), *Proceedings of Semantics and Linguistic Theory (SALT) 21*. Ithaca, NY: CLC Publications. 592–608.

Rubio-Fernández, P. (2007). Suppression in metaphor interpretation: differences between meaning selection and meaning construction. *Journal of Semantics*, 24, 345–71.

Rubio-Fernández, P. (2016). How redundant are redundant color adjectives? An efficiency-based analysis of color overspecification. *Frontiers in Psychology*, 7, 153.

Rubio-Fernández, P., Cummins, C., and Tian, Y. (2016). Are single and extended metaphors processed differently? A test of two Relevance-Theoretic accounts. *Journal of Pragmatics*, 94, 15–28.

Rundblad, G., and Annaz, D. (2010). The atypical development of metaphor and metonymy comprehension in children with autism. *Autism*, 14(1), 29–46.

Sag, I. A., and Liberman, M. (1975). The intonational disambiguation of indirect speech acts. *CLS-75*. University of Chicago. 487–98.

Schegloff, E., and Sacks, H. (1973). Opening up closings. *Semiotica*, 8(4), 289–327.

Schiffer, S. R. (1972). *Meaning*. Oxford: Oxford University Press.

Schumacher, P. (in press). Metonymy. To appear in C. Cummins and N. Katsos (eds), *Oxford Handbook of Experimental Semantics and Pragmatics*. Oxford: Oxford University Press.

Schwarz, F. (2007). Processing presupposed content. *Journal of Semantics*, 24(4), 373–416.

Schwarz, F. (in press). Presuppositions, projection and accommodation. To appear in C. Cummins and N. Katsos (eds), *Oxford Handbook of Experimental Semantics and Pragmatics*. Oxford: Oxford University Press.

Scott, R. M., and Baillargeon, R. (2017). Early false-belief understanding. *Trends in Cognitive Sciences*, 21(4), 237–49.

Scott-Phillips, T. C. (2014). *Speaking Our Minds*. London: Palgrave Macmillan.

Searle, J. R. (1975a). Indirect speech acts. In P. Cole and J. Morgan (eds), *Syntax and Semantics 3: Speech Acts*. New York: Academic Press.

Searle, J. R. (1975b). A taxonomy of illocutionary acts. In K. Gunderson (ed.), *Language, Mind, and Knowledge*. Minneapolis, MN: University of Minnesota Press. 344–69.

Sedivy, J. C., Chambers, C., Tanenhaus, M. K., and Carlson, G. (1999). Achieving incremental semantic interpretation through contextual representation. *Cognition*, 71, 109–47.

Shannon, C. E., and Weaver, W. (1949). *The Mathematical Theory of Communication*. Urbana, IL: University of Illinois Press.

Shanon, B. (1976). On the two kinds of presuppositions in natural language. *Foundations of Language*, 14, 247–9.

Sheldon, A. (1974). The role of parallel function in the acquisition of relative clauses in English. *Journal of Verbal Learning and Verbal Behavior*, 13, 272–81.

Simons, M., Tonhauser, J., Beaver, D., and Roberts, C. (2010). What projects and why. In N. Li and D. Lutz (eds), *Proceedings of Semantics and Linguistic Theory (SALT) 20*. Ithaca, NY: CLC Publications. 309–27.

Singh, R., Fedorenko, E., Mahowald, K., and Gibson, E. (2016). Accommodating presuppositions is inappropriate in implausible contexts. *Cognitive Science*, 40(3): 607–34.

Smyth, R. (1994). Grammatical determinants of ambiguous pronoun resolution. *Journal of Psycholinguistic Research*, 23, 197–229.

Sperber, D., and Wilson, D. (1981). Irony and the use–mention distinction. In P. Cole (ed.), *Radical Pragmatics*. New York: Academic Press. 295–318.

Sperber, D., and Wilson, D. (1986). *Relevance: Communication and Cognition*. Oxford: Blackwell.

Stevenson, R. J., Crawley, R. A., and Kleinman, D. (1994). Thematic roles, focus, and the representation of events. *Language and Cognitive Processes*, 9, 519–48.

Stivers, T., Enfield, N. J., Brown, P., Englert, C., Hayashi, M., Heinemann, T., Hoymann, G., Rossano, F., De Ruiter, J. P., Yoon, K.-E., and Levinson, S. C. (2009). Universals and cultural variation in turn-taking in conversation. *Proceedings of the National Academy of Sciences of the United States of America*, 106(26), 10587–92.

Strawson, P. F. (1950). On referring. *Mind*, 59, 320–44.

Strawson, P. F. (1964). Identifying reference and truth-values. *Theoria*, 30(2), 96–118.

Sudo, Y. (2012). On the semantics of phi features on pronouns. PhD thesis, Massachusetts Institute of Technology.

Sun, C., Tian, Y., and Breheny, R. (under review). Scale homogeneity and local enrichability affect scalar diversity.

Swinney, D. A. (1979). Lexical access during sentence comprehension: (re) consideration of context effects. *Journal of Verbal Learning and Verbal Behavior*, 18(6), 645–59.

Tanenhaus, M. K., Spivey-Knowlton, M. J., Eberhard, K. M., and Sedivy, J. C. (1995). Integration of visual and linguistic information in spoken language comprehension. *Science*, 268(5217), 1632–4.

Thomson, B. (2010). Statistical methods for spoken dialogue management. PhD thesis, University of Cambridge.

Tiemann, S., Schmid, M., Bade, N., Rolke, B., Hertrich, I., Ackermann, H., Knapp, J., and Beck, S. (2011). Psycholinguistic evidence for presuppositions: on-line and off-line data. In I. Reich, E. Horch, and D. Pauly (eds), *Sinn und Bedeutung 15: Proceedings of the 2010 Annual Conference of the Gesellschaft für Semantik*. Saarbrücken: Saarland University Press. 581–95.

Tomlinson, J. M., Bailey, T. M., and Bott, L. (2013). Possibly all of that and then some: scalar implicatures are understood in two steps. *Journal of Memory and Language*, 69(1), 18–35.

Tonhauser, J. (2016). Prosodic cues to speaker commitment. In M. Moroney, C.-R. Little, J. Collard, and D. Burgdorf (eds), *Proceedings of Semantics and Linguistic Theory (SALT) 26*. Ithaca, NY: CLC Publications. 934–60.

Traum, D. (1999). Speech acts for dialogue agents. In M. Wooldridge and A. Rao (eds), *Foundations of Rational Agency*. Dordrecht: Kluwer. 169–201.

Van der Sandt, R. (1988). *Context and Presupposition*. London: Croom Helm.

Van Tiel, B., Van Miltenburg, E., Zevakhina, N., and Geurts, B. (2016). Scalar diversity. *Journal of Semantics*, 33, 137–75.

Von Fintel, K. (2004). Would you believe it? The King of France is back! Presuppositions and truth-value intuitions. In M. Reimer and A. Bezuidenhout (eds), *Descriptions and Beyond*. Oxford: Oxford University Press. 315–41.

Ward, G., and Birner, B. (2004). Information structure and non-canonical syntax. In L. R. Horn and G. Ward (eds), *Handbook of Pragmatics*. Oxford: Basil Blackwell. 153–74.

Warren, M. (2006). *Features of Naturalness in Conversation*. Amsterdam: John Benjamins.

Warren, P. (2016). *Uptalk: The Phenomenon of Rising Intonation*. Cambridge: Cambridge University Press.

Webber, B., Joshi, A., Miltsakaki, E., Prasad, R., Dinesh, N., Lee, A., and Forbes, K. (2006). A short introduction to the Penn Discourse TreeBank. *Copenhagen Studies in Language*, 32(9).

Weber, A., Braun, B., and Crocker, M. W. (2006). Finding referents in time: eye-tracking evidence for the role of contrastive accents. *Cognition*, 49(3), 367–92.

Wellman, H. M., Cross, D., and Watson, J. (2001). Meta-analysis of Theory-of-Mind development: the truth about false belief. *Child Development*, 72(3), 655–84.

Wilson, D. (1975). *Presuppositions and Non-Truth-Conditional Semantics*. New York: Academic Press.

Wilson, D. (2012). Relevance theory, communication and cognition. Retrieved from <http://www.gist.ugent.be/file/374> (last accessed 16 July 2018).

Wilson, D., and Sperber, D. (2002). Relevance theory. *UCL Working Papers in Linguistics*. 249–87. Retrieved from <http://ftp.phon.ucl.ac.uk/home/PUB/WPL/02papers/wilson_sperber.pdf> (last accessed 16 July 2018).

Wimmer, H., and Perner, J. (1983). Beliefs about beliefs: representation and constraining function of wrong beliefs in young children's understanding of deception. *Cognition*, 13(1), 103–28.

Winograd, T. (1972). Understanding natural language. *Cognitive Psychology*, 3(1), 1–191.

Wittgenstein, L. (1953). *Philosophische Untersuchungen* [Philosophical Investigations]. Oxford: Blackwell.

Zeevat, H. (1992). Presupposition and accommodation in update semantics. *Journal of Semantics*, 9(4), 379–412.

Zehr, J. (2015). Vagueness, presupposition and truth value judgments. PhD thesis, Institut Jean Nicod, École Normale Supérieure de Paris.

Zipf, G. K. (1949). *Human Behavior and the Principle of Least Effort*. Cambridge: Addison-Wesley.

Index

accommodation, **76**–8, 80–2, 84–5,
    97–8, 114
  global accommodation, **88**, 96
  local accommodation, **88**, 94, 96
addressee, **5**
adjacency
  adjacency pairs, **201**–3, 207–8
  clausal, 178
adjectives, 49, 118–19, 125–6, 177
AI, 103, 195–6
ambiguity, 2, 6, 17, 24, 85, 101–5,
    109–10, 114–16, 131–2, 134–5,
    147, 165–6, 176, 181–3, 201,
    207–8
anaphora, 81, 101–3, 181–3
and, 44
Antithesis, 171–2
artificial dialogue systems, 199–200,
    203, 205–8
assertives, 204
at-issue/not at-issue, **80**, 88–9, 90
attention, 34–5
Attribution (relation), 173
audience design, **120**–1
Auditor's Economy, 24
autism spectrum disorder (ASD), 11,
    131, 149–52

backchannel, **200**
Background (relation), 173
backgrounding, 76–**80**, 85–6
bandwidth, 20–1
BDI, 195–6
bottleneck *see* bandwidth

cancellation, **3**, 41, 48, 83
class inclusion, 137–40, 143,
cognitive effects, 29–30, 34, 50, 123, 149
cognitive effort, 29–30, 123
Cognitive Principle of Relevance,
    29–30
coherence, 103, 155–83
colour, 125–6, 127, 177
comment, **157**
commissives, **204**
common ground, 113–**15**, 116–19
Communicative Principle of
    Relevance, 30
community co-membership, 116–17
competence, (pragmatic), **9**–11
compositional semantics, **2**, 132
conceptual pacts, **113**
Concession, 171
conditional perfection, **49**
conditionals, 49, 75–6, 87–8, 161
context, **5**–9, 27–9, 33–4, 41, 51, 56,
    70, 80, 89–90, 93–4, 96–8, 100–1,
    115–16, 133–4, 160, 166
contextualism, **53**–6, 58, 62, 69–70
contrastive inference, 125–6, 178
Cooperative Principle, **16**–19, 41–2
  opting out, 41–2
coordinating discourse relations, 173,
    175, **178**–9
cues, 134, 136, 177, 181, 199–203, 205,
    207

DAMSL, 205
Defaultism, **53**–6, 58, 60, 63–70

220